The Canadian
Legislative System

Books
in the
Series

Canadian Controversies Series

Canadian political commentators have adopted the full range of political styles, from cold detachment to partisan advocacy. The Canadian Controversies Series is disciplined by the idea that, while political analysis must be based on sound descriptive and explanatory modes of thought, social scientists should not abnegate the role of evaluating political systems. Such evaluations require a conscious approach to the interrelationships between facts and values, empirical and normative considerations in politics.

Each theme in the series has been chosen to illustrate some basic principles of Canadian political life and to allow the respective authors freedom to develop normative positions on the related problems. It is thus hoped that the volumes will stimulate debate and advance public understanding of some of the major questions which confront the Canadian political system. By treating the enduring themes and problems in Canada, the authors will also illustrate the important contribution that social science can offer politics in terms of facts, ideas, theories, and comparative frameworks within which meaningful controversy can take place. Creative political thought must not be divorced from the political fabric of a country but form an integral part of it.

ROBERT J. JACKSON
General Editor

The Canadian Legislative System: Politicians and Policymaking

Second, Revised Edition

Robert J. Jackson
and
Michael M. Atkinson

Canadian Controversies Series

Macmillan of Canada

Canadian Cataloguing in Publication Data

Jackson, Robert J.
  The Canadian legislative system

(Canadian controversies series)
Includes index.
ISBN 0-7705-1848-6 pa.

1. Canada — Parliament.   2. Canada — Politics
and government — 1963-   *I. Atkinson, Michael M.
II. Title.   III. Series.

JL136.J32 1980   328.71   C80-094217-5

Printed in Canada for
The Macmillan Company of Canada
70 Bond Street
Toronto, Ontario
M5B 1X3

Contents

Preface to the
Second Edition

Since the first edition of this book was published, several changes have been made in the legislative system, some of them in keeping with our criticisms and suggestions. The House of Commons is now broadcast and televised, some Commons committees have launched important investigations, and the salaries of MPs are automatically adjusted with inflation. Unfortunately, none of these changes has been guided by a thorough diagnosis of the ills of parliamentary government and in the meantime further complications have appeared. Ministerial indiscretions, ineffective expenditure controls, and uninformed parliamentarians are just a few of the unpleasant features of parliamentary government in Canada that can be traced in part to the unwillingness of politicians to reform their role in the process of public-policy formation.

The second edition of this book, like the first, is aimed at a description, analysis, and criticism of this process. Since 1974, however, new research has appeared which makes the task easier and more rewarding. In the area of parliamentary organization and procedure, we have been fortunate to be able to draw on John Stewart's *The Canadian House of Commons*. Our own firsthand impressions of parliamentary institutions have been strengthened by a collection of papers authored by parliamentary interns and entitled *The House of Commons Observed*. In the study of legislative behaviour, Allan Kornberg and William Mishler's *Influence in Parliament: Canada* and Colin Campbell's *The Canadian Senate: A Lobby From Within* have provided new data and analysis.

Our understanding of the organization and behaviour of central policymaking institutions has been enhanced by the work of R. M. Punnett and William Matheson on the prime minister and cabinet and by Colin Campbell and George Szablowski's book, *The Superbureaucrats*. The work of Douglas Hartle on the expenditure budgetary process and of Richard Phidd and Bruce Doern on economic policy have contributed immensely to our understanding of the bureaucratic context in which politicians must operate.

There have also been several conferences and reports which bear on politicians in the House of Commons and the Senate. The reports of the Auditor General and the Royal Commission on Financial Management and Accountability are foremost, but the Institute for Research on Public Policy has held conferences on a variety of issues including legislative reform and the evaluation of public expenditures and the Study of Parliament Group has sponsored conferences on accountability, the budgetary process, and the Senate. For academics, the most significant conferences may have been those held in 1977 at York University and in 1979 at Simon Fraser University.

In response to these and other contributions to the study of the legislative system we have reconsidered each part of our original work and have added some sections and substantially changed others. This second edition includes, for example, a new section on the prestige of parliament, an expanded consideration of subordinate legislation, new data on the government's legislative programs, and a preliminary evaluation of the Clark cabinet. Parliamentary committees are scrutinized in greater detail and more attention is devoted to the consideration of financial measures. The final chapter of the book expands on our original reform proposals and calls once again for sweeping changes. Indeed, this entire edition has been reorganized, rewritten, and updated to focus attention on the need for comprehensive change.

Neither our colleagues nor our students have hesitated to comment on our work and we are grateful for all of their observations. We have reinterviewed many of the people mentioned in the preface to the first edition, and have held discussions with Joe Clark, Mark MacGuigan, James Gillies, Stanley Knowles, Walter Baker, Bill Neville, Greg Fyffe, Jim Hurley, Jean-Pierre Gaboury, Alistair Fraser, Marcel Pelletier, Graham Eglington, and all of the recent parliamentary interns. Mary Kastellic, Greg Kozicz, and Liz Rickerby provided much appreciated research assistance.

We are very grateful to the secretaries at McMaster University: Marlene Moore, Darlene Jones, and particularly Lori Hill. They deciphered our writing, corrected our errors, and made the project much easier. Virgil Duff and Dave Marshall of Macmillan provided invaluable encouragement and editorial assistance.

Finally, we would like to thank our wives, Doreen and Pam, who have tolerated for years our interest in politicians and legislatures on the condition that we hold our discussions in interesting places.

ROBERT J. JACKSON
MICHAEL M. ATKINSON
Berlin

Preface to the First Edition

This volume is disciplined by the philosophy of the Canadian Controversies Series that political analysts should not abdicate the role of evaluating political systems. *The Canadian Legislative System: Politicians and Policymaking* combines descriptive, analytic, and evaluative statements about the polity. It places the legislative system within the framework of Canadian culture and dissects the major institutions in the inner circle and parliament in order to ascertain the role played by politicians in the policymaking process. The volume concludes that major adjustments are required if Canadian parliamentarians are to secure a major position in the system.

There has been a considerable amount of research on the Canadian political system and many of our perspectives have been based on this work. The contributions of Peter Aucoin, Bruce Doern, David Falcone, David Kwavnick, John Meisel, Khayyam Paltiel, Robert Presthus, John Porter, Michael Stein, Michael Whittington, and Richard Van Loon on Canadian politics in general were invaluable. Detailed examinations of legislative behaviour by Allan Kornberg, David Hoffman, and Norman Ward provided important information for the various sections on political actors. The institutional and procedural research of William Dawson, Thomas Hockin, Ned Franks, J. R. Mallory, Roman March, Michael Rush, Denis Smith, John Stewart, and Paul Thomas underlies many of the descriptive statements about parliament and its committees.

We have been blessed with the editorial assistance of Diane Mew. As executive editor of this series on Canadian politics and society Diane's encouragement and technical competence have played a major part in bringing our book to fruition.

The bulk of the material in the book is designed to express opinions the authors developed during work undertaken for the Canadian government over the past several years. In this respect, we are grateful for opportunities provided to witness parts of the inner circle in operation and to study the detailed functioning of the House of Commons. We are indebted to those senior officials who generously answered specific and general questions about the legislative system. Among those who deserve special thanks are Gerard Bertrand, Michael Butler, Henry Davis, Peter Dobell, Michael Kirby, Philip Laundy, Marcel Massé, André Millar, Robert Miller, C. R. Nixon, Michael Pitfield, Jim Ryan, Eric Spicer, Donald Thorson, and Len Trudel.

In terms of the development of our perspective on reform we have been aided by politicians and their appointees. These include members or former members of parliament — Allan J. MacEachen, John Reid, Mark MacGuigan, Douglas Fisher, Gordon Blair, Gordon Fairweather, Stanley Knowles, Grant Deachman, Jim Jerome, Lloyd Francis, and Robert Kaplan. The political assistants include Brian Bruce, Gloria Kunka, Sandy Blue, Jerry Yanover, Robert Wright, Jim Davey, and Peter McGuire.

The academics, bureaucrats, and politicians are responsible neither for the facts we have cited nor for the judgments put forward. Many of them, however, are in positions to weigh the evidence and decide whether or not there is a case for restructuring the role of politicians in the policymaking process. We hope that our book will contribute to such a reassessment.

ROBERT J. JACKSON
MICHAEL M. ATKINSON
Tabarka, Tunisia

The Canadian
Legislative System

1. Perspectives on the Canadian Legislative System

During the past decade there has been a resurgence of criticism of Canada's parliamentary institutions. Public commentators have called for a more responsive parliament, defenders of the private sector have clamoured for tighter financial controls, academic analysts have suggested clear guidelines for ministers, and politicians have demanded more powers and responsibilities. Why, then, has Canada not embarked on a comprehensive restructuring of the role of elected representatives in governmental and parliamentary institutions?

This simple answer is that no institution, political party, or individual has been able to offer an instrument of change sensitive to the competing interests of government, opposition, and the public. This book explains some of the reasons why it is difficult to achieve such a reform. Many politicians are sceptical of the virtues and possibilities of comprehensive change, but we remain optimistic that an acceptable, balanced package of reforms can be struck. Reforms can be made acceptable to most political participants as long as partisanship is accepted as part of the democratic foundations of our system of government.

It would, however, be unwise to overlook the limitations on reform. In parliament, politicians tend to protect revered institutions. Any increase in institutional autonomy, for example, is frequently regarded as a challenge to the parliamentary form of government. Neither backbenchers nor ministers seem particularly inclined to conceive of parliament as a feedback mechanism to the executive or to consider the functions the legislative system may perform in society. And yet reform proposals must be premised on a strengthening of these relationships.

These problems are compounded by an absence of continuity in the recruitment and promotion of Canadian politicians. In Canada, politics sometimes appears to be an ephemeral sport engaged in by those who have the available time and resources. The rate of attrition (about 40 per cent) among Canadian members of parliament remains very high by British and American standards, so Canada lacks an adequate core of experienced parliamentarians. In liberal democracies, schemes to improve the calibre of politicians are frowned upon, but it is rather utopian to expect a reforming zeal and a commitment to parliamentary institutions from politicians whose relationship to the legislative system is often shortlived.

The attitudes and values of bureaucrats also constitute an obstacle to reform. Officials have a distinctive and necessary policymaking role in the legislative system, but they remain protective of their realms of authority. Employing the canons of administrative secrecy and guarding their "territory" is a preoccupation of officials even at the highest echelons of government.

The inertia in Canadian politics is compounded by the behaviour of political parties and interest groups. In a political system where interest-group demands are highly valued, public policymaking often deteriorates into the negotiation of private-group claims. Detailed knowledge of particular policies and the authority acquired from their membership permit interest-group leaders to make representations to the government that may be more compelling than those of members of parliament. Political parties similarly overshadow elected representatives. For many observers the ritualistic imposition of party discipline has robbed parliament of an independent capacity to affect contemporary events.

Reform of the legislative system in Canada has been a spasmodic affair. When the strains of workload and antiquated procedures finally appear to lower performance levels, the government reacts with reforms designed to alleviate the immediate causes. This penchant for short-term amendment can be traced in part to electoral necessity. Policies are almost always evaluated in terms of their electoral appeal and politicians are understandably reluctant to think beyond the next election. Minority governments, in particular, focus attention on survival and the short term. Parliamentarians are normally resistant to change but, in minority situations, governments are especially reluctant to further complicate relationships by reforms that affect the rules of the game.

These rather negative observations are not intended to deaden enthusiasm for reform. Reform proposals must be premised, however, on a recognition of the problems outlined above. These problems in turn have their roots in the complexity of relationships which prevail in a parliamentary democracy. This book will endeavour to bring some order to these relationships by offering a conceptual framework which integrates executive and legislature in a larger "legislative system," and by providing a detailed understanding of the way in which this system presently operates. The remainder of this chapter is devoted to a brief overview of parliamentary development in Canada and a review of recent reform efforts. It sets the stage for a critical interpretation of existing arrangements.

EVOLUTION OF THE LEGISLATIVE SYSTEM

It is fashionable nowadays to forecast the kind of institutions and resources that society will have in the year 2000. This is normally accomplished by statistical models which project current trends into the future. If such is attempted for the Canadian legislative system one point seems certain of discovery—it will not become more important! Increased governmental activity, the significance of federal-provincial arrangements, and the ascendancy of the prime minister and his office will continue to prevent the growth of parliamentary influence.

The question of weak legislative power is not unique to Canada. In the United Kingdom, the United States, and other democracies, critics have professed that their political systems have not achieved a proper balance of constitutional and political force. While in the American case this judgment is normally concluded from an examination of the intentions of the founding fathers, scholars in parliamentary systems of the British type often refer to a "classic" and harmonious period from which parliament has declined. The legislature constantly emerges as the weak partner in the constitutional balance.

The list of indictments against the Canadian parliament is impressive, as we will attempt to show. Yet it would be presumptuous to argue that in the Canadian political system parliament has "declined." The relative authority and power of legislatures is a complex question. To begin an assessment requires above all a clear conception of the purposes of parliament in the political system. Part of our concern in this book is to characterize and assess some of the activities parliament is expected to perform. Our task is also to set the Canadian parliament within the larger legislative system. In fact, this comprehensive framework is our main concern, since relations among elements such as cabinet, parliament, and bureaucracy determine the kinds of functions each can be expected to undertake. The role of politicians can be properly assessed only when parliament is integrated with the other institutions in the policymaking process.

Unfortunately, no comprehensive study of the relations between the Canadian parliament and the executive exists to guide an appraisal of the legislative system. Canadians tend to measure their institutions against the positive features of the British model and against the dangers assumed to be inherent in the American congressional system. This perspective has limitations as well as advantages. To some extent the Canadian experience does parallel the British and many of the criticisms of parliamentary government apply to both. But the Canadian legislative system has some peculiar burdens and in our opinion its capacity for flexibility has never been very impressive.

An appreciation of the evolution of the Canadian legislative system can best be obtained by a brief comparison with British constitutional development. The paramount political question in Britain during the eighteenth and first half of the nineteenth centuries was the quest for parliamentary democracy. The gradual absorption of democratic ideals in the culture was mirrored by the growing importance of parliament in society. In the second half of the nineteenth century, democratic reformers concentrated on extending the franchise from property owners to all male citizens and eventully to females. Westminster institutions were exported to the colonies in the belief they would provide the same stable foundations they had in Great Britain.

During the embryonic stages of the British parliament the government did not dominate in the development of legislation. The private act of parliament was the normal vehicle for lawmaking. This was congruent with the type of society and government that existed in Britain. Walkland put it this way: "Procedure by Private Bill was natural to a society which wished to make marginal adjustments to the reigning state of affairs, but which could not conceive of consciously-directed broad social and economic reform."[1] However, the consensus on limited government did not persist indefinitely. New constitutional arrangements were emerging in the latter part of the eighteenth and early nineteenth centuries and these would eventually contribute to the more active intervention of government in society.

The Reform Act of 1832 acknowledged the existence of a new and delicate balance of constitutional forces. The distinction between the function of governing and that of controlling the governors emerged as the key to understanding the new developments.[2] The responsibility of ministers to parliament was confirmed and defeat in the House of Commons on important legislative proposals required the government to resign. Parliament thereby increased its capacity to require the executive to account for its direction of the nation. At the same time, however, parliamentary interference with administrative responsibilities diminished.

By the 1860s, the constitutional balance had been changed again. Political parties had become national organizations which could command the support of the electorate. Most candidates had to rely on the parties for electoral success. At the same time, governments began to accept responsibility for a legislative program. In the face of new societal demands the public act of parliament became the main legislative instrument and private bills declined to insignificance. In parliament procedure began to solidify, generally in the direction of increased governmental control. The significance of cabinet continued to grow and the civil service showed a remarkable ability to remain in touch with modern developments.

Procedural development in parliament had to reflect competing requirements. On the one hand, rules and procedures were needed which acknowledged the existence of partisan interest; on the other hand, the privileges of private members had to be respected. The codification of procedures ensured that the national interest could be defined and that the equality of individual members of parliament would be preserved.

While governments in Britain were tightening their control over parliament and parliamentary procedure, the first few decades of the Canadian Confederation more closely approximated earlier periods of British constitutional development.[3] Although government-sponsored legislation has always been important in Canada, private bills and private members' bills played a relatively large role in parliament during the twenty years following Confederation.[4] Parliamentary leadership relied on the extensive patronage at its disposal to attract and secure the support it needed. Gradually, parliamentary parties became identifiable, but until 1878 members of parliament could not always be relied upon to maintain their party loyalties. During this period, John A. Macdonald suffered several defeats in parliament without submitting his resignation. At the same time, the need for wholesale government intervention in the economy was not generally accepted — except, of course, for the promotion of railways as a stimulus to economic development.

By the end of the nineteenth century, Canadian political parties were becoming national in scope.[5] They were not the mass organized parties that had come to dominate the British political system, but they had begun to aggregate demands and to organize the vote in the electoral process. The parties began to limit the independence of MPs and to extinguish any desire for wholesale changes in the relations between the executive and parliament. Patronage was by no means unknown, but it was limited by the creation in 1908 of a Civil Service Commission and subsequently by the growth of a permanent civil service.

With the expansion in the economy came immense growth in government expenditure and activity. In 1913 the executive began the slow process of establishing control over the consultative process and decisionmaking. A procedure to terminate debate — closure — was introduced at this time, and other rules guaranteed that the government's expenditure proposals would be discussed more regularly.

On a general level the institutions of the Canadian legislative system developed in the same direction as those in Britain. Cabinet's responsibility for initiating public policy became undisputed, parties replaced patronage as the means of securing legislative support for the executive, and periodic procedural changes provided governments with more opportunities to realize their legislative programs. However, the Canadian legislative system has never corresponded exactly to the British. Each system has had unique institutional arrangements. The speakership and the operation of parliamentary committees, for example, have differed markedly from the British. More important, perhaps, have been the differences in the institutional and cultural context of parliamentary government.

Parliamentary institutions in Canada have not been stabilized and strengthened by a comparatively homogeneous political culture as they were in Britain. Religious, linguistic, and regional cleavages have deterred politicians from the task of building centalized political institutions. Canadian parliamentary institutions have not become arenas for the disposal of local, provincial, and regional claims.[6] Instead, new institutions capable of sustaining intergovernmental liaison had to be created to satisfy these demands of the federal system.[7]

Societal cleavages fragmented the party system in Canada and affected parliamentary organization. The existence of minor parties has complicated the legislative process and created some impediments to reform. Minority government is perhaps the most significant legacy of minor parties. While little research has been undertaken on the impact of minority government, it is clear that party leaders prefer not to seek procedural changes during periods of parliamentary instability. Furthermore, reform requires some degree of consensus on the role of parliament in the political system and alternating minority-majority situations may militate against such agreement.

REFORM AND REFORMERS

Disillusionment with existing parliamentary institutions and scepticism about the democratic process is not limited to Canada. In most developed democracies, scholars lament executive dominance, administrative despotism, and parliamentary decline: they continually stress the insignificant role of the backbencher in policymaking.[8] Everywhere the demands placed on the time of legislators are mounting. The necessity for personal specialization and more legislative expertise engulfs most parliamentarians.[9] At the same time, interest groups rather than political parties have become prominent participants in the creation and administration of public policy. The role of the representative is being questioned and specific problems like administrative secrecy and political corruption have acquired new urgency. There has also been a general weakening in acceptance of the rational model of democracy, in which voters are expected to influence policy decisions by their electoral choices. Empirical research on voting and legislative behaviour has increased doubts about linkages between citizen preferences and legislative decisions.[10] In short, once the battle for representative assemblies had been won, many critics found that the new institutions could not satisfy all their democratic expectations.

In response to these alleged deficiencies in liberal democracies, some democrats have demanded a reconsideration of the basic organization of government. One school of thought calls for a reassessment of the concept of representation with the intention of strengthening the capacity of citizens to make actual decisions.[11] A second school demands a restructuring of representative institutions in the expectation that organizational changes can improve the impact of individual legislators and promote executive accountability.

Advocates of participatory democracy believe that the decentralization of authoritative decisionmaking will produce better citizens and improve decisions. Suggestions from this school run from romantic proposals to have electronic voting machines installed in the home of every citizen through to more standard devices such as referendums.

Contrary to popular opinion, the practice of holding referendums is not entirely foreign to our system of government. Canada has held two major referendums at the national level. Both were called plebiscites because they were considered to be only advisory and were not necessarily to result in law. As a result of the advisory nature of these two referendums, each received a different response. In 1898 the federal government proposed a plebiscite on prohibition and, although a small majority voted in favour of it, the prime minister, Sir Wilfrid Laurier, did not feel that it was strong enough to warrant a federal prohibition law. In the better-known conscription crisis case of 1942, Prime Minister Mackenzie King decided to proceed with a conscription law after the plebiscite had received an affirmative vote of 62 per cent. In addition to these national consultations, numerous provincial and municipal experiments have been made with referendums in Canada.

Referendums are therefore relatively infrequent but not unknown to Canada. Since democracy implies a reasonable degree of citizen participation, the demand for an increase is bound to be well received. However, several problems are involved in elevating even further direct citizen participation to the summit of the hierarchy of democratic values. First, advocates of participatory democracy are usually unclear about the precise meaning of participation or about the degree and type which is most desirable. Second, they have been unable to suggest what mechanisms or structures would actually improve the individual's access to policymaking machinery. Mechanical devices such as referendums alone are rarely acceptable to participatory democrats. Third, they have been unable to demonstrate convincingly that citizens wish to assume the burden of continual involvement in national decisionmaking. Most citizens seem content to engage in the political process through elections and occasionally through the traditional devices of direct participation such as referendum and sometimes initiative and recall.

The orthodox response to criticisms of representative democracy has come from those who support the reform of parliamentary institutions. From the most trenchant critics have come some of the most vigorous proposals for change. Occasionally, romantic allusions are made to more glorious days of parliament,[12] but such reformers have generally concentrated on procedural changes and the enhancement of particular parliamentary institutions. Unfortunately, procedural reforms are often piecemeal and regarded as ends in themselves. When such reforms are contemplated, ultimate objectives are seldom paramount and the consequent incrementalism has occasionally led to inconsistent proposals. Furthermore, it is by no means clear which of these reforms will actually have an impact on the effectiveness of representative institutions. And the evaluation of all reforms is impossible in the absence of a coherent philosophy about the functions of the legislative system and the institutions which comprise it.

When the House of Commons embarked on reform in the 1960s, most commentators agreed on the advisability of a review.[13] Institutional reform and attitudes toward procedures had not kept pace with changes in the volume and complexity of the nation's business. One expert has suggested that, prior to these reforms, procedures in the Canadian parliament were reminiscent of those at Westminster before the reforms of the 1880s.[14]

Reform proved to be a long and sometimes disjointed process. Its history illustrates how far Canadian parliamentary institutions had lagged behind other policymaking structures and how a vast overhaul was bound to elicit grievances and suspicions from some individuals and, from others, hope for more extensive change. The Special Committees on Procedure throughout the 1960s offered proposals designed to modernize antiquated methods to make greater use of institutions such as parliamentary committees.[15] After these reforms were finalized in 1968, some academics began to argue that they constituted an unnecessary strengthening of the executive and were evidence of the prime minister's presidential aspirations.[16] But as soon as this period of reform was complete, many MPs began to request the extensive support facilities that had long been associated exclusively with the American congressional system.

The detailed criticisms of the legislative system contained in this book and the reform package offered in the last chapter are firmly in this "reform of parliament" tradition. Our framework of the legislative system and description of particular institutions are designed to integrate criticisms and proposals. To guide our discussion, however, it is useful to outline a set of reform priorities based on a preliminary evaluation of Canada's experience with parliamentary institutions.

First, the balance of power between parliament and the executive must be reconsidered. In Canada the executive too often assumes a posture of complacency toward the legislature. This posture can be attributed in part to parliament's inability to hold the executive responsible for the ever-increasing scope of government activities. Between 1960 and 1978 the total expenditures of the federal government grew from $6.5 billion to more than $47 billion, but parliament failed to acquire the resources to fully comprehend an expenditure budget of this magnitude. Similarly, parliament has not acquired the means to control commitments made at federal-provincial conferences and to compete with the personalized politics of the prime minister. In the House of Commons the governing party continually supports executive action, while the opposition parties cannot be relied upon to offer a comprehensive alternative. The weakness of parliamentary institutions is accentuated when the bureaucracy, the cabinet, and the prime minister establish direct links of communication with the public. To some extent task forces, royal commissions, and public-opinion polls have replaced parliamentarians as feedback mechanisms for the executive.

Second, the image of backbenchers is one of powerlessness. The member of parliament ought to become a more important participant in the legislative system. In part, this ideal means improving the backbencher's role in policymaking and strengthening the links between citizen and representative. The gulf which presently separates representatives and their constituents should be narrowed by an improvement in parlimentary communications. Traditional executive-legislative divisions need to be reevaluated; as far as cabinet is concerned, the principle of ministerial responsibility must be clarified, especially in sensitive areas such as the relationship between the solicitor general and the RCMP.

Third, parliamentarians and academics should reconsider the relations between the legislative system and Canadian society. In particular, attention ought to be paid to the general feelings Canadians have about their parliamentary institutions. Legislatures in industrialized nations do not always command universal support and it is by no means certain that all Canadians have a benevolent view of legislative activities. If the Canadian legislature lacks prestige, part of the problem may be traced to an inability to canvass the various alternatives of public policy. It must compete with other political structures which are more proficient in the generation and communication of new political ideas. In order to attract public support, parliament will have to function as a forum where members assemble, not merely to pass legislation but, as Walter Bagehot declared, to inform, teach, and express the nation.

In the next chapter a conceptual framework of the legislative system in a parliamentary setting is outlined and the relationships among the legislature, the executive, and society are discussed in general terms. Only when attention is directed toward these complex interrelations is it possible to achieve an adequate perspective. The linkages between the environment and the legislative system are discussed in Chapter 3. In this case, precision is hampered by the lack of research on the relations among interest groups, parties, political elites, and public policy. Chapter 4 focuses on the preparliamentary part of the legislative system. Among those structures examined are the cabinet and the central agencies. Chapters 5 and 6 concentrate on the parliamentary part of the system, its operation, and some of the obstacles to a more adequate performance of its functions. Research on Canadian legislators is examined in Chapter 7, particularly the aspirations of Canadian members of parliament and their opportunities for personal initiative. The problems of evaluating the Canadian legislative system are considered in Chapter 8 and Chapter 9 outlines the essentials of a reform design.

NOTES

1. S. A. Walkland, *The Legislative Process in Great Britain* (London: Allen and Unwin, 1968), pp. 9 and 14.
2. For an authoritative discussion, see M. J. C. Vile, *Constitutionalism and the Separation of Powers* (London: Oxford University Press, 1967), Chapter 8.
3. This theme is developed by Ronald Blair in ''What Happens to Parliament?'', in T. Lloyd and J. McLeod (ed.), *Agenda: 1970* (Toronto: University of Toronto Press, 1968), pp. 217-40.
4. John B. Stewart, *The Canadian House of Commons: Procedure and Reform* (Montreal: McGill-Queen's University Press, 1977), pp. 198-201. Differences in types of bills are discussed in detail in Chapter 5.
5. See Escott M. Reid, ''The Rise of National Parties in Canada,'' in Hugh Thorburn (ed.), *Party Politics in Canada*, 4th ed. (Scarborough: Prentice-Hall, 1979), pp. 12-20; Hugh Thorburn, ''The Development of Political Parties in Canada'' in *ibid*., pp. 2-11; and George M. Hougham, ''The Background and Development of National Parties,'' in *Party Politics in Canada*, 1st ed., pp. 1-13.
6. Garth Stevenson, *Unfulfilled Union: Canadian Federalism and National Unity* (Toronto: Macmillan of Canada, 1979) and Donald Smiley, *Canada in Question: Federalism in the Seventies*, 2nd ed. (Toronto: McGraw-Hill Ryerson, 1976).

7. The incompatability of federal and parliamentary forms of government is discussed in Richard Simeon, *Federal-Provincial Diplomacy* (Toronto: University of Toronto Press, 1971), pp. 25-31.

8. There is an enormous literature on parliamentary reform and the following list is by no means exhaustive. On Britain: S. A. Walkland and Michael Ryle, *The Commons in the Seventies* (London: Fontana, 1977); Bernard Crick, *The Reform of Parliament* (London: Weidenfeld and Nicolson, 1964); A. H. Harrison and B. Crick (ed.), *Commons in Transition* (London: Fontana, 1970); and P. G. Richards, *The Backbenchers* (London: Faber and Faber, 1973). On the French Parliament: Andrè Chandernagor, *Un Parlement, Pour Quoi Fair?* (Paris: Gallimard, 1967); J-Ch. Maout and R. Muzellec, *Le Parlement sous le Ve Republique* (Paris: Colin, 1971); Pierre Avril, *Les Français et leur Parlement* (Paris: Casterman, 1972); Jean-Luc Parodi, *Les Raports entre le Legislatif et l'Executif sous la Cinquieme Republique* (Paris: Colin, 1972). On developing countries: Abdo Baaklini and James J. Heaphey (ed.), *Comparative Legislative Reforms and Innovations* (Albany: State University of New York, 1977), and G. R. Boynton and Chong Lim Kim (ed.), *Legislative Systems in Developing Countries* (Durham: Duke University Press, 1975).

9. Among the comparative works which stress these and related matters see Gerhard Lowenberg and Samuel C. Patterson, *Comparing Legislatures* (Boston: Little, Brown, 1979); M. Mezey, *Comparative Legislatures* (Durham, N.C.: Duke University Press, 1979); V. Herman and F. Mendel, *Parliaments of the World* (London: Macmillan, 1976); and, J. Blondel, *Comparative Legislatures* (Englewood Cliffs, N.J.: Prentice-Hall, 1973).

10. Seminal works in the field of voting behaviour include: A. Campbell, P. E. Converse, W. E. Miller, and D. E. Stokes, *The American Voter* (New York: John Wiley and Sons, 1960), and David Butler and Donald Stokes, *Political Change in Britain* (Toronto: Macmillan of Canada, 1969). On the relationship between constitutents and legislators, see Warren Miller and Donald Stokes, "Constituency Influence in Congress," *American Political Science Review*, Vol. 57, no. 1 (March 1963), pp. 45-56, and Kenneth Prewitt and Heinz Eulau, "Political Matrix and Political Representation: Prolegomenon to a New Departure from an Old Problem," *American Political Science Review*, Vol. 63, no. 2 (June 1969), pp. 427-41. This subject is considered briefly in a comprehensive book on Canadian elections: Harold D. Clarke *et al.*, *Political Choice in Canada* (Toronto: McGraw-Hill Ryerson, 1979).

11. Participatory democracy is normally discussed in the context of democratic theory. One of those who places emphasis on the need for increased participation is Peter Bachrach. See *The Theory of Democratic Elitism: A Critique* (Boston: Little, Brown, 1967). A balanced collection of views can be found in Terrance E. Cook and Patrick M. Morgan (ed.), *Participatory Democracy* (New York: Harper and Row, 1971).

12. See, for example, Andrew Hill and Anthony Whichelow, *What's Wrong With Parliament?* (London: Penguin Books Ltd., 1964).

13. Thomas Hockin, "Reforming Canada's Parliament: The 1966 Reforms and Beyond," *Canadian Bar Review*, XVI (1966), pp. 326-45; Donald Page, "Streamlining the Procedures of the Canadian House of Commons," *Canadian Journal of Economics and Political Science*, 33 (February 1967), pp. 27-49; C. E. S. Franks, "The Reform of Parliament," *Queen's Quarterly*, 76 (Spring 1969), pp. 113-17; Pauline Jewett, "The Reform of Parliament," *Journal of Canadian Studies*, 1 (1966), pp. 11-16; Philip Laundy, "Procedural Reform in the Canadian House of Commons," in R. S. Lankster and D. Dewol (ed.), *The Table: Being the Journal of Society of Clerks-at-the-Table in Commonwealth Parliaments for 1965*, 34 (London: Butterworth, 1966); Trevor Lloyd, "The Reform of Parliamentary Proceedings," in Abraham Rotstein (ed.), *The Prospect of Change: Proposals for Canada's Future* (Toronto: McGraw-Hill, 1965), pp. 23-39; J. A. A. Lovink, "Who Wants Parliamentary Reform?" *Queen's Quarterly*, 79 (Winter 1972), pp. 502-13; and J. A. A. Lovink, "Parliamentary Reform and Governmental Effectiveness," *Canadian Public Administration*, 16 (Spring 1973), pp. 35-54.

14. Laundy, "Procedural Reform in the Canadian House of Commons," p. 20.

15. Special Committee on Procedure, *Third Report* (Ottawa: Queen's Printer, 1968).

16. Denis Smith, "President and Parliament: The Transformation of Parliamentary Government in Canada," in O. Kruhlak *et al.* (ed.), *The Canadian Political Process* (Toronto: Holt, Rinehart and Winston, 1970), pp. 367-82. For a critical analysis of the Smith approach consult R. M. Punnett, *The Prime Minister in Canadian Government and Politics* (Toronto: Macmillan of Canada, 1977). On the need for further parliamentary reform, see Canada, Royal Commission on Financial Management and Accountability, *Final Report* (Ottawa: Supply and Services, 1979), Part 5; The Canadian Study of Parliament Group, *Budgetary Process* (Ottawa: Queen's Printer, 1977) and *Accountability to Parliament* (Ottawa: Queen's Printer, 1978); Stewart, *The Canadian House of Commons*, Chapter 10; T. d'Aquino *et al.*, *Parliamentary Government in Canada* (Intercounsel, 1979); and Allan Kornberg and William Mishler, *Influence in Parliament: Canada* (Durham, N.C.: Duke University Press, 1976). Two compendiums have emerged from conferences on the Canadian legislature: W. A. W. Neilson and J. C. MacPherson, *The Legislative Process in Canada: The Need for Reform* (Montreal: The Institute for Research on Public Policy, 1978), and Special Issue, *Legislative Studies Quarterly*, 3 (November 1978).

2. Policymaking and the Legislative System: An Overview

The problems in the legislative system are intimately related to other processes and parts of society. The task of this chapter is to provide an overview of the legislative system which will be sensitive to the fact that legislatures do not operate in isolation from other societal or political processes and that they may produce results or outputs unnoticed by formal-legal methods of analysis. In Canada, much of the analysis of parliament has been inward looking and, although the evolution of our institutions has been studied, we have failed to examine the legislative system as a whole or to see trends and anticipate problems.

To help place legislative analysis and problems in a comparative and manageable perspective we rely on four concepts: system, process, policy, and function. These four broad notions focus attention on the totality of government activities and away from the important, but narrow, examination of the rules of procedure in legislative institutions. They provide the building blocks for a more comprehensive understanding of the role of legislatures in their societies.

Much of the common wisdom and many of the value judgments about Canada's legislative institutions need to be reconsidered. It may appear from our description of the evolution of these institutions in Chapter 1 that parliament is extremely weak. This conclusion is warranted if and only if the analysis remains within a narrow legalistic conception of power. The argument and conclusion alter markedly if one considers the formal and informal links which connect cabinet, parliament, and society. Students of public administration began this trend away from the study of legal structures to the use of other concepts during the 1960s. In the study of the Canadian parliament, our analysis also has to be raised to broader relationships and processes.

Degrees of influence within any political system are extremely difficult to gauge. Anticipatory actions, in which individuals engage before influence or power are exercised, make it difficult to demonstrate who has power or influence. The subtle behind-the-scenes exercises of power and the executive's anticipation of parliamentary activities cannot be examined in studies of parliamentary procedure. Nor does study of the formalities of the legislative system aid in understanding the oscillation of parliament's power in particular circumstances, such as during minority governments or during the passage of particular types of legislation. These considerations, among many others, require a reformulation of some of the language used to study parliamentary power in Canada.

THE POLITICAL SYSTEM

Practitioners of systems analysis in political science endorsed the concept of the political system after becoming uncomfortable about discussing politics exclusively in terms of formal institutions and legal procedures. In Canada, politicians and political scientists are still often inclined to view legislative elements in isolation and to treat their problems as legal and inherently different. The concept of system, on the other hand, is illuminating primarily because it presumes the interconnectedness of parts and depicts the elements on that basis. This approach is not the only way of examining politics, but systems analysts have demonstrated that it can facilitate understanding of complex processes and provide a complement to traditional constitutional descriptions. It is in the context of facilitating understanding that we bring this concept to bear, first on politics in general and then on the Canadian legislative system.

In their preliminary examinations of the political system, academics use almost exclusively the model developed by David Easton. This approach is based on a biological analogy which seeks to portray the whole as more than the sum of its parts. In the political system the parts are not individuals, but subsystems, roles, and structures. The idea of a system suggests relationships between these parts and the whole. In Easton's approach the political system is seen as only one part of the social system and the study of politics is essentially the study of the authoritative allocation of values for society. His approach focuses attention on the input-output exchange which links the political system and its environment. The key elements are depicted in Figure 2-1, with the exception of stress which is communicated to the system through fluctuations in the level of inputs.

Figure 2-1
THE POLITICAL SYSTEM

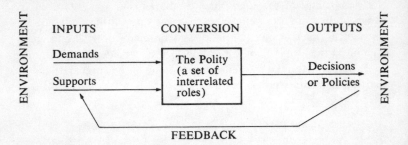

SOURCE: Adapted from David Easton, *A Systems Analysis of Political Life* (New York: John Wiley and Sons, 1965), p. 32.

Inputs from the environment may be described very generally as demands or supports. The model suggests that demands are made on the polity, but demands also originate within the polity itself. The campaigns for better housing and increased social welfare which have been prevalent in postwar Canada are examples of demands on the polity. Demands which arise within the policymaking structures (such as the public service or cabinet) are sometimes referred to as within-puts. The nature of each demand is rooted firmly in the culture and the economic and social structure of the environment. Successful conversion of demands into outputs depends upon such factors as the acceptance of demands in the environment, the importance of the originators of the demands, the timing of the demands, and the means by which demands are pressed upon the political system. In theory, one could create a demand schedule and estimate the likelihood of success for each demand or group of demands.

Demands are regulated by "gatekeepers" in the system. In Canada, structures such as parties, interest groups, and communications networks operate as gatekeepers by selecting and conditioning which demands will be processed by the political system. Since every demand cannot be satisfied by the resources available, it is important that not all become issues. Such a situation would undoubtedly over-tax the system's capacity and result in unmanageable stress.

Basic to the continued activity of the democratic system is the support directed toward the three components of the polity: community, regime, and government. Citizens must be willing to settle differences through peaceful action: this solution presumes their acceptance of the political community. Support must also be directed toward the regime — that is, the rules of the game through which resources are authoritatively allocated. Finally, support may be directed toward the government — that is, the individuals who hold the highest offices in the regime and are responsible for its decisions and policies.

The level of overall support determines the system's capacity to process demands. Supports include actual material resources such as money, time, and labour. The taxes paid to government as well as the time and energy used in participating in political parties are examples of this form of input. Support also consists of those actions or attitudes which affirm allegiance to the political system. The pro-regime attitudes expressed in a public-opinion poll in October 1970, when the government employed the War Measures Act, may be taken as a general example of this type of support. On the other hand, the support for Premier René Lévesque's desire for "sovereignty-association" for the province of Quebec must be seen as reducing overall acceptance of the institutions of the Canadian parliament.

Different political cultures provide different types and degrees of support, but the level of support is also affected by the outputs and extent to which demands are satisfied by the political system. The attitudes and norms which individuals adopt toward the political system are transmitted continuously through the socialization process. Coercion will, of course, provide some degree of compliance in a political system, but alone it can never be sufficient. The political stability of the system requires a degree of moral consensus in addition to central coercive mechanisms.

It is easy to recognize that outputs from the political system could have an effect on the level of support the system enjoys. The most important outputs are the policies adopted in reaction to the issues which have entered the system. Policies determine future decisions and structure the nature of future system outputs. The decision to build a railway across Canada required a commitment regarding how resources and support would be mobilized for decades. The reversal from a high public spending philosophy in the 1950s and 1960s to fiscal restraint in the late 1970s indicates a new general direction which may determine other policies and decisions for many years. While some outputs allocate and mobilize tangible resources, others are symbolic. Symbolic outputs would include the adoption of a national flag for Canada and a new national anthem.

The idea that legislative activity generates support for the political system is widespread. Recent empirical research moderates this assumption. Kornberg *et al.* found that 21.6 per cent of a national Canadian sample had negative feelings toward the government, 16.9 per cent were neutral, and the remaining majority were positive. The authors, however, discovered a negative correlation between the public's interactions with MPs and its support for the regime. They concluded that the public-legislators-regime support relationship may be "premature."[1]

THE LEGISLATIVE SYSTEM

Implicit in traditional writing about politics is the assumption that the legislature is the keystone of democracy. In this book, however, the legislative system is seen simply as a major subsystem of the political system. It competes with interest groups, parties, the bureaucracy, and provincial governments in the importance it plays in the political system.

The legislative system must be distinguished from the courts, administrative agencies, and other governmental activities. All may force citizens to comply with laws and regulations. Without determining here the specific activities within its sphere or the exact nature of the outputs involved, the legislative system can be said to include those structures and interrelated roles involved in the initial creation of a legislative program through to those which provide the formal proclamation of laws. The term *process* will be used to refer to the ongoing linear means of creating these products of the system. While such definitions aid in the identification of institutions and behaviours which are important in the legislative system, they do not exhaust the activities that take place in the structures. For example, surveillance of the administration and communication with the public are activities of the legislative system which are not specifically part of lawmaking.

The legislative system should be considered part of what has been called the *policymaking process*. Policies are grand and general in scope. In academic discourse they are distinguished from decisions by the requirement that they set the parameters of future decisions by developing a long-term perspective in issue areas. Of course, decisions may constitute policies, either singly or cumulatively. However, not every decision should be considered a policy. The decision to provide particular grants for youth or local initiatives is not a policy, but the decision to establish such programs is a policy decision. Policymaking is the activity of arriving at these types of significant decisions.

In the study of the legislative system the language of policymaking has some advantages over the use of the word *lawmaking*. Since all the components of a policy may be present without the formalities attached to passing a bill in parliament, the word *policy* can be used to apply to almost any government action. Such policies as bilingualism in the public service and multiculturalism required no legislation as such. Money may be appropriated for programs through votes on the estimates without the passage of a substantive bill. Many policies, such as reorganization within government departments and a vast number of regulations which are made and applied by the bureaucracy, are not even discussed in parliament.

The study of policymaking has produced several competing "theories" of how the process operates.[2] Students of policymaking use them sometimes to describe the process and sometimes to suggest how the process ought to work. Important among these are the decisionmaking theories and their attendant models: the incremental, the rational, and the mixed-scanning models. Most Canadian students of policymaking seem to agree that at least until 1968 the process at the federal level was best represented by the incremental model, which emphasizes the creation of new policy by the piecemeal modification of past activities. However, there have been recent efforts to consciously create the institutions of rational policymaking in Canada. In his early days in office, Pierre-Elliott Trudeau appeared to believe that the needs of Canadian society could best be met by the establishment of new institutions for the efficient pursuit of generalized goals. By the middle of the 1970s, he and his government reduced their public commitment to this form of policymaking and reverted to the *ad hoc* incrementalism of earlier governments. Prime Minister Joe Clark has done little to dismantle the structures associated with rational policymaking, but he and his cabinet have avoided the rhetoric of the early Trudeau years.

The contents of policies differ remarkably and various attempts have been made to categorize these political outputs and to relate them to other variables. In the classic formulation of his typology, Theodore Lowi classified public policies as distributive, redistributive, or regulatory.[3] Distributive policies are those which confer benefits individually on groups in the political system. The distributed resources are disaggregated and dispensed in small units, like patronage. Only by accumulation are such decisions considered policies. Canadian examples include the choice of post-office sites and the building of federal airports and wharves. Redistributive policies are those which require governments to indulge one major group in society and deny another. In Canada such policies are not aimed directly at individuals but at social categories or classes. Examples include policies, such as the progressive tax system, which are designed to alleviate economic inequality. Regulatory policy tends to be the residue of overt group conflict for benefits all cannot share. The conflict which characterizes this type of policymaking is based on shifting coalitions of groups. The anticombines legislation, which has been successfully opposed by large manufacturing concerns, affords a good example of Canadian regulatory policy and the conflict it inspires.

Another type of output may be called positional policy. Such policy is intended to have an impact on political actors, the structures, or the dominant values of policymaking. Its importance for the political system cannot be exaggerated. In Canada, efforts to restructure federal-provincial relations or to rewrite the British North America Act would be major positional policies, since they could be interpreted as attempts by some groups to enhance their position *vis-à-vis* others in the political system. Struggles to reform structures in the Canadian legislative system may also be viewed as positional policies and are therefore subject to the same constraints present in the development of any positional policy. Examples include the setting up of the Federal-Provincial Relations Office within the bureaucracy and the strengthening of the Auditor General's Office in 1977.

Unfortunately, the utility of the concept of policy has been diminished by analysts who use it to refer to everything governments do, intended or otherwise. The concept is also rendered vacuous when it is employed to avoid arguments that decisions are "politically motivated," "class-based," or infused with ideological bias. In this latter case the term "policy" gives the illusion of scientific respectability when the "policies" of governments are no more devoid of politics than the distribution of patronage.

The replacement of the term *lawmaking* with that of *policymaking* and the development of concepts (such as those outlined above) almost appear to relegate parliament to the status of an inconsequential actor as attention is directed toward executive-bureaucratic structures. Some Canadian writers conceive of the policymaking process almost exclusively in terms of the executive.[4] This attention to the executive-bureaucratic structures of policymaking was a legitimate reaction to the paucity of Canadian literature on policy outputs and the internal dynamics of policymaking. This approach wastes little energy with institutions which appear to have no major impact on policy, while at the same time channelling attention to structures previously ignored. The need for this type of attitude became even more acute with the advent of new policymaking structures in the Canadian political system after Trudeau became prime minister in 1968.

Executive-bureaucratic structures do not operate in a vacuum, however. Somehow demands must be channelled into the system, but policymaking models have been unable to accommodate the influence of political culture and such environmental structures as political parties and interest groups. Public policies are shaped by groups and individuals who make claims—legitimate or not—on the political system. Until the policymaking models are equipped to discuss the making of claims and the power configuration of society, students of legislative systems may be well advised to treat executive decision-making structures as offering only a partial description of policymaking. Moreover, there is very little hard evidence that changes in policymaking structures have demonstrable consequences for the actions of governments.[5]

Until recently the most obvious structure ignored by academic policymaking models has been the Canadian parliament. It is crucial, in our opinion, to reintegrate the study of policymaking and the traditional study of representative institutions. For example, it is unsatisfactory to separate all preparliamentary stages of bills and other matters from the parliamentary process. In the nineteenth century, Walter Bagehot's conception of the cabinet as the link between the executive and the legislature helped to dispel the tendency to separate the two structures. Today there is a multitude of linkages and the idea of two closed systems distorts reality. Would-be reformers of the Canadian political system have avoided any approach which would bring parliament face to face with the executive-bureaucratic structures of government. If the initiation and refining of legislation were seen as part of one analytic system, the patterns of communication and influence might be more difficult to disentangle but would accord more with reality. Figure 2-2 depicts the legislative system as a combination of preparliamentary institutions such as the prime minister, cabinet, cabinet subject-matter and legislation committees, the Privy Council Office, the drafting office of the Department of Justice and the other departments, plus the normal parliamentary institutions which include the House of Commons, the Senate, and parliamentary committees.

Figure 2-2
THE LEGISLATIVE SYSTEM IN A PARLIAMENTARY SETTING

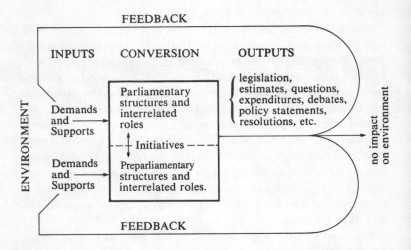

The diagram shows the legislative system in a parliamentary setting. It attempts to depict the complexity of relationships among the parts, to trace the flow of power and influence, and to indicate that legislative outputs are not the product of a simple, linear process. There are several reasons for adopting this perspective. Final approval of laws, expenditures, and taxes are the result of a tangled web of influence and power relations. Ideas are transmitted from MPs to ministers to bureaucrats and in the opposite direction. Participants throughout the system anticipate the reaction to initiatives before they are advanced. The cabinet anticipates parliamentary behaviour before it decides on a course of action; parliamentarians consider the views of ministers and the implications of behaviour for their own careers. Opposition spokesmen in parliament calculate both the advantages to be gained by adopting a line of questions or debate and the problems involved in appearing obstructive and uncooperative. Bureaucrats weigh and employ the ideas expressed in earlier political and parliamentary debates before they develop their position papers and cabinet documents.

It may be satisfying—but highly simplistic—to trace the origins of proposals to the private deliberations of bureaucrats. Ministers, ordinary members of parliament, public servants, and scientists function in a similar intellectual environment. This environment is composed of developments in public opinion, the attitudes of attentive publics, economic and international crises, and changes in science and technology. A very long time perspective indeed is needed to trace these currents in a country's history.

Individuals throughout the legislative system struggle within this environment to determine the public-policy agenda and to shape its contents. Normally the placing of new ideas on this agenda is a long process: the incubation may occur in any organization or combination of institutions. An understanding of the collective culture and behaviour of all these individuals is therefore crucial to an appreciation of the role politicians play in policy formulation.

The fusion of the legislative and the executive branches of government distinguishes this model from that developed for the investigation of legislative behaviour in the American Congress. Unfortunately, much of the investigation of politicians' behaviour and government output in Canada has been premised on the assumption of a division between the executive and legislature. Researchers concentrate on cabinet and the bureaucracy or on parliament, rarely both. As we shall see, however, legislation is not drafted in parliament and government policies are rarely determined on the floor of the House of Commons. A series of political and bureaucratic forces are brought to bear on pieces of legislation, the legislative program as a whole, and the schedule for their introduction in the House long before bills are actually introduced. On the other hand politicians, employing the rights and privileges of parliament, are often able to delay, amend, and even jettison legislative proposals which originate with cabinet and the public service. The nebulous relation between the preparliamentary and the parliamentary structures may be depicted by the word *initiatives*. Such initiatives may take the form of bills introduced by the government or resolutions sent from parliament to the executive, as well as host of other legal relationships and influence possibilities. The results of these activities (regardless of their origin) are processed through parliament.

Legislation is perhaps the most obvious output of the system. While an act of parliament cannot always be distinguished analytically from the general directive of an administrative agency or the decision of a court, it is usually more general and more future oriented than other modes of authoritative decisionmaking. Delegated legislation — through which the executive exercises statutory authority to formulate regulations — is also an output of the legislative system. Other outputs include expenditure approvals, resolutions, and symbolic action such as questions and debates.

Outputs from the legislative system may or may not have an effect on the environment. Those outputs that do penetrate into the environment help to restructure the schedule of demands and supports for the political system by way of a feedback loop. And, as much as the political system affects the policies which are developed, the content of the outputs helps to structure the nature of the system itself.

While the legislative-system approach orients investigations largely in parliamentary terms, not all the tensions outlined in Chapter 1 deal exclusively with parliament. In fact, even those which appear to originate in the legislature often deal with relationships between the legislature and other elements in the political system. We therefore contend that the resolution of difficulties cannot be satisfactorily accomplished by a reform of isolated structures. The reform of parliament with little regard for other parts of the system will raise problems even more enigmatic and complex than those which already exist.

FUNCTIONS OF THE LEGISLATIVE SYSTEM

The use of the language of systems analysis in the examination of politics could lead to the conclusion that the legislative system can be understood almost entirely by an appreciation of the external pressures placed on it and by an examination of system outputs. But, from the point of view of reform, it is inadequate to conceive of the legislature simply as a mechanism which reacts to environmental influences. The system perspective implies effectiveness and persistence, yet in some societies the legislative system may be ineffective and fail to survive. On the other hand, some social scientists maintain that the study of legislatures is primarily the study of the behaviour of legislators.[6] This approach concentrates analysis on individual behaviour and gives only minimal consideration to the environment. Neither perspective considers in precise terms the consequences of activity in the legislative system for the political system as a whole.

To organize the discussion of this latter dimension we will employ the *function* and suggest several functions that may be performed by the legislative system. In social science the term *function* has a variety of meanings. It is used here simply to denote the impact which activity in the legislative system may have for the political system. The Canadian legislative system does not differ dramatically from those of other countries. Among the functions attributed to them in the standard literature have been the following: lawmaking, surveillance, representation, and electoral conversion. Political sociologists have added to this list: recruitment, socialization, and training; conflict management; integration; and legitimation.[7] It must be stressed that the legislative system does not enjoy a monopoly on the performance of these functions. Not all those who hold important political offices are recruited through the legislative system, nor does the creation of legislation exhaust all lawmaking. In some countries legislatures are constitutional decorations, legislation is not the major expression of lawmaking, and recruitment and socialization are carried on by the military and police forces.

The legislative system in Canada performs all of the above functions to some degree, but it is most often associated with the function of lawmaking. The initiation of bills is practically monopolized by the cabinet and structures in the preparliamentary part of the legislative system; parliamentary initiatives normally require cabinet approval or acquiescence. Of course, the formal processing of government-initiated legislation is accomplished in the House of Commons and Senate. Only by adopting a comprehensive legislative system approach can sense be made of the interrelationships required to perform the lawmaking function. Moreover, an adequate performance of the lawmaking function in both parts of the system is necessary for the successful accomplishment of other societal requirements, such as integration and conflict management.[8]

In the study of legislative institutions the term *surveillance* refers to the array of activities undertaken by the legislature in an attempt to supervise and control the executive. The most important of these activities is the examination of the executive's budgetary requirements, but the concept may also be employed to describe such procedures as the supervision of delegated legislation, Oral Question Period, and the budget debate. When the Canadian parliament reviews the report of the auditor general, it is also performing a surveillance function.

The legislative system performs an important representation function. Few citizens are in close and continuous contact with the political system through their daily lives. Elections are infrequent and individuals seldom choose to participate actively in political parties. The legislative system may provide an access point for individuals whose relationship to the political system would otherwise be tenuous and spasmodic. The member of parliament is given opportunities to publicly articulate the interests and views of constituents. Cynics may call some of this activity simply "errand running," but many legislators see this representation function as the central aspect of their role as parliamentarians. It is true, however, that intermediary groups are providing much of the effective representation of national interests. Many political interests are sponsored by interest groups which interact with the executive-bureaucratic structures rather then the legislature. The ability of the legislative system to perform an effective representation function ought to be reassessed in the light of this fact.

In some forms of government the electorate's choice is automatically translated into the choice of a government. In the parliamentary form the legislature is involved in an electoral conversion function. This occurs when the legislature has an impact on converting the general election results into general decisions about the composition of cabinets. On occasion, parliamentary parties may have a precise role in the selection and dismissal of governments. Moreover, in Canada the lack of majority-party control in the House of Commons and the practical inability to form coalition governments have often forced political leaders to adopt stopgap solutions to essential political problems. This situation may be dysfunctional for the Canadian political system and may eventually require a reassessment of the electoral laws and perhaps the development of new norms about cabinet composition.

Parliament performs an important activity when it recruits members for other prestigious positions in the political system. The effective performance of this function and the related activities of training and socialization are usually aided in other legislatures by a period of apprenticeship and the existence of regular pathways to other roles. Unfortunately, the turnover rate of the Canadian House of Commons hovers around 40 per cent, so few individuals have an opportunity to obtain wide experience. Parliament has not always been the recruiting ground for prime ministers, cabinet members, or party leaders. Both Pierre Trudeau and Robert Stanfield were recruited with almost no experience in the Canadian legislative system. Stanfield walked into the House of Commons as Leader of the Opposition on his first day on Parliament Hill; Trudeau, after three years as an MP, became prime minister because of his victory at a Liberal party convention. Joe Clark had only three years of parliamentary experience before he was chosen leader of the Progressive Conservative party in 1976.

When the activities of the legislative system produce acquiescence by members of the political system in the moral right of the government to rule, political sociologists say that the legislative system is performing a legitimation function. This function is performed in a manifest manner when the legislature meets to debate and vote on legislative proposals. Unless we appreciate the importance of this function, it is difficult to understand the often lengthy debates, votes, and rituals that are brought to bear on initiatives which have been taken elsewhere. In crisis situations such as the FLQ affair of 1970 or disasters such as Hurricane Hazel, the *Arrow* oil pollution, or Manitoba floods, the legislature debated the events only after executive action had been taken. But in each case parliament legitimated the government's behaviour. The legislature also legitimates government decisions in a latent manner. When the legislature meets ostensibly to perform lawmaking functions the meeting itself bestows a degree of legitimacy on government.

When the legitimation function is successfully performed, the legislature is able to generate support for itself and transfer support to other parts of the political system. These relationships are described as feedback in our model of the legislative system discussed on page 22. The support accorded to the legislative system may be either specific or diffuse. Specific support is the product of favourable attitudes toward those outputs which are responses to specific demands. Diffuse support is a more general and continuous phenomenon best described as a reservoir of good will engendered by the past performance of the system.

To some extent the legislature embodies or symbolizes the prevailing values in society about how the government should operate. Some of its support comes through the process of political socialization by which attachments are transferred to it from other figures such as the queen, the governor general, and the prime minister. There is also evidence that the legislature may be a direct "contact point" between the child and the political system.[9] However, rather than viewing the legislature solely as a recipient of support, we believe that it may be able to generate diffuse support for other parts of the political system.[10] This support occurs when the legislature enhances the legitimacy of the government, the military, the courts, or the bureaucracy. Of course, it should be added that a legislature can detract from legitimacy as well as contribute to it. To perform the legitimation function well, a legislature must command considerable support itself. It is possible that a legislature will even embark on a public-relations campaign, as did the *Bundestag* in modern West Germany. The mere existence of the Canadian parliament is not enough to secure a role for it in generating or transmitting support. Parliament must ensure that the legitimation function is performed and act to protect its own position in the legislative system.

NOTES

1. Allan Kornberg, Harold D. Clarke, and Lawrence LeDuc, "Some Correlates of Regime Support in Canada," *British Journal of Political Science,* 8 (April 1978), pp. 199-216.
2. For a summary discussion of the strengths and deficiencies of these "theories" see Peter Aucoin, "Public Policy Theory and Analysis," in G. B. Doern and P. Aucoin (ed.), *Public Policy in Canada* (Toronto: Macmillan of Canada, 1979), pp. 4-12.
3. Theodore Lowi, "American Business, Public Policies, Case Studies, and Political Theory," *World Politics,* XVI (July 1964), pp. 677-715.
4. See, for example, Doern and Aucoin (ed.), *The Structures of Policymaking* (Toronto: Macmillan of Canada, 1971). These authors maintain that "an understanding of how policy is made in the Canadian political system requires that the focus of attention be placed on the executive-bureaucratic arena" (p. 267).
5. See the comments of Richard Simeon, "Studying Public Policy," *Canadian Journal of Political Science,* IX (December 1976), pp. 548-80.
6. The amount of literature in this field can only be described as vast. The seminal work on American legislatures is John Wahlke *et al., The Legislative System* (New York: John Wiley and Sons, 1962). On Canada, see Allan Kornberg, *Canadian Legislative Behaviour: A Study of the 25th Parliament* (New York: Holt, Rinehart and Winston, 1967).

7. Robert A. Packenham, "Legislatures and Political Development," in Allan Kornberg and Lloyd D. Musolf (ed.), *Legislatures in Developmental Perspective* (Durham, N.C.: Duke University Press, 1970), pp. 521-82, and John D. Lees and Malcolm Shaw, *Committees in Legislatures: A Comparative Analysis* (Durham: Duke University Press, 1979); Murray Edelman, *The Symbolic Uses of Politics* (Urbana: University of Illinois Press, 1964).

8. Two authors advise that the legislative system may collapse if the functions of integration and conflict management are not performed. See Malcolm Jewell and Samuel Patterson, *The Legislative System of the United States,* 3rd ed. (New York: Random House, 1978).

9. David Easton and Jack Dennis, for example, report that near the end of elementary school, children "increasingly tend to see government with Congress at its centre [and] law as its most visible produce." *Children in the Political System: Origins of Political Legitimacy* (New York: McGraw-Hill, 1969), p. 120. A collection of essays which address this issue in the Canadian context may be found in Jon Pammett and Michael Whittington (ed.), *Foundations of Political Culture* (Toronto: Macmillan of Canada, 1976).

10. Considerable support exists for this position in the literature of comparative legislatures. See for example, Gerhard Loewenberg, "The Influence of Parliamentary Behaviour on Regime Stability: Some Conceptual Clarifications," *Comparative Politics,* 3 (1971), pp. 177-200; Paul R. Abramson and Ronald Inglehart, "The Development of Systemic Support in Four Western Democracies," *Comparative Political Studies,* 2 (1970), pp. 419-42; and S. C. Patterson *et al., Representatives and Represented: Bases of Public Support for the American Legislatures* (New York: John Wiley and Sons, 1975).

3.   External Influences:
             The Environment
             and Structures

The legislative system exists in a complex and changing environment, but some important regularities help to maintain continuity. As Chapter 2 has shown, political scientists have attempted to organize their discussion of the environment by using broad concepts like demands and supports. The viability of the system is maintained when it reacts to demands in such a manner as to secure support. But these general ideas do not exhaust our appreciation of the environment or its influences. The environment may also be considered in terms of attitudes toward the legislative system, in terms of social and economic resources, and in terms of the issues which dominate political discourse. Our discussion begins with an elaboration of these factors in the Canadian context and then concentrates on structures in the environment, particularly parties and interest groups. While these institutions stand outside the legislative system, they act as intermediaries conveying both demands and supports. Parties and interest groups manifest conflict over issue positions and their continual activity draws together the environment and the legislative system.

POLITICAL CULTURE

The attitudinal dimension of the environment is referred to as political culture. It consists of general public orientations toward the political system and toward government-related activities in the system. The models of governing that Canada inherited from the United States and Britain have fostered certain types of attitudes and behaviour and discouraged others. The most important of these are attitudes toward political participation and governmental authority.

Although the data are limited, they indicate that Canadians participate very readily in electoral politics.[1] About 75 to 80 per cent of eligible Canadians vote regularly in federal elections. By comparison with many countries, therefore, Canada may be considered to have a "participant" political culture. But the act of voting does not necessarily entail more than passive contact with the political system. Many Canadian citizens who vote regularly take little interest in politics and have a low estimation of their ability to influence political authorities.[2]

William Mishler has even concluded that Canada conforms "more closely to the elitist rather than the classical or representative model of democracy."[3] He estimates that less than one-third of the public — and perhaps as few as 10 to 15 per cent — have ever participated in more demanding political activities. Only 4 to 5 per cent of the Canadian electorate participate continuously in political parties or hold elected public office. These individuals usually possess more social, economic, and political resources than individuals who participate only passively in the system.

Vested authority and the laws have rarely been questioned in Canadian history.[4] Authority patterns in Canada seem to exhibit a strong element of deference toward political elites. Federal politicians and administrators usually command respect; enforcement agencies (such as the RCMP and the military) have not been viewed as symbols of oppression as they have in some countries. Even when it was alleged that some members of the RCMP security service had been engaged in unlawful activities in Quebec (including barn burning!), most Canadians were steadfast in their support for the force.

The Task Force on Government Information found that after indexing responses to two questions on faith in the federal government, only 19 per cent of respondents expressed no confidence on both counts.[5] When asked how often one can trust the government to do what is right, 58 per cent of respondents in both the 1965 and 1968 election studies said "always" or "most of the time."[6] In the 1974 election study the mean score for "Canada" on a thermometer scale was 84, "indicating a very warm feeling."[7] When it came to estimating personal efficacy, only about 25 per cent of Canadians had a low estimation of their capacity to influence governmental authorities.[8] In English Canada, deferential attitudes have been traced to the early impact of the United Empire Loyalists; in French Canada, to the strength of traditional elites and the lack of a tradition of democratic institutions on the part of the mass public. Robert Presthus has examined the literature and the data on authority patterns in Canada and adds that deferential attitudes may also result from a combination of monarchical rule, elitist education, pervasive class distinctions, and highly bureaucratized institutions.[9]

The combination of "passive" participation and deference to authority may be the cornerstone of the attitudes which underlie the viability of the Canadian political system and one reason that strong commitment to coherent ideology is not reflected in the mainstream of political life. In fact, with the exception of nationalism issues, intense feeling is rarely found. One explanation for the lack of competing ideologies is the presence of a strong liberal philosophy in English Canada and an absolutist tradition in French Canada.[10] The geographic proximity to the United States and the economic dependence on its markets provided an impetus for Confederation; since then, Canadians have only periodically had an eruption of nationalist fervour. However, nationalism has been a constant feature of Quebec politics during the twentieth century. The new nationalism of the Parti Québécois is based more on the urban, educated secular classes of society than earlier forms, but its importance in political dialogue resembles earlier types.

Canadian political culture is not homogeneous and several lines of cleavage occasionally find political expression. Of particular importance are the sometimes hostile relations which prevail between Canada's two charter groups, the French and the English. To some extent, ethnic and linguistic divisions have been reinforced by federal arrangements which were designed in part to guarantee the persistence of cultural diversity. Immigration policy tended to further reinforce ethnic differences because Canada required large numbers of European immigrants, first to initiate frontier life and later to develop an industrial base.

Regional cleavages have also been prominent in Canadian history. Differences in economic status have combined with regional loyalties to produce a society of rich and poor provinces divided over the type and extent of central-government interference required in the economy.[11] Recent findings indicate significant regional differences in levels of trust, efficacy, and involvement that suggest the existence of regional political cultures.[12] These cleavages seem to have diminished prospects for class conflict in Canada, but a possibility remains that the Canadian political culture will eventually be strongly affected by the process of industrialization.[13]

The cohesion found in the Canadian political culture has been strong enough to permit division and conflict without the eruption of widespread and constant violence. The peaceable-kingdom concept of

Canada is an inaccurate one, but what violence does exist is sporadic and not a prominent feature of enduring political divisions.[14] This lack of violence has meant that while societal cleavages constantly threaten the country, politicians can rely on deep-seated attitudes to maintain the independence and authority of the legislative system. Canadian modes of participation and attitudes toward authority have generated at least enough support to permit politicians to make piecemeal adjustments in public policy in response to specific demands.

SOCIAL AND ECONOMIC DETERMINANTS

When the environment is viewed primarily in terms of political culture, it is difficult to assess the environment's impact on the legislative system. In an attempt to resolve this problem, some policy analysts have developed concepts and statistics to show the relations between the socioeconomic context of a nation and its policy output. This methodology requires the use of quantifiable variables such as percapita income, age distribution of the population, and level of industrialization as ''environmental'' indicators. For the most part ''policy output'' is defined very generally as whatever the government does: many of the data used are outputs from the legislative system, namely legislation. By finding indicators for each of these types of variables and by systematically examining relationships, researchers have isolated those variables which have a significant, independent effect on policy output.

In such studies the impact of political variables (such as legislative apportionment and type of party system) on public policy is usually found to be insignificant. Instead, the system's social and economic characteristics are found to have the greatest impact on policy output. At the extreme, some researchers, interested in American state politics, claim that environmental factors can account for most changes in public policy and that politicians and legislatures have very little, if any, effect on the outputs of the political system.[15] In Canada the analyses of public policy have also yielded unflattering results for the importance of political variables. A comprehensive study of 27 Canadian parliaments has indicated that there is a strong direct link between environmental factors and public policy. But characteristics of the Canadian legislative elite and aspects of political change (political variables) have little independent relation to policy output.[16]

Despite its appeal, this approach has not provided a satisfactory answer to some important questions about the relationships among environmental factors, the legislative system, and policy outputs. The most significant point is that, even if the pattern of output is accurately modelled, the procedure offers no satisfactory explanation of *how* these patterns are achieved or *how* conversions are accomplished. While environmental factors are obviously significant for public policy, it is difficult to find, quantify, and (especially) weight some environmental variables. Similarly, the political variables chosen do not always seem appropriate. None of these models provide for the dynamism found in politics and not all take into consideration the impact of the legislative system on particular types of policies. Furthermore, even among technicians in this field there is agreement that much of the variance remains to be accounted for statistically. It is this unexplained variance which is most important to political scientists. Even if policy analysts were to claim that Canada's unemployment-insurance policies are environmentally determined (e.g., the level of GNP indicates that the country will have such a policy), its details may not be — and these details may alter attitudes toward all of the unemployment policy, and possibly aid in producing a new one. Gross-data analysis does not (and without extensive refinement cannot) account for the choices made among policies, amendments to legislation, or the timing of legislative outputs. And these are policymaking and legislative roles which politicians consider important and which students of legislatures cannot ignore.

POLITICAL ISSUES

The environment, defined either as political culture or as the social and economic context of society, places constraints on public policymaking and hence on the substantive outputs of the legislative system. Political authorities cannot dispose of resources they do not have, nor can they afford to consistently violate patterns of behaviour which are valued by the mass public. When major problems are confronted, environmental factors limit the number of policy alternatives available to politicians. Ideally, it is the politician's role to transform the demands which emerge from the environment into debatable issues, to outline the alternatives, and to endorse a course of action. In this way, politicians can claim a unique role in the political system.

Recent Canadian examples illustrate the emergence of issues from the environment. The ethnic-linguistic cleavage has produced questions such as whether or not the province of Quebec should be allowed to separate and the degree to which the federal public service and other federal bodies should consist of bilingual personnel. Emerging from the regional cleavages have been issues such as unemployment, agricultural subsidies, differential tariffs, and the distribution of oil revenues. Cleavages are not always the source of problems, but they usually aggravate them. The Roman Catholic–Protestant cleavage has complicated the abortion issue in Canada and since 1969 federal politicians have been reluctant to permit an open debate in parliament.

While such issues create tensions in political parties and give rise to demands on the legislative system, it is not entirely clear how parliamentarians perceive and interpret these issues. In *Political Choice in Canada*, Harold Clarke and his colleagues have shown how difficult it is to relate issues to voting behaviour. They argue persuasively that if an issue is to have important effects it must be salient, linked to a party or parties, and based on opinion skewed in a single direction so that there is a firm consensus on an issue's resolution. On examination of four issues — foreign investment, bilingualism, majority government, and inflation — the authors found that none met all three tests.[17] Even when an issue was highly visible in the media it did not necessarily have an overall effect on the results of the 1974 General Election.

Even if political parties were committed to faithfully reflecting the preferences of citizens, the results of elections constitute a most uncertain guide to action. Moreover, politicians are not always appreciative of explicit direction. To establish the actual empirical link between the public's perception of issues and how politicians behave is tortuous. On the highly salient issue of capital punishment, for example, only the NDP took a party position. For the most part, party lines dissolved both in parliament and in the country.[18] But it is not always possible for governments to avoid adopting an explicit stand on issues. Aggregating institutions such as interest groups and political parties shape alternatives and demand responses to contemporary issues. The legislative system responds by determining the agenda for the decision or nondecision about these concerns.

INTEREST GROUPS

Implicit in the argument that the environment is the source of issues for the legislative system is the idea that means exist to convey these issues in the form of demands to political authorities in the system. Those structures which exist to transmit these inputs must be compatible with the political culture. In Canada, interest groups generally meet this requirement. They are successful in marshalling support for issues and providing ideas for public policy without displacing the decisionmakers themselves. Their activities assist the legislative system to perform the multitude of functions ascribed to it. It has even been suggested that the Canadian political culture contains an organic view of society which nurtures the corporatist idea that most important interactions in the political system ought to transpire between major social groupings.[19]

Beyond the fact that interest-group activity is an accepted part of the political system, three basic facts about group life in Canada need to be mentioned. First, there are many different types of interest groups with different resources, tactics, and goals. They range from promotional groups such as the Canadian Temperance Society through to self-interested groups such as the Canadian Manufacturers' Association; from groups active in the legislative system, such as the Canadian Labour Congress, through to those like the Canadian Institute of Nursing whose connection with the legislative system is, at most, transient. The differences among interest groups have repercussions in the political system primarily because they seem to have a strong influence on the success or failure of group objectives. The report of the Royal Commission on Corporate Concentration summed up these inequalities: "There is little doubt that the representatives of major corporations can and do have greater access to both politicians and public servants than do other individuals through trade associations, their own professional representatives and perhaps most effectively, private conversations between corporate officers and those involved in the policymaking and legislative process."[20]

The second general point is that the interaction between interest-group leaders (and lobbyists), bureaucrats, and politicians is permeated by the ethos of mutual accommodation. This means that the interaction involving interest groups in the political system is characterized by cooperation in which each party is considered by the others to have a legitimate share in the making of public policy. The accommodation depends upon all parties receiving enough satisfaction that continued interaction is deemed worthwhile. Nowhere is the phenomenon of mutual accommodation more apparent than in clientele relations established between interest groups and government departments. Examples have included the close affinity developed between the Canadian Federation of Mayors and Municipalities and the Ministry of Housing and Urban Affairs, and between the Canadian Legion and the Department of Veterans' Affairs.

Thirdly, the legislative system is not the only focus on interest-group activity. Interest groups often devote a great deal of time to decisions of an administrative nature. It is sometimes more important and often easier to affect the substance of a policy at the earliest stages of policy formulation or at the stage of its implementation rather than in the legislative system. This is one reason for the frequent criticism that interest-group leaders bypass parliament in their attempts to influence policy.

When groups do attempt to influence decisions in the legislative system, access to decisionmakers at important stages becomes a necessary condition of success. The existence of an access point is not a guarantee of influence, but without access almost nothing else is possible. Of equal importance is the fact that access is heavily influenced by the institutional and procedural structure of the legislative system. Initially, influence may depend on the extent to which groups are able to participate in the politics of mutual accommodation. Beyond this, groups must succeed in adapting to the legislative system and using the access points provided.

Successful access to bureaucrats and politicians hinges in part on the type of group, its status, and its organizational resources (such as membership size, finances, and the quality of its personnel). According to Robert Presthus, religious, educational, and business groups seek access primarily through the cabinet, welfare groups through the bureaucracy, and labour through the legislature.[21] Given their styles and resources, groups are continually attracted to particular parts of the legislative system. This tendency is accentuated by the fact that certain policies receive consideration primarily in one arena. In the early 1970s, groups interested in obtaining a continuation of Local Initiatives Projects, for example, concentrated more attention on the preparliamentary part of the legislative system. Parliament, on the other hand, had more attraction for those groups interested in pursuing such topics as the return of capital punishment and the reform of abortion laws.

There are a limited number of access points, so few groups can afford to continually ignore any possibilities for influence. Only the most marginal and violent of groups fail to adapt to the access points available in the legislative system. Eventually, interest groups employ every tactic and approach every available target of influence. Among the tactics used are personal representations to members of the legislative system, public-relations activities, the enlisting of membership for mail campaigns, and the presenting of briefs which contain expert opinions and information. The stress on particular tactics depends largely on the group's resources and the types of issues involved. As a tactic, for example, personal representation or lobbying is most often employed by business groups in Canada, while enlisting membership support is a tactic employed by professional groups such as the Canadian Medical Association.

In the preparliamentary stages of the legislative system the norms of secrecy influence the style and content of interactions.[22] Even when a policy has been agreed on, groups are not always made aware of the decision or the policy details. Ali ministers may be vaguely aware of an interest group's demand, but only the minister responsible and perhaps one or two with strong regional or constituency interests will even read (or have their officials read) the letters and briefs which are sent by interest groups. In principle, interest-group representatives are not informed of the content of cabinet decisions or given the text of a bill before it is introduced in the House of Commons. However, in the preparliamentary stages of the process, cabinet takes the position that the minister responsible for a new policy should give an audience to interested parties. Groups may be requested to provide information or advice on the subject area without being advised of the exact nature of the government's intentions. Such an atmosphere allows ministers and senior public servants to achieve some independence from interest groups and permits the cabinet to act as a collective decisionmaking body.

These characteristics of the legislative system stifle access, but others tend to break down this atmosphere. Public servants, among others, cannot afford to alienate interest groups on whom they depend for some of the expert opinions they provide their ministers. Also, because legislation (as we will discuss more fully) is often returned to departments for reconsideration, the process is opened up: consultation must resume and groups which wish to block proposals may have further opportunities to lobby bureaucrats. Groups which lobbied against the government's initial proposals for a new tax system in the late 1960s were given — and took — every opportunity afforded in the legislative system to raise objections. Interest groups are not always concerned with blocking proposals, but the complexities of the legislative system and the rough landscape of Canadian politics give some indication of why it is generally considered easier to block or slow down proposals than to initiate them. In the case of competition legislation, Warren Allmand — a former minister of Consumer and Corporate Affairs — complained that, ''In their lobbying efforts, I think the powerful opponents have taken advantage of the complexity of the economic issues underlying effective competition legislation and, by clouding the real issues, by oversimplifying and sometimes intentionally distorting them they have managed on occasion to confuse and sidetrack the public understanding of this vital area of public policy.''[23]

By the time it enters the parliamentary part of the system, legislation has usually undergone a significant input from interest groups. The views of most groups have been given a hearing. At this stage policy is well formed, but it is not irreversible. Interest groups which have been unable to secure access to the cabinet or the bureaucracy, or have been dissatisfied with the results of consultation, often find that more than one opportunity exists to influence the passage of legislation in parliament. Caucus, the meeting of a party's MPs, usually affords the first opportunity. Before a bill is introduced in the House, an outline of the new policy direction is given to the government caucus. At the weekly meetings which follow, caucus members are given opportunities to express the sentiments and grievances of interest groups. Even when the bill has been introduced for first reading in the House, caucus continues to debate the bill and sometimes prevents the moving of second reading.

When bills are before the House, a multitude of devices exist for retarding their process. Many of these procedures are too complicated for the public to gain much of an appreciation of what has actually transpired in parliament. Moreover, the passage of legislation is often a lengthy process and only the most devoted parliament watcher can follow the machinations of politicians as they manoeuvre to escape the wrath of major interest groups. The controversial Drug Bill was first introduced in the House in 1962 but did not secure passage until 1968. By that time its contents were well known, two governments had been in power, and interest groups had been given extensive opportunities to renew lobbying and to conduct public-relations campaigns. In the case of the latest comprehensive tax bill, the process began with Mr. Diefenbaker's decision to set up the Carter Commission in 1962; the bill did not receive final approval until 1972. The last-minute amendment which favoured the cooperatives was the direct result of interest-group pressure combined with provincial support, backbench approval, and the government's desire either to prevent a showdown or to be conciliatory in order to get the bill through the committee stage. Similarly, the mining industry obtained provincial cooperation in its successful campaign for a reintroduction of favourable tax arrangements which had been opposed by the Carter Commission.[24] Interest groups are given added opportunities for access when the government prolongs the process by introducing legislation, like the Competition Act of 1972, for the prime purpose of having its contents subjected to interest-group criticism. This tactic sometimes amounts to little more than a manipulation of the legislative system to help solve policy difficulties in the governing party.

In the parliamentary part of the system, interest groups may lobby members of parliament individually or they may seek to publicize their views before the committee system of the House of Commons. In either case, the efforts often appear hopeless. On their own, individual members are usually of little consequence unless they command special knowledge or are in a tense minority government situation. Nevertheless, interest-group leaders continue to discuss policy issues with members of parliament. One of the main reasons is that cabinet members are, to a large degree, recruited from the ranks of the government backbench and neither they nor opposition members can be made to feel isolated or ignored. Both groups have significant potential influence. Members may also become good public-relations agents for various interests.

Although most members do not acknowledge much interest-group influence in their own elections, there are strong possibilities for group activity in those constituencies where group interests are concentrated. But the major reason for constant pressure on the backbench may be the belief that a changed opinion there may force an alteration in cabinet's position. Generally, cabinet opinion prevails when the caucus, the provinces, or the relevant interest groups can be attracted to cabinet's side. Cabinet has the least chance of imposing its views when all three of these elements resist its direction. Major interest groups will therefore attempt to affect a coalition of at least some antigovernment forces, the backbench included, in cases where cabinet and interest-group opinion diverge. In minority situations, opposition attitudes become another element which weighs heavily in the equation and draws attention from interest groups.

Legislators seem to regard the committee system as the most important forum of interest-group influence in parliament.[25] It is attractive from the interest-group point of view because individuals with different perspectives are assembled for the primary purpose of listening to and commenting on interest-group arguments. Committee meetings afford an opportunity to present briefs to the government and to obtain at least limited publicity for interest-group endeavours.

It is clear, however, that lobbying both the individual legislator and the committee system represents long-term interest-group investment. In majority governments and even in minority situations, individual legislators are unable to dramatically alter the course of public policy. Throughout the legislative system, responsibility and control of legislators rests in the hands of the government. The Canadian parliament, as we have already suggested, does not initiate laws, it passes them. Policies, bills, and expenditures are at least partially woven together and it is difficult for cabinet to permit adjustment of single policies or bills without destroying the delicate compromises that have been made in the whole legislative program. In other words, legislators and committees rarely act on policies soon enough to make a substantial impact.

The mutual accommodation which prevails between interest groups and actors in the political system can now be further elaborated. Interest groups offer to political actors invaluable information about the state of the political environment. They also make it possible for politicians and bureaucrats to understand the environment by communicating consolidated attitudes. Information costs for the system are thus diminished. In recent years the Department of Agriculture, for example, has been encouraging farmers to unite under the umbrella of one organization primarily for this purpose. Interest groups provide a reservoir of expert skills which can be made available to government. Of some importance also is the actual personnel which groups provide to the legislative system, usually to the bureaucracy but sometimes to parliament and the cabinet.

Participation in the legislative system provides interest groups with two major advantages. First, it provides several discrete points of access to one part of the policymaking process, a benefit which enables interest-group leaders to claim that they are succeeding in pressing for their groups' interests. Not only is this a necessary consideration for attaining goals, but interaction within the system also serves as a bulwark against threats to the organization. When interest groups use points of access, they can rely on established patterns of consultation, the frequent support of public servants, and a reasonable degree of privacy in their interactions. On occasion these patterns shift. Until 1973 the federal government's relations with the oil industry were extensive and cordial. Consultation with the oil industry and the Canadian Petroleum Association was of paramount importance. Swift and unilateral government action during the energy crisis signalled a change in relations. According to Glyn Berry, the oil industry "seems to have reluctantly accepted the greater role that government will play in its affairs. It will now seek to ensure that the intervention will be as consultative and non-coercive as possible."[26]

The second major benefit is perhaps more abstract. Interest groups are often able to obtain legitimacy by their interactions within the legislative system.[27] Legitimacy may be thought of as the quality of moral acceptability which is believed to accompany political action. To be able to influence the course of policy formation and application, interest groups must have legitimate claims to make and be considered legitimate vehicles for the expression of such claims. Interaction within the legislative system permits interest groups to obtain a high degree of legitimacy. Thus, by hearing annual representations and considering the briefs from such large interest groups as the Canadian Labour Congress and the Canadian Chamber of Commerce, cabinet is able to accord some degree of legitimacy to their goals and methods of attaining them. However, legitimacy is also a quality traceable to societal standards. It is possible for the cabinet, the bureaucracy, or the legislature to confer legitimacy on the activities of groups only if the goals and tactics of the group are compatible with standards present in Canadian political culture. Thus, rival groups compete for recognition to enhance their legitimacy, but the nature of some groups, such as the Front de Libération du Québec, makes their recognition in the legislative system highly unlikely.

The general problems in the legislative system, discussed in Chapter 1, are aggravated by certain aspects of interest-group activity. Representation—and hence participation in the Canadian legislative system—is supposed to be achieved through the electoral process which is founded on a somewhat ambivalent application of the one-man, one-vote principle.[28] However, this form of representation, which is based on the views of individual constituents, has been replaced to some degree by what can be called *functional representa-*

tion. According to this perspective, interest groups constitute a major legitimate form of political representation. It is argued, implicitly, that groups are perhaps the most important interests deserving of representation and that the constituency form of representation is unable to meet the demands of groups in the political system. Furthermore, the requirements of a modern welfare state make the representation of interest groups a necessary adjunct to government activity. Without the eventual cooperation of doctors, for example, the Canadian government would probably have failed in imposing medicare. In Canada, the increasingly high ratio of government expenditure to GNP may make cooperation an even more common requirement in expensive social-policy fields.

The advocacy of functional representation depends on an exalted view of the role groups ought to play in the formation of public policy. The proliferation of advisory councils attached to government departments, such as the National Welfare Council, is one indication of the appeal of this type of representation. The reluctance of governments to insist on setting standards for professions such as medicine and law suggests that certain groups enjoy an exalted status in the political system. The implications for democratic accountability are clear. The drainage of public authority to interest groups, which is implied in this notion of representation, erodes political responsibility in a representative democracy.

It may be that members of parliament were never able to represent constituents in anything but the Burkean fashion with its emphasis on independent judgment. But if representation is also to mean the offering of broad policy guidelines, then even here interest groups, or advisory committees attached to departments, are presently offering a significant proportion of the information and the arguments. As long as arrangements exist to accommodate such policy advice from interest groups, then there is strong justification for demanding that elected representatives be given more opportunities to affect the content of public policy.

It has already been mentioned that groups differ substantially in their style, tactics, and resources. Groups with large operating budgets and a prestigious membership, for example, seem to possess a greater means of achieving and maintaining access in most situations. No simple correlation exists between resources and success, but most observers have found at least some relationship. However, structure and resources are not the only conditions of effective access. As shown above, interest groups must also succeed in identifying their own goals with dominant values in the political culture. In Canada, organized labour has not had the success in this regard which it seems to have achieved in Britain and the United States. To some degree its goals stand outside the dominant belief system, a situation reinforced by the existence of close relations between labour and the NDP which has been unable to achieve power at the federal level.[29] In Canada, labour has not constituted the electoral power it has in Britain, nor has it been identified with one of the larger parties.

Unlike other groups which suffer a lack of legitimacy, labour organizations have tried to adjust to the accepted norms of interaction in the legislative system. On the other hand, some organizations have employed tactics which violate accepted norms. For example, on occasion governments have cancelled projects for groups which publicly demonstrated in an effort to have their grants extended. The norms of mutual accommodation exclude the type of ultimatum conveyed by demonstrations. In Canada the standard practice is negotiation of individual group claims, a rule which is violated at a group's peril. Thus, the legislative system demonstrates a certain rigidity in relations with interest groups.[30]

The most obvious example of this rigidity can be found in the lack of response to the unorganized. Along with other largely unorganized interests in society, consumers and pensioners do not possess the resources to sustain mass organization. Decisions such as those to lower the drinking age or to raise annual income supplements for the elderly are often made in the absence of pressure from those directly affected. So complete is the spirit of accommodation and consultation among organized groups that the unorganized are placed at an overwhelming disadvantage. The institutions of the legislature system should be developed to respond to this challenge.

POLITICAL PARTIES

The difficulties of group politics may be resolved by the activities of political parties. While interest groups enjoy pervasive influence, they are usually unable to overcome their narrow interests or to articulate all the demands of a society. According to classical democratic theory, political parties, by their role in elections, are supposed to respond to such deficiencies in the articulation and aggregation of societal demands.[31] In Canada, however, political parties have achieved only partial success in ameliorating the problems created by our system of interest-group politics.[32]

Political parties are organized to contest elections for the attainment of political office and the realization of generalized goals. Such purposes require a specificity of roles and structures. In Canada the activities of all four political parties which contest federal elections are based on a relatively small membership core. The Liberal, Progressive Conservative, and Social Credit parties rely on the direct participation of committed party workers. The New Democratic party similarly depends on a membership core, although it can claim the indirect membership of union affiliates. In all parties the relationships between constituency, provincial, and federal structures are more weakly articulated than in the United Kingdom. The lines of communication between the components are intermittent except during election campaigns. With the exception of the NDP, whose workers are more inclined to participate at both the federal and provincial levels, party organization in Canada is strongly influenced by the federal system of government. Provincial units are not inferior wings of the party and many party members are content to pursue political careers at only one level of the political system. By defending either provincial or federal interests, party leaders are occasionally required to assume policy positions which oppose those of the same party at a different level, whether provincial or federal.

In addition to being decentralized, Canadian political parties must face electors whose psychological identification with particular parties may be quite volatile. According to the authors of *Political Choice in Canada*, about 62 per cent of voters did not have strong, stable identities with one political party in the 1974 survey.[33] Such voters are prepared to change their votes according to election issues and the personalities of local candidates and party leaders. As well, a significant proportion of Canadian voters support one party at the provincial level and another at the national level. Despite this volatility, there is continuity in the electoral process with few dramatic reversals in national voting trends. Only the Progressive Conservatives and the Liberals have ever held federal office in Canada, while neither the New Democratic nor the Social Credit parties have ever received more than one quarter of the votes cast in a federal election.

Political parties should be able to accomplish at least three basic tasks for the legislative system: aggregate demands from society, provide decisionmakers, and offer practical and systematic policy contributions on a continuing basis.

Parties are gatekeepers in the political system, channelling some demands directly to decisionmakers while eliminating and combining others. Electoral success in Canada has depended on an efficient performance of this function. The Conservatives and Liberals have achieved office primarily by forging a broad coalition of interests, particularly ethnic and regional. In the employment of this strategy these parties have contributed to political integration. Furthermore, success in interest aggregation has permitted the Liberals and Conservatives to provide managers and decisionmakers for the legislative system. Cabinet composition, with its emphasis on regional representation, also symbolizes a compromise of interests. On the other hand, parties which have attempted to capture public office with a program based on a single principle or ideology have been unsuccessful either in aggregating interests or in providing decisionmakers. In recent years even the New Democratic party has been prepared to alter its program in the pursuit of national office, a strategy which illustrates the fundamental importance of interest aggregation for electoral success in Canada.

There are limitations on the extent to which political parties may have an independent policymaking role and make major policy contributions in the legislative system. A party program, at minimum, is a set of coordinated and consistent policies designed to achieve goals with which the parties are identified. Only the NDP and Social Credit have had even moderate success in generating such programs. Because the two major political parties do not have distinguishable programs, it is difficult for either of them to insist on the resolution of issues according to the dictates of party principle. Once in office such parties regularly adopt the programs of their opponents and even reverse policy positions announced during election campaigns. The aggregation function that the Liberals and Conservatives perform so singlemindedly impedes the development of comparable programs. Parties that attempt to mediate diverse and sometimes inconsistent demands in order to achieve electoral victory cannot afford the rigidity which firm policy commitments imply.

It may be argued that, even though political leaders are primarily conscious of winning elections, this need not interfere with the party's role as an agent of policy development. Elected representatives, according to this view, are held accountable in a democracy by elections in which their policies are confirmed or rejected. However, electoral research has indicated that voters have considerable difficulty distinguishing among the contesting parties on matters of policy. The parties are therefore unable to extract clear policy directives out of election results. Elections are rarely a source of policy communication and political parties cannot transform general feelings into specific policy alternatives which are the substance of the legislative system. With rare exception, individual parties cannot claim—even with an electoral majority—that the votes cast on their behalf illustrate the electorate's commitment to one or all of their policies. This fact does not mean that issues are not important or that ideas are not developed for election campaigns. Politicians design policies to cater to imperfect notions of electoral attitudes and many policies are constructed in a random fashion during the frenzy of election campaigning. In the 1972 general election both the Conservatives and the Liberals scrambled to respond to the "corporate rip-off" issue pressed by the New Democrats. In the 1974 election it was the NDP and the Liberals who were forced to organize their campaign in reaction to the Conservative "wage and price freeze." In the 1979 campaign the Conservative proposals of tax deductions for interest on mortgage payments influenced much of the campaign rhetoric. None of the major parties appear committed to substituting a comprehensive, programmatic approach for the present pattern of electoral campaigning.

Do party organizations in Canada act as policy stimulants between elections? The answer is mixed. The acknowledged role of the party organization in Canada is to achieve the party's electoral victory. Workers and organizers seem to demonstrate more concern over their party's slogans than over the details of its policies. Part of the reason lies in the importance of the electoral battle from the participants' point of view. The emphasis parties place on electoral victory complements the attitudes of many party workers who display little interest in politics except during the excitement of election campaigns.

Canadian party leaders recognize that their members are not primarily concerned with policy questions. They provide infrequent opportunities for members to contribute to policy formation. All parties have been experimenting with periodic policy conventions in recent years (the NDP biannually; the Conservatives and Liberals every two to four years) but their impact on the party leadership is uncertain. The relatively high degree of intraparty democracy which these conventions demonstrate cannot be equated with a significant policy input. The status of convention policy statements is ambiguous, even in the NDP. There is an unmistakable feeling on the part of rank and file members in the governing party that the cabinet politely entertains the policy ideas of the party organization, but expends most if its energy attempting to avoid embarrassing inconsistencies in party and government policy. This is a matter for interpretation.[34] In the 1968 Liberal government, Trudeau initiated the practice of appending Liberal convention resolutions to every cabinet document. Ministers were therefore made aware of the relationship between party positions and government decisions. Cabinet debate sometimes centred on the discrepancies and occasional attempts were made to reconcile conflicting views. This meant that some convention issues received a second hearing in the inner circles of government. It did not mean, however, that all convention resolutions were discussed by cabinet.

From the point of view of the party as an organization, policy is perhaps best conceived as an instrument rather than as a goal. The party must have a policy if it is to mobilize electoral support, and some policies are designed to do little more than that. On most occasions the so-called thinkers' conferences have also been used for this purpose. In recent decades the Conservative party has clambered over the obstacles of French-Canadian nationalism in its search for policies with which to attract the Quebec electorate, while the Liberals have sought policies with which to appease the West. Policies may also be used to sanctify political positions which are adopted for pragmatic purposes. The fact that the party organization tends to follow rather than lead makes this tactic an easy and convenient one. Finally, policy may be used to recruit new personnel into the party organization. Although party activists tend to continue their participation for social and personal reasons, the initial participation of many members is often prompted by policy considerations of a very general nature. Politicians cannot afford to adopt policies which might alienate large numbers of weak identifiers or individuals who occasionally lend active support to the party.

In the legislative system itself the bureaucracy tends to exercise a modifying effect on those policies which do emerge from the mass party organization and the electoral battle. The party *qua* government inherits a public service which advised its predecessor and seems inexhaustably capable of offering objections, financial or technical, to proposals whose merits seemed quite obvious in party circles. Added to this is the basically incremental nature of public-policy formation in Canada: new polices, as we have mentioned, tend to emerge out of the old ones and party policies are often not attuned to this fact.

Since Canadian political parties are not well organized for the task of policy formation, it would seem that they should have little influence in the legislative system. However, the influence of political parties seems to be ubiquitous. The most independent of politicians and the most disinterested of bureaucrats must, on occasion, take into consideration the view of parties. However, it is not the mass party which has much influence but the senior officers of the central party organization and the members of the parliamentary party. At high political levels the overlap of personnel, access, and self-interest in party success necessitates close liaison.

In the early years of the Trudeau administration, formal arrangements were established to provide a continual dialogue between the government and the Liberal party. Regular meetings were held between PMO staff, the president of the Liberal Federation, and the parliamentary secretary to the prime minister. Regional officers linked the prime minister and the PMO to party organizations and group interests throughout the country. Perhaps the most important expression of influence was the operation of "troikas" which consisted of the senior minister from a region, a member of the parliamentary party, and a nominee of the Liberal Federation. In concert these individuals exercised some authority where the government had discretionary powers to make appointments, select contractors, or affect strictly regional changes.

Senior party officials meet with cabinet members and caucus semi-regularly. In the Progressive Conservative party, the national director was continually invited to meetings with Robert Stanfield and occasionally attended caucus meetings. During Joe Clark's period as leader of the opposition, the organizational structure of the Conservatives in parliament was thoroughly disciplined and became the party's major policy-setting structure. Within the Conservative caucus, groups were organized to orchestrate Question Period, develop long-term policies, and even to determine Clark's short-term tactics — including speeches and appearances. At the same time, the national director was Clark's closest political friend and confidant.

In 1970 the Liberal party organized a "political cabinet," which was a special meeting of cabinet usually attended by party officials.

While the political cabinet was developed primarily for campaign purposes, the congruence of government policy and campaign interests was also determined in these meetings. The Election Expenses bill, 1971-72 vintage, was discussed in detail with at least one financial officer of the National Liberal Party Federation. On occasion the national director attended formal cabinet committee meetings to discuss policy matters, and the schedule of legislative proposals was amended on his initiative. Senior party officials may therefore find themselves actually taking part in cabinet policymaking.

The governing party exercises another form of control over policy because of the nature of the parliamentary system. In Canada the private meeting of each parliamentary party is referred to as caucus. The support of the government caucus is crucial for cabinet survival. While not a policy initiator, caucus does exercise a broad control over the government's policies and legislative program. As a body, it must occasionally be appeased. The parliamentary party is afforded opportunities to discuss almost all policy matters before they are discussed in the House of Commons. In 1972, for example, the Liberal party caucus alone prevented the government from moving second reading of an amendment to the British North America Act which would have altered electoral distribution and caused Quebec members some embarrassment in their own province. During the 30th Parliament the Liberal caucus also succeeded in softening gun-control legislation, in convincing cabinet to send the Green Paper on Immigration to a parliamentary committee rather than to an outside body, and in forcing a ministerial resignation during the "Judges Affair." In 1979, Joe Clark organized several backbench caucus committees before the opening of the 31st Parliament so that his supporters might offer advice on a variety of matters. The formula for backbench success is the same as that for interest groups: if a coalition of provincial, interest-group, and backbench interests can be formed, the cabinet's power to command adherence to its policies is severely limited.

Canadian parliamentary parties cannot always be considered consensual bodies of opinion on policy. By comparison with the radical right of the British Conservative party and Labour's left wing, Canadian parties have not experienced the type of backbench dissension necessary to maintain full-fledged factions, but there are "tendencies" in all parties. Several reasons exist. The major parties, as we have mentioned, are aggregating parties and, as a result, the issues with which they identify are diverse and therefore provide much scope for criticism. The regional nature of many political issues and of political representation occasionally force the cabinet to assuage certain backbench policy tendencies. But internal conflict over policy is even more apparent in programmatic parties. Both the NDP and the Social Credit party have experienced considerable dissension on policy issues.

The nature of the legislative system may also affect harmony on policy matters. The norms of cabinet secrecy mean that the cabinet may take government backbenchers into its confidence on policy issues only after the major decisions have been taken. Yet cabinet seems to recognize that it is an advantage to have backbench opinion channelled into cabinet discussions as early as possible in the policymaking process and changes in caucus organization have attempted to achieve some measure of backbench influence. With such procedures, cabinet can take advantage of its own secret operations to determine which policy path will avoid conflict among its supporters. Whether the communication links will actually yield benefits, either for cabinet control or backbench influence, also depends on the effectiveness of other organizations. It is well known that the Trudeau government improved communication between the government bureaucracy and the cabinet by strengthening the Privy Council Office. But the PCO has been purposely excluded from other interaction with such obviously "political" bodies as caucus. It was perhaps envisaged by some Liberals that an expanded PMO would provide the necessary liaison. But its activity suggests that it was more likely to have an affinity with the PCO than with party stalwarts in the House of Commons. Prime Minister Clark appointed a defeated Conservative candidate, Jean Pigott, to the PMO and assigned her the specific task of relations with the party caucus.

The ineffectiveness of mass party control over policy formation is demonstrable but, as we have shown, many opportunities exist for senior party bureaucrats and backbenchers to be involved in policymaking. When interest-group pressures, provincial concerns, and backbench intransigence combine, there is a likelihood of government appeasement either on the policy itself or, more likely, on the timing of its implementation. The inner circle may be the apex of decisionmaking in Canada, but its policy options are narrowed as it attempts to reconcile the limitations of finance, the demands of cultural norms, and the claims of provinces, groups, party bureaucrats, and caucus. Nevertheless, when the prime minister can develop consistent policies and legislation, the weapons at the disposal of the inner circle are formidable.

NOTES

1. Rick Van Loon, "Political Participation in Canada: The 1965 Election," *Canadian Journal of Political Science*, 3 (September 1970), pp. 376-99.
2. *Ibid.*, pp. 393-96.
3. William Mishler, *Political Participation in Canada: Prospects for Democratic Citizenship* (Toronto: Macmillan of Canada, 1979), Chapter II.
4. See, for example, Seymour Martin Lipset, "Revolution and Counter-Revolution: The United States and Canada," in O. Kruhlak, R. Shultz, and S. Pobihushchy (ed.), *The Canadian Political Process* (Toronto: Holt, Rinehart and Winston, 1970), pp. 13-38.
5. *Task Force on Government Information*, Vol. II (Ottawa: Queen's Printer, 1969), p. 70.
6. Reported in Robert Presthus, *Elite Accommodation in Canadian Politics* (Toronto: Macmillan of Canada, 1973), p. 45.
7. Harold D. Clarke *et al.*, *Political Choice in Canada* (Toronto: McGraw-Hill Ryerson, 1979), p. 70.
8. Adapted from Van Loon, "Political Participation," p. 393.
9. Presthus, *Elite Accommodation*, p. 29.
10. Kenneth D. McRae, "The Structure of Canadian History," in Louis Hartz (ed.), *The Founding of New Societies* (New York: Harcourt, Brace and World, 1964), pp. 219-72.
11. David J. Bercuson (ed.), *Canada and the Burden of Unity* (Toronto: Macmillan of Canada, 1977).
12. Richard Simeon and David J. Elkins, "Regional Political Cultures in Canada," *Canadian Journal of Political Science*, 7 (September 1974), pp. 397-437.
13. Indeed, Dale Posgate and Kenneth McRoberts argue that this phenomenon has already taken place in Quebec. See their *Quebec: Social Change and Political Crisis* (Toronto: McClelland and Stewart, 1976). See also John Wilson, "Canadian Political Cultures: Towards a Redefinition of the Nature of the Canadian Political System," *Canadian Journal of Political Science*, 7 (September 1974), pp. 438-83.
14. Robert J. Jackson *et al.*, "Collective Conflict, Violence and the Media in Canada," *Learning from the Media* (Toronto: Government of Ontario, 1977).
15. The literature in this field has been summarized in J. Fenton and D. W. Chamberlayne, "The Literature Dealing with the Relationship between Political Processes, Socio-Economic Conditions and the Public Policies in the American States: A Bibliographic Essay," *Polity*, 2 (Spring 1969), pp. 388-94. See also T. R. Dye, *Politics, Economics and the Public: Policy Outcomes in the American States* (Chicago: Rand McNally, 1966).
16. Allan Kornberg, David Falcone, William T. E. Mishler II, *Legislatures and Societal Change: The Case of Canada* (Beverly Hills: Sage Publica-

tions, 1973). For research on the provinces that asserts the importance of political variables, including legislative development, see William Mishler and David Campbell, "The Healthy State: Legislative Responsiveness to Public Health Care Needs in Canada, 1920-1970," *Comparative Politics,* X (July 1978), pp. 479-97.

17. Clarke *et al.*, *Political Choice in Canada*, pp. 243-72.
18. Diane Pothier, "Capital Punishment in Canadian Politics" (Unpublished M.A. thesis, Carleton University, 1978).
19. Presthus, *Elite Accommodation*, pp. 28-37. For criticisms of corporatism in Canada, see Leo Panitch, *The Canadian State* (Toronto: University of Toronto Press, 1978).
20. Canada, *Report of The Royal Commission on Corporate Concentration* (Ottawa: Supply and Services, 1978), p. 338.
21. Presthus, *Elite Accommodation*, Chapter 6. It should be noted that Presthus's data were collected in the provinces as well as at the federal level, and frequently the data are presented without these distinctions.
22. A. Paul Pross, "Pressure Groups: Adaptive Instruments of Political Communication," in A. Paul Pross (ed.), *Pressure Group Behaviour in Canadian Politics* (Toronto: McGraw-Hill Ryerson, 1975), p. 19.
23. Cited in W. T. Stanbury, "Lobbying and Interest Group Representation in the Legislative Process," in W. A. W. Neilson and J. C. MacPherson (ed.), *The Legislative Process in Canada* (Montreal: Institute for Research on Public Policy, 1978), p. 207.
24. M. W. Bucovetsky, "The Mining Industry and the Great Tax Reform Debate," in Pross, *Pressure Group Behaviour*, pp. 89-114.
25. Robert Presthus, "Interest Groups and the Canadian Parliament: Activities, Interaction, Legitimacy and Influence," *Canadian Journal of Political Science*, 4 (December 1971), p.452.
26. Glyn Berry, "The Oil Lobby and the Energy Crisis," *Canadian Public Administration*, 17 (Winter 1974), p. 635.
27. For an extended discussion of legitimacy and related concepts, see David Kwavnick, *Organized Labour and Pressure Politics* (Montreal: McGill-Queen's University Press, 1972), Chapter 1.
28. T. H. Qualter, *The Election Process in Canada* (Toronto: McGraw-Hill, 1970), Chapter 3.
29. For a discussion of NDP-labour complexities see Desmond Morton, "Labor's New Political Direction," *Canadian Forum*, LVII (October 1977).
30. Peter Aucoin, "Pressure Groups and Recent Changes in the Policy-Making Process," in Pross, *Pressure Group Behaviour*, p. 183.
31. H. B. Mayo, *Introduction to Democratic Theory* (New York: Oxford University Press, 1960).
32. John Meisel, "The Decline of Party in Canada," in Hugh G. Thorburn (ed.), *Party Politics in Canada*, 4th ed. (Scarborough: Prentice-Hall, 1979), pp. 119-35.
33. Clarke *et al.*, *Political Choice in Canada*, Chapters 5 and 10.
34. Stephen Clarkson, "Democracy in the Liberal Party," in Thorburn, *Party Politics in Canada*, pp. 154-60.

4.   The Inner Circle

In a democracy, institutions are established to convert societal demands into satisfactory political outputs. From the prime minister to the smallest municipal officeholder, individuals are prepared to assume leadership roles in every Canadian institution. This chapter is devoted to an examination of those institutions and individuals responsible for sorting out demands and setting priorities at the highest national level. In our parliamentary form of government the constitution provides for the fusion of executive and legislative powers by requiring overlapping membership in the cabinet and parliament. This type of fusion centralizes governmental authority in the hands of any individual or group who can maintain the loyalty or acquiescence of a majority of Canada's elected representatives. Buttressed by mass party organizations and a permanent public service, the prime minister, cabinet, and senior officials have acquired the responsibility for authoritative decisionmaking and the power to behave as an inner circle in the Canadian legislative system.[1]

PRIME-MINISTERIAL GOVERNMENT

These considerations have provided the foundation for arguments that Canada has developed a prime-ministerial government,[2] led by an all-powerful "super group" somehow out of step with the requirements of parliamentary democracy. This complex question has too often suffered from superficial treatments.[3] In Canada's composite government, influence and power are widely dispersed throughout the country and conflict is inherent in the major policymaking institutions. Within the legislative system a constant exchange of opinions and sentiments occurs between actors in the preparliamentary and the parliamentary sectors. As we will see in this and later chapters, the prime minister cannot exercise personal power in parliament independent of the views of either his supporters or his antagonists. Not even in the inner circle can he hope to be effective if he fails to anticipate the reactions of his closest colleagues. On substantive issues he and his advisors must guide the cabinet toward the policy path which avoids a coalition of hostile interests capable of blocking government initiatives. No prime minister (or super group) can embark on a new policy direction without securing the loyalty of his followers and anticipating obstacles in both parts of the legislative system.

Discussion about the existence of prime-ministerial government in Canada is confused by arguments about the location of power in the political system. While theorists of decisionmaking have discarded the idea that a "lump of power" exists anywhere, Canadian commentators persist in using the concept of power in this unique spacial manner. The prime minister's power, however, is not like currency: it cannot be located spacially or spent conceptually. Power ought to be employed as a relational concept which links together two or more actors, with different political resources, in a situation involving a multitude of influences, including severe losses for noncompliance.[4] When academics have examined the evolution of individual bills for power configurations, for example, they have always found that a myriad of influences were at work, including phenomena as disparate as political culture and the idiosyncracies of individual members of parliament. Participants generally respond to persuasion rather than threats—hence, the concept of power is of little use. A more helpful concept may be that of "anticipatory reactions." According to Carl Friedrich, individuals anticipate the reactions of others before they act in the first place and this conditions their behaviour.[5] At the most general level, that is precisely what politicians—especially prime ministers—do.

Comparing the power of individuals requires insuring that situations are comparable. This is a complex but indispensable task which few Canadian commentators have been inclined to undertake. The great Canadian debate about whether or not Trudeau inaugurated prime-ministerial government in 1968 owes as much to a journalistic conception of power, as it does to some misunderstandings about the detailed relations among the parts of the legislative system.

In *The Prime Minister in Canadian Government and Politics*,[6] R. M. Punnett posits four possible models of cabinet organization:

1. Prime-ministerial model: decisions are taken by the prime minister with individual ministers acquiescing.
2. Ministerial model: departments initiate proposals.
3. Cabinet model: members of cabinet make decisions collectively.
4. Inner-group model: subgroups of cabinet or informal groups of ministers make decisions.

No government is characterized exclusively by one or another of these models; prime ministers employ all of them for different purposes. Punnett argues, however, that the inner-group mode of decisionmaking, where decisions are entrusted to an informal, partial cabinet, best describes the Canadian experience. Under Trudeau, for example, cabinet delegated numerous collective responsibilities to smaller groups of ministers; under Clark an effort has been made to institutionalize and solidify the inner-group model by creating an inner cabinet.

The political resources of the prime minister and the executive are undeniably extensive. The constitutional prerogatives of the executive to introduce legislation, spend money, and make appointments are among the important available resources. But the importance of the prime minister does not derive from the exercise of these prerogatives in isolation. Only occasionally, as in the case of federal-provincial relations in the Trudeau years, will a prime minister identify himself firmly with an issue and demand that his views take precedence over all others. The prime minister's influence stems from an ability to command the maximum possible amount of information about the political environment and to use this resource in persuading political actors to follow his policy initiatives. Administrative secrecy and collective ministerial responsibility permit the executive to acquire requisite political knowledge without revealing conflicts or divisions which may occur within its ranks. However, the ability to conceal the process of decisionmaking at this level in government has sustained the erroneous idea that the executive works in isolation from parliamentary influence and has contributed significantly to the impression that the government acts independently of public opinion.

The prime minister's resources will differ from problem to problem and all attempts to enumerate his prerogatives and equate them with his power will founder. What is required is an accurate understanding of the influences at work on the prime minister and how they structure the deployment of his resources. This chapter provides the basis for an assessment of the influence of various actors in the inner circle by outlining cabinet's organizational basis, describing the atmosphere of its deliberations, dissecting the policymaking prism, and analyzing the linkages between the inner circle and parliament. An accurate conception of the inner circle is required prior to a discussion of parliament and the roles actors assume in both parts of the legislative system.

THE ORGANIZATIONAL BASIS OF CABINET

The constitutional authority of the prime minister and cabinet derives from the fact that the cabinet is a committee of the Queen's Privy Council for Canada and, as such, tenders advice to Her Majesty's representative, the governor general. Membership in the Privy Council itself is for life, but it meets only on rare ceremonial occasions. When the crown lost most of its political importance, the cabinet, though not mentioned in the BNA Act, remained the agent of executive authority. The legal instruments of cabinet are called *orders-in-council*. In 1975 about 3000 were approved.

As the head of the cabinet, the prime minister embodies governmental leadership between and during election campaigns and is the political figure who has the greatest saliency for the public. Members of the governing party accept his preeminent position because their survival as members of parliament depends to a large degree on his personal electoral appeal. His control over ministers, even deputy ministers, is more complete since both are appointed and dismissed on his personal authority as prime minister. His exceptional powers also include the ability to dissolve parliament and to organize central government. His appointment powers, which include the right to appoint senators, judges, and senior public servants, are vast.

Cabinet members are usually chosen from the House of Commons, but at least one is selected from the Senate to direct the government's affairs in the upper house. In the minority government of 1979, Prime Minister Clark found it necessary to supplement his French-speaking representation by appointing three cabinet ministers from the Senate. Almost all cabinet ministers are given individual responsibility for administering a department of government or a ministry of state. However, since the enactment of the Ministries and Ministers of State Act, five categories may be discerned: departmental ministers; ministers with parliamentary responsibilities, ministers of state for designated purposes (eg., the Minister of State for Science and Technology); Ministers of State to assist a departmental minister; and ministers without portfolio. The Parliamentary Secretaries Act of 1970 provides for the appointment of an equivalent number of secretaries to assist ministers. They are appointed by the prime minister, hold office for a year, and have no statutory responsibilities.

While policy derives from a multitude of sources, government departments predominate in providing specific policy initiatives. The development of a welfare state requires a modern bureaucracy which can understand and respond to new demands. Politicians cannot hope to duplicate the expertise which derives from administration, or the information which comes from permanent contact with groups in the environment. And yet only a minister may carry forward departmental requests to the cabinet or defend departmental policies in the House of Commons. Such a relationship between a minister and his department protects departmental officials from public attack and, in theory, concentrates approval or disapproval on the responsible "political" head of the department. As a unit, the ministers act to adopt orders-in-council or to advise the prime minister. Such deliberations are private, individual opinions are not publicly voiced, and ministers speak or act only in the name of the entire 30 members of cabinet. Such an arrangement provides cabinet with a protective cloak of secrecy and theoretically allows it to approach each political situation as a collective body.

In constitutional dictum, ministers are "responsible" or "accountable" to parliament for the activities of their departments. In practice, this prescription is difficult to follow. There are problems in determining which activities a minister should be required to acquaint himself with in the department. He cannot be expected to be responsible for all the technical and administrative activities of departmental officials. In some situations it may be more important to withold information from ministers than to preserve the integrity of the concept of ministerial responsibility. It is by no means obvious, for example, that the solicitor general should be made aware of all operations of the RCMP. As a democratically chosen head of a department he must be held responsible but, on the other hand, too much control might justifiably be called political control of the police. It is up to parliament to demand that ministers define the range of their responsibilities and, at a minimum, answer publicly for the actions of their subordinates. Of course, the final accountability in a democracy must come from the electorate. In both senses ministerial responsibility is deeply imbedded in the Canadian parliamentary system.

The increased prominence of cabinet and the prime minister in the policymaking process has been accompanied by a conscientious effort to maximize the efficiency of individual members and the cabinet as a whole. The evolution and improvement of the cabinet committee system is the most obvious manifestation of this concern. As late as the Pearson administration, full cabinet was the main vehicle of cabinet decisionmaking and, though it met somewhat irregularly, it debated and reviewed almost every decision taken in committee. After Trudeau came to office in 1968, cabinet and committee meetings were scheduled regularly. More important, committees were practically given the right to make decisions, not just provide opinions for cabinet consideration. By the end of the Trudeau period there were two agendas: one cited items which had been processed by a committee and which required only perfunctory confirmation by cabinet; the other listed subjects on which conflict had been expressed by noncommittee members or which the committee proposed be reexamined in cabinet.

At any one time the Trudeau cabinet divided into two to 12 committees. Each committee was chaired by the minister who held the cabinet portfolio most directly associated with its subject matter. There were five operations committees, each of which handled questions of specific policy content: External Policy and Defence, Economic Policy and Programs, Social Policy, Culture and Information, and Science and Technology. Over the years special committees were established to solve problems associated with strikes, tax reform, grain sales, and security. Planning committees included such illustrious committees as Priorities and Planning and Treasury Board as well as Legislation and House Planning, Federal-Provincial Relations, Government Operations, and the less prominent special council which passes routine orders-in-council. The coordination of the legislative system has been the responsibility of Priorities and Planning, Legislation and House Planning, and Treasury Board. Priorities and Planning, chaired by the Prime Minister and composed of the chairmen of cabinet's standing committees, was concerned with providing an orderly timetable for government activities. Its domination of long-term policy development resulted from its responsibility to develop goals and priorities for Canada and its status as the prime minister's committee.

On assuming office in June 1979, Joe Clark appointed an 11-member "inner cabinet" whose composition appeared to conform to no strict guidelines. It was charged with "establishing the over-all priorities of the Government" and according to early reports would meet more often than full cabinet and actually take some final decisions without full cabinet's approval. Full cabinet was to consist of 30 members and to be divided into five policy committees, each chaired by a member of the inner cabinet. The policy committees were Economic Development, Social and Native Affairs, External Affairs and Defence, Federal-Provincial Relations, and Economy in Government. The decision to make a clear distinction between "inner" and "outer" members of cabinet was based on Mr. Clark's desire to institutionalize a formal hierarchical system—a judgment based to some degree on his M.A. political science research on the Diefenbaker cabinet.

The composition of cabinets in Canada has always been a matter of intense deliberation and debate. Faced with two major languages and extreme regional division, prime ministers usually seek to provide language, cultural, and regional representation at the highest levels of government. If it is difficult to achieve a proper balance in a cabinet of 30 members, it is practically impossible to replicate this balance in an inner cabinet of 11 members. Within weeks of forming his new government Prime Minister Clark was confronted with intense back-bench criticism from British Columbia MPs who complained that no member from their province had been selected for the inner cabinet. Mr. Clark capitulated and appointed the twelfth member from British Columbia.

Under the new Clark system, the policy (or subject-matter) committees of cabinet are chaired by ministers who hold "horizontal" portfolios which bridge departmental responsibilities. The influence and status of these ministers have been further augmented by placing them in the inner cabinet. Inner cabinet reviews the decisions of the subject-matter committees and discusses the general priorities of the government. If inner cabinet overturns the decision of a subject-matter committee, members of this committee may raise the issue in full cabinet after giving 48 hours' notice. The Clerk of the Privy Council, a member of his staff, and a representative of the Prime Minister's Office normally attend the meetings of inner cabinet.

There are two other important coordinating committees. The leader of the government in the House of Commons, who is given the title of President of the Privy Council to provide a place for him in cabinet, chairs Legislation and Housing Planning. From this perspective he can develop a detailed appreciation of the legislative program as it appears in both parts of the legislative system. Treasury Board has responsibility for the general supervision of government spending and for monitoring new program commitments. Its secretariat prepares economic analyses and expenditure forecasts which are forwarded to cabinet for use as general guidelines in the preparation of legislative items. Together these two committees and the inner cabinet provide ministers with an opportunity to plan and coordinate the preparliamentary stages of the legislative system and to link them to parliamentary activities. In November 1978 the Trudeau government felt compelled to create yet another body of ministers—the Board of Economic Development Ministers—to coordinate industrial and economic development.

The administrative and political support for the prime minister and his cabinet has grown immensely since A. D. P. Heeney initiated the development of a cabinet secretariat during the Second World War. This growth in the Prime Minister's Office and the Privy Council Office has contributed both the cabinet's efficiency and to arguments about the covert influence of these bodies in the policymaking process. The PMO is filled through personal appointment by the prime minister, while the PCO is staffed by permanent public servants. In 1979, the PMO had about 90 professional employees and a personnel budget of approximately $3 million. Under the direction of the Principal Secretary, the PMO acts as a liaison between the prime minister and the bureaucracy via the PCO. It also staffs the "political cabinet," which is the organizational expression of cabinet's political and electoral interests. The Clerk of the Privy Council and Secretary to Cabinet directs the PCO which coordinates cabinet activities by setting agendas, taking the minutes of cabinet meetings, and conveying cabinet decisions to the bureaucracy.[7]

Both the PMO and the PCO brief the prime minister on issues and alert him to possible ministerial differences. Together they monitor all the information flow within what we shall describe as the policy prism. Plainly these officials do not lack access to the centres of policymaking. The prime minister meets officials from the PMO and the PCO every day to plan his activities; other officials from these offices attend all high-level planning sessions, participate in interdepartmental committees, and have continual access to ministers during cabinet meetings. They can command prime-ministerial and cabinet attention. With some notable exceptions, PMO appointees are not specialists in policy areas and the short tenure of PCO officials (except the clerk and deputy secretaries to cabinet) renders them unable to perform the substantive task of policy review carried out in the United States by the Executive Office or in the United Kingdom by the new Central Policy Review Staff.

Individual cabinet ministers are also provided with staff. In 1979 each minister could spend up to $200,000 for assistance. In that year the parapolitical bureaucracy consisted of 180 to 190 aides to ministers. Like members of the PMO they are appointed on the personal authority of their minister and are not subject to normal recruitment regulations of the public service. While it is questionable how much influence these aides wield in the inner circle, there is no doubt that they "play a fundamental and legitimate role at the executive level of the governmental process."[8] As a body, the assistants are a source of future members of cabinet and other high offices in the inner circle. Blair Williams has calculated that one-third of the cabinet ministers in 1979 had been at one time a member of another minister's staff.[9]

Besides the role of the parapolitical bureaucracy and the central coordinating agency of the Privy Council Office, three other agencies are closely associated with the policy prism. In 1975 a portion of the PCO, the Federal-Provincial Relations Office, was created as a separate department under the prime minister. The FPRO coordinates federal government activities with similar offices in the provinces. After the election of René Lévesque and the Parti Québécois in 1976 it was given special responsibilities for Quebec.

The final two agencies control the financial activities of government. The Department of Finance supervises all matters relating to financial affairs, revenue, and the expenditures of the government. It provides revenue forcasts and predictions of general economic and social conditions. In 1966 a Treasury Board Secretariat was carved out of the Department of Finance. As mentioned earlier, it controls the allocation of expenditures and resources within the government.[10]

CABINET IN ACTION

Cabinet and its committees are assembled regularly. In 1978 cabinet met 56 times; its committees, 207 times. Through the operations of the PCO, the prime minister exercises control over cabinet's agenda, although committee chairmen are always consulted about the scheduling of committee items. This heavy workload has prompted ministers to complain that they have assumed too much responsibility for matters that might be attended to by public servants. Mitchell Sharp, a former minister under both Pearson and Trudeau, has estimated that the collegial style of decisionmaking which characterized the Trudeau cabinet resulted in ministers spending as many as 15 hours a week in cabinet meetings.[11]

Although small groups of ministers may take decisions on behalf of cabinet, all items are placed before cabinet in the form of cabinet papers, signed or approved by a minister. The volume of cabinet documents increased rapidly after the Second World War to approximately 2000 a year by 1972. In January 1977 the entire system for the production and circulation of cabinet papers was revised. A basic distinction was made between types of cabinet submissions. Memoranda to cabinet are tightly worded statements containing specific proposals and a brief outline of the issue. Discussion papers contain background information and, unlike memoranda, are not deemed to contain confidences of the cabinet. In 1978, cabinet was presented with 483 memoranda, 226 discussion papers, 89 draft bills, while 731 records of cabinet decisions were taken. The new rules for cabinet papers were established both to relieve ministers of work and to anticipate the demand for the release of documents.

Even though a document may be directed toward a single committee for decision, it is usually circulated to all cabinet ministers. Each cabinet document is given a number and a security classification. The desire to uphold cabinet secrecy has infused this process with a measure of ritual where even the use of unauthorized paper or pens has delayed submissions to cabinet. Informal communication by telephone and personal conversations about cabinet business add immeasurably to the complexity of cabinet interaction.

All ministers, including the prime minister, are expected to bring substantive policy questions before cabinet. As each document comes forward, the responsible minister is required to explain and defend its contents. A deputy minister or a senior official may represent his department at cabinet meetings and occasionally speak on a specific point, but he does so only at the request of his minister. In practice, each minister is allowed at least one major policy area, some legislative proposals, and the opportunity to place at least one topic on cabinet's list of priority problems. Cabinet cohesiveness, like that of any group, is maintained by encouraging each minister to believe that he will succeed in persuading his colleagues to accept some of his proposals. Even if cabinet conflict emerges over a minister's ideas, they will rarely be totally rejected. Instead, the minister will be provided further opportunities to revise and resubmit his document. While policies are, of course, unequal in their significance for the political system, each minister's ability to initiate and obtain agreement on his legislation affects both his evaluation of his cabinet colleagues and his personal esteem in the inner circle.

On some matters, such as national security and the budget, cabinet deliberations are very restricted. With the exception of the prime minister, ministers are not made aware of the budget, for example, until it is too late to make any changes to its proposals. Mitchell Sharp has related that as minister of finance he spoke to the prime minister personally three weeks in advance of the budget, conferred with his colleagues over the alternatives two weeks before budget day, but only described in detail the tax changes on "the day before the budget presentation."[12]

The "balance of influence" within a cabinet varies enormously. Some prime ministers such as Mackenzie King and R. B. Bennett were quite authoritarian, while others encouraged full and open discussion. The latter category includes most recent prime ministers such as Lester Pearson, John Diefenbaker, Pierre-Elliott Trudeau, and Joe Clark. Under some prime ministers (such as Trudeau) cabinet deliberations were extremely formal, while others such as Pearson insisted on informality.

Today decisions are rarely taken by a systematic rendering of opinion. As in other social contexts, guides or hints are communicated about expected behaviour (a process sometimes referred to as "cue reading") and chairmen manage meetings by advancing through cabinet documents unless dissent is expressed. Prime ministers quickly learn that they intimidate their ministers if they state personal opinions before others have been given a chance to express their ideas. Prime Minister Trudeau usually chaired cabinet by providing each minister the opportunity to develop a personal perspective on each issue and only asserted his authority as chairman to indicate that a cabinet consensus had been attained or a division was apparent. Contemporary cabinet deliberations cannot be compared to a meeting between an all-powerful head of state and his courtiers. They bear closer resemblance to the relationship which might exist between a feudal baron and his independently powerful vassals. In this case the participants are united for the group's interests — especially political survival.

THE POLICY PRISM

The policy prism is a concept we employ to denote the operations of central institutions in the coordination of policies and the explication of their legislative details and ramifications for parliament and the public. Like a light prism, these operations convert undifferentiated phenomena into an organized and recognizable pattern. Within the policy prism the relationships among political goals, governmental activities, budgetary requirements, and legislative initiatives are determined. Policies are the culmination of these activities. They provide a long-term governmental perspective in issue areas and structure specific decisions in the legislative system.

In recent years, academic students of policymaking have revealed major structural changes in the policy prism. Under Lester Pearson a well-developed system for coordinating departments or formulating priorities within the government did not exist. Pierre-Elliott Trudeau installed a more orderly system of decisionmaking. Cabinet was organized to reflect the essentials of rational policymaking—the efficient pursuit of predetermined goals. In theory, goals would be established and the government would develop policies designed to attain them. Policies would be chosen on the basis of the resources required for their implementation and their relation to other commitments.

Many of these changes were accomplished by adopting for cabinet's use those elements of rational policymaking which had already found expression in the introduction of Program, Planning, and Budgeting techniques (PPB) in the public service. This type of budgeting procedure is based on priorities which are set at the cabinet level and communicated to departments via the Treasury Board. Departments are obliged to frame their budgetary requirements in terms of goals and objectives. They are also expected to provide a program forecast which will enable cabinet and Treasury Board to improve government planning in subsequent years. PPB was buttressed by a series of new managerial techniques including systems analysis, benefit/cost analysis, and management by objectives. Together these techniques constituted a trend toward greater collegiality in decisionmaking and a reinforcement of the collective responsibilities of cabinet. They also increased the power of central agencies, especially the PCO and Treasury Board Secretariat, by providing them with information about the options available and hence more opportunities to exercise control.[13]

The new structures of rational policymaking were implemented most thoroughly in the lower levels of the bureaucracy and less completely in the upper echelons. During the Trudeau administration the Cabinet Committee on Priorities and Planning did develop a set of goals which it wanted to achieve for Canada. In recent years these general goals included such vague concepts as social justice, national unity, and quality of life. The Committee also developed a list of priority problems such as regional economic expansion, bilingualism, participation, and pollution and assigned extra resources to their resolution. Such goals and priority areas were used to prod departments into making new policy proposals and to initiate interdepartmental committees where no clear departmental interest had been established or where more than one department could claim an expertise. Hartle summarized the changes in this fashion: "Under the Trudeau government, there seems to have been some shift of power to the centre from departments, a substantial shift in power from the bureaucracy to Ministers, greatly increased formality in decisionmaking processes and procedure, and greater emphasis on longerrange problems."[14]

Goals and priorities exert an influence on government spending and on the legislative program. In the budgetary process the inner cabinet receives information from the Treasury Board and the departments about program forecasts. When this information is combined with the fiscal framework from the Department of Finance and cabinet's goals and priorities, the inner cabinet is able to develop expenditure guidelines which the Treasury Board applies in its assessment of departmental budgetary proposals. By developing these new methods of financial regulation, politicians in the inner circle have strengthened their control over existing programs. The government also attempts to use goals and priorities in the development of a legislative program. This assumes that, given the proper structures, politicians will be able to relate their party's philosophy to the items they intend to introduce in parliament.

The rationalist approach underlying these assumptions has not proven as successful in relating goals to items in the legislative system as it has in the budgetary process. Adherence to a rational model of decisionmaking necessitates that decisionmakers in the inner circle strive for clear and consistent goals. Such clear policy direction has rarely, if ever, been present in Canada. Goals are difficult to establish at any time and recent government experience indicates that they are usually so nebulous as to be virtually useless. It is politicians who must assume much of the responsibility for the failures of rational policymaking. Without political parties which are devoted to specific legislative programs, a rational model holds only limited promise for actors within the inner circle. No rational technique will help to make choices among goals or to determine how much government expenditure should be devoted to defence as opposed to social welfare measures. In Canada the government has developed organizations and categories based on some aspects of a rational model, but politicians have been unable to adhere to the assumptions inherent in the approach.

The relationship between the legislative program and the government's goals demonstrates some of the difficulties. When the legislative program is being developed, each item is categorized under one of cabinet's goals or priorities. The relationship between the goals, the priorities, and the legislation is broadly intuitive. Ministers do not develop their legislation in response to the government's goals, but use the goals as rhetorical categories to justify their legislation. The relationship between goals and bills is sometimes so tenuous that when legislative proposals arrive at the PCO, officials merely group bills haphazardly under one of the government's goals or priorities. Many senior politicians, sceptical of the so-called rational structures, do not believe it would be advisable to do otherwise.

In Canada we have created the structures of rational policymaking, but incrementalism predominates within them. While the central organs of policymaking, buttressed by the techniques of PPB, have attempted to drive governmental goals into the departments, they have faced ministerial and departmental intransigence. There are three fundamental reasons why prime ministers have experienced limited success in "top down" policymaking.

First, Canadian governments have been unclear about the goals they wished to achieve. Even when the government has attempted to articulate goals, it has discovered that policies cannot be extracted from ringing phrases. Before goals can be used to construct policies, politicians must agree on their meaning and their relevance — and they must be accompanied by clear operational goals, detailed information, and adequate program evaluations. This is an extremely demanding array of requirements which few governments have been able to meet. For example, it is virtually impossible for the Department of Finance to provide a reliable fiscal framework, complete with expenditure and revenue forecasts, for a fiscal year which will not commence for 15 months. As far as program evaluation is concerned, the creation of the Office of the Comptroller General in 1977 was an acknowledgment of the government's previous inability to come to grips with the problems of evaluation.[15]

Second, Canadian governments have often been forced to set aside long-term considerations in the face of short-term contingencies. Rational planning structures could anticipate and manage critical events in an orderly fashion, and the government has given some indication of its willingness to create such structures. Nonetheless, the nature of crises is such that government response cannot always be assessed against existing goals and priorities. On August 1, 1978, Prime Minister Trudeau suspended the standard budgetary cycle and announced substantial cuts in federal government spending. This event was another step in the progressive dilution of the priority-setting process in the late 1960s. The October Crisis in 1970 and the election of René Lévesque in 1976 transformed another part of the priority-setting process into a *post hoc* search for programs designed to achieve national unity. The minority government period of 1972 to 1974 focused attention on the government's survival and ''the imposition of the October 1975 anti-inflation program relegated most of the 1975 priority exercise to the dustbin.''[16] Finally, the original structures have been supplemented by *ad hoc* appointments and committees, such as the group of ten deputy ministers (DM 10) established to oversee the post-controls period.[17] Vague misgivings about the usefulness of formal decisionmaking structures have given way to positive pressure for pragmatic and flexible responses.

Third, individual ministers must be allowed to develop their own legislative priorities or the mutual trust which cements cabinet will erode. The prime minister's need to assure every cabinet member at least limited personal success requires that goals and priority areas be moulded to satisfy ministerial and departmental aspirations. The development of a legislative program based on the need to satisfy stipulated goals is continually plagued by traditional political constraints. Many ministers dislike the rational process and prefer *ad hoc*, piecemeal personal decisionmaking. As one senior minister put it: ''The only time I feel I'm doing something is when I make a decision about an individual appointment or decide an immigration question.'' In an attack on the collective approach to decisionmaking, A. W. Johnson has argued that creativity in policy development is best achieved when responsibility is assigned to individual ministries which are not obliged to compromise endlessly in an effort to find the lowest common policy denominator.[18]

The government's inability to achieve all the requirements for rational policymaking has led some academics to suggest that a mixed scanning model more closely approximates actual policymaking behaviour. In such a model, fundamental policies and incremental policies are differentiated by decisionmakers. Incremental policymaking is transferred to relatively low levels in the system, while the energies of senior policymakers are concentrated on those policies selected for intense examination. Ideally, all policy areas would eventually be examined and incremental policies could ultimately be related to fundamental ones. But the government's ability to satisfy even the requirements of this model with its selective application of rational planning is suspect. New institutional devices are required to develop the legislative program into a coherent and comprehensive instrument for the achievement of government goals.

THE LEGISLATIVE PROGRAM

By tracing the process for producing legislation, the various components of the policy prism can be identified and their contributions assessed. The construction of the legislative program spans activities from the acknowledgment of societal needs through to the assembly of specific legislative items for introduction in parliament. The successful coordination and scheduling of these activities requires institutions that are sensitive to Canadian values, political realities, and the procedures and demands of the whole legislative system.

The first operation in the development of a legislative program occurs when the Clerk of the Privy Council writes to heads of departments and agencies to request their list of proposed legislation and details about the availability and urgency of each item. This preparatory step normally occurs approximately one year before the parliamentary session for which these items are intended. When they arrive in the PCO, the legislative proposals are classified according to government goals and priorities. The initial analysis of the proposals is made by an *ad hoc* committee of officials from the PCO, the PMO, the Department of Justice and, more recently, the Office of the President of the Privy Council. Departments which submit proposals may prefer to believe that they are in a constant state of readiness to pursue them, but it is intended that this committee should review departmental proposals in terms of practical impediments such as drafting deadlines, administrative requirements, and parliamentary feasibility. Although the committee does not meet again to review this list, its participants advise the leading political actors in the policy prism about the progress of each item in both parts of the legislative system.

The reformulated list of legislative proposals is forwarded to the prime minister and, under Trudeau, the Cabinet Committee of

Priorities and Planning. Together they establish the political criteria on the basis of which items are chosen from the list. Either the Cabinet Committee on Legislation and Housing Planning or an *ad hoc* committee selects the specific items which will be developed by departments. The process of the cabinet committee meetings is somewhat similar to that suggested by the mixing scanning model in that politicians examine some of the proposals in detail while other proposals receive only a brief mention. Relatively minor bills and departmental housekeeping items are of little interest to ministers. On occasion some of these bills have been included on future legislative programs even though no one outside the department knew anything about them. The selection process has become so undisciplined that a legislative item has been chosen even though it had low ministerial and departmental priority. When cabinet finally settles on the content of the program, the PCO employs the decision to prod departments into bringing forward legislation, and the PMO uses it to write the first draft of the speech from the throne.

The development of this list of legislative proposals provides, in practical terms, the most important occasion for significant political contribution to the whole program. This list instructs departments and agencies about overall cabinet preferences and in the year prior to an election it also becomes part of the government's total campaign strategy. Since at least a year is required from the construction of this program to the writing of policy memos, the drafting of bills and, finally, the introduction of legislation in parliament, there is little scope for the addition of items except for emergencies. The constraints of time make it extremely important, therefore, that when the cabinet's decision on the content of the program is circulated to departments, the government's political thrust be at the heart of it. Such emphasis on the government's philosophy is often missing in the face of the demands on the program emanating from items carried over from an earlier session of parliament, statutory requirements, departmental aspirations, and recommendations and reports of task forces and royal commissions. As we have pointed out, the presence of a political thrust in the legislative program requires ministers, or the prime minister, to have a clear conception of what the government wishes to achieve. If there is no commitment to espoused goals, ministers will be forced to negotiate, individually, with groups in the legislative system and may find they are unable to withstand special interests or the conservative forces in the public service.

In addition to the difficulties inherent in relating the legislative program to the government's predetermined goals, the central coordinating agencies have not devised adequate means of forcing individual departments to respond to the legislative program, nor have they succeeded in coordinating the multitude of stages involved in both parts of the legislative system. On occasion, the government has even run out of legislation to place before the House of Commons and at other times there have been so few draft bills available that cabinet has been unable to enjoy the luxury of a selection.

The development of the legislative program imposes a framework and a timetable on departmental formulation of pieces of legislation. The sources of legislation are numerous. Political parties, interest groups, the provinces, and occasionally members of parliament suggest legislative initiatives, but it is the administration and evaluation of existing programs which provides the inspiration for most ministerial and bureaucratic measures.

If a minister merely wishes to make minor administrative amendments to the law, he is likely to submit a legislative proposal which may be channelled quickly through the system. If, on the other hand, he intends to change government policy or emphasis he will be required to follow a more difficult route. He must first submit a policy memorandum to cabinet. The prime minister through the PCO will determine which subject-matter committee will receive the memorandum and when it will be placed on their agenda. Prior to the original submission it is likely that interdepartmental committees will have attempted to ensure that the new policy is coherent and consistent with other government activities. It is also their task to anticipate and resolve ministerial conflict which could emerge in cabinet. At the cabinet committee meeting, two perspectives will be brought to bear on the policy memorandum. It will be placed in its widest possible setting and discussed in terms of its political impact. Discussion will also concentrate on the details and technical requirements of the policy. Policies are usually so long in the developmental stages, often being returned to departments for reconsideration, that experienced ministers have been thoroughly briefed by their own officials, been approached by interest groups, and been engaged in lengthy discussions with caucus and individual members of parliament.

When the complex process of achieving a cabinet decision on the policy memorandum is completed, different governmental structures become involved.[19] Cabinet first approves the legislative proposal for drafting. At this stage the sponsoring department is supposed to provide a comprehensive set of instructions to the drafting office of the Department of Justice so that drafting in both official languages may begin. Usually, however, the original policy memorandum serves as the basis for drafting and, because of its general nature, draftsmen often encounter inconsistencies and situations in which policy details have not been related to existing Canadian statutes. In the discussion between drafting officials and the sponsoring department, minor policy is made in the resolution of these difficulties. Some officials consider that the final policy impact is influenced almost as much by these details as by the original policy memorandum. ''You can have the policy, leave the details to me'' has been the philosophy of at least some senior administrators. Moreover, in their quest to provide unity to Canadian law, the draftsmen also make what might be called ''legal policy inputs.''

If drafting considerations were made an integral part of policy formation, perhaps some of the practical difficulties could be anticipated and the legal details could be made to serve the general policy intention. In the United Kingdom, preliminary drafts of bills are circulated to all departments to provide extensive opportunities for senior officials to comment on the legal and administrative ramifications. In Canada the actual bill is discussed only between the sponsoring department and Justice. This solicitor-client system prevents officials in other departments from commenting on the deficiencies of legislation until the bill is in parliament. At that stage it is too late.

When the sponsoring minister accepts the draft legislation, it is returned to cabinet via the Committee on Legislation and House Planning. This committee, chaired by the President of the Privy Council, attempts to examine the draft bill clause by clause to ascertain if it accords with the policy memorandum and to determine the reception it is likely to receive in the House of Commons. In the minority situation following the 1972 election, cabinet ministers used this setting to inform their colleagues of discussions they had held with opposition spokesmen about the passage of their bills. Nevertheless, this committee tends to be preoccupied with the legal expression of government policy. In recent years, departments have appended an explanatory memorandum to the draft bill to aid ministers in the discussion of its technical and legal aspects. The chairman is briefed by officials in his own office and by the Legislation and House

Planning Secretariat of the Privy Council Office. Draftsmen are always in attendance and lawyers on the committee furnish much of the debate.

If the committee is generally dissatisfied with the draft legislation, it is returned to a subject-matter committee. Normally, however, the committee makes only minor changes, approves the bill, and relays it to cabinet for inclusion on the agenda for items requiring only perfunctory approval. The draft bill is then submitted to the prime minister for his signature. The formal transmittal to parliament occurs when the draft bill, signed by the prime minister, is sent to the clerk of the appropriate House for introduction. At this stage, parliamentary strategy and tactics become paramount and the structures which link the preparliamentary and the parliamentary stages of the system go into operation. In this way some 60 to 80 bills are introduced each year into parliament. This does not end cabinet's legislative role either in parliament or after the successful passage of the bill. Most statutes require the government to develop detailed regulations for the administration of the general provisions and these are given legal authority by orders-in-council. Moreover, many laws require cabinet to set a date for the proclamation. This can be quite long: the Pest Controls Product Act, for example, was passed in June 1969, but not brought into force until November 1972. For practical purposes some Acts may never be proclaimed.

Coordination of the legislative system has occasionally suffered from inadequate attention to the time required to complete the various stages of the process. On some occasions the government may be without sufficient parliamentary time to handle its available legislation and on others it overtaxes institutions in the preparliamentary stages in order to obtain a minimum number of bills. The difficulties may be illustrated by an incident related among members of the Department of Justice. In replying to a command for the immediate production of a very difficult bill, a senior official told the prime minister that it reminded him of a story. A young child, after having been promised a baby brother by Christmas, was told by his mother that there was no longer enough time available. Somewhat dejected, he suggested that his mother do what his father would do: "Hire more men!" When cabinet shifts priorities to cope with emergencies or to introduce new ideas, the time difficulties are understandable. But when the government runs out of legislation or demands that parliament work overtime, it is often due to a lack of coordination in the legislative system that could be corrected by an overhaul of some of the structures.

LINKAGES WITH PARLIAMENT

In a parliamentary form of government it is necessary to remember that the executive and the legislature in combination form the legislative system. In Chapter 2 we treated conceptually the links between the executive and the legislature and outlined the functions this system performs. The structures that actually link the institutions in the inner circle with parliament have often been underestimated in descriptions of the organization of Canadian government. The crucial factor in this linkage is the requirement that members of cabinet hold a position in the House of Commons or the Senate. This simple requirement structures the activities of virtually every institution and the behaviour of every actor in both parts of the legislative system. Neither the legislature nor the executive could operate democratically if ministers did not have to defend in parliament their legislative proposals and account for the actions of their departments before their parliamentary peers. Bagehot's classic description of cabinet as "a hyphen which joins, a buckle which fastens" may fail to appreciate the contemporary role of the prime minister, but it remains the most appropriate metaphor to describe the nature of the executive-parliamentary link.

In recent years the effectiveness of this link has come under attack. Ministers still answer questions in the House and appear before parliamentary committees to explain and defend the actions of departmental officials, but the pretense that ministers can be responsible for all of the activities that take place in a department, to the point of resigning in the face of a serious administrative error, has been abandoned. In fact, ministers have expressed increasing reluctance to defend public servants. In 1972 Jean Chretien, then Minister of Indian Affairs and Northern Development, publicly described a report prepared by officials in his department as "a shabby piece of research."[20] In 1978 Jean-Pierre Goyer, Minister of Supply and Services, criticized the work of officials in his department and argued that ministerial responsibility does not extend to the defence of gross negligence. Opposition calls for the resignation of ministers who are unwilling to shoulder the burden of responsibility for administrative decisions are met with silence. Unless public servants have acted on the explicit instructions of a minister, or unless a minister's conduct is patently unethical, resignation is highly unlikely.

The tendency for ministers to disclaim responsibility has been accompanied by a decrease in the anonymity of public servants. The doctrine of ministerial responsibility, it should be remembered, requires public servants to give confidential advice in private, to implement policies regardless of personal conviction, and to refrain from partisan political activities. While it cannot be said that public servants have renounced these values, they have been drawn more and more into the public eye. In part this has occurred because senior public servants are now obliged to appear before parliamentary committees. Beyond this, Kenneth Kernaghan has argued that public servants are simply less circumspect than they once were in their meetings with groups and individuals.[21] This infusion of candor might be considered refreshing were it not for the fact that public servants still expect to have their anonymity preserved on other occasions.

Critics maintain that these developments have created a gap in the responsibility system.[22] Ministers are willing to accept responsibility only for certain, ill-defined departmental activities and public servants continue to expect their anonymity to be protected. Under these circumstances parliament finds it difficult to identify responsibility for maladmininstration. This has been aggravated by the refusal of Prime Minister Trudeau to appear — or permit his Clerk of the Privy Council to appear — before parliamentary committees. What remains of the doctrine of ministerial responsibility is the requirement that ministers appear in parliament to answer questions and defend departmental policy. Question Period in particular is a source of concern for both ministers and officials. In a survey conducted by the Lambert Commission, almost 80 per cent of the deputy ministers who responded agreed that "Question period keeps us sensitive to our departmental responsibilities."[23] Ministers and opposition critics will continue to argue about the limits of responsibility, but when administrative errors or transgressions occur the real penalty is public political embarrassment.

It is possible that controversy regarding the scope of ministerial responsibility will result in the emergence of stronger links between the inner circle and parliament. H. V. Kroeker concluded his study of the government's expenditure process with the recommendation that departments appoint accounting officers who, as senior departmental officials, would appear before the Public Accounts Committee of parliament to assume personal responsibility for the propriety, efficiency, and economy of departmental expenditures.[24] The Lambert Commission endorsed this proposal, arguing that, by focusing responsibility for administration on the deputy minister, ministers would be relieved of "the burden of operational detail without removing final responsibility for policy development and implementation."[25] How ministers can be held accountable to parliament is an issue to which we return in the final chapter.

The link between cabinet and parliament is strengthened when experience in the House of Commons is considered a valuable or even necessary attribute for promotion to the cabinet. In Britain it is routine for members to spend 15 to 20 years in the backbenches before being elevated to cabinet. Partly because of the rapid turnover among members, this tradition of a lengthy apprenticeship has never been fully established in Canada. Among recent prime ministers, only John Diefenbaker has recruited heavily from trusted parliamentary veterans. John Courtney calculates that one-third of Liberal ministers appointed in the period between 1921 and 1970 had spent less than a year in parliament when appointed to the cabinet.[26] Prime ministers themselves have had less prior legislative experience since 1919 than they had in the 1867-1917 period.[27] Joe Clark spent three years in parliament before achieving the Conservative leadership and four years before becoming prime minister. However, members of his cabinet had an average of 8.17 years of parliamentary experience on appointment and only one cabinet minister was appointed with no exposure to parliament whatsoever. This compares favourably with the latter years of the Trudeau government when ministers' prior parliamentary experience was less than four years on average. Ministers with limited experience often find it difficult to adjust to the nuances of parliamentary life and their knowledge of and respect for parliamentary tradition is often less than adequate in the eyes of the opposition.

In addition to the pervasive influence of overlapping membership, several devices exist to bridge activities in both parts of the legislative system. The results of these linkages are reminiscent of open covenants, secretly arrived at. The throne speech, which is read by the governor general in the Senate chamber at the beginning of every session, outlines what has been prepared in the inner circle for presentation to parliament. It is considered by cabinet to be the most important public statement of its political intentions. It forms the basis for all parliamentary business and as such should be used in evaluating cabinet's performance in governing the country. The throne speech consists of a rather vague statement of government goals and the legislative program which the government will place before parliament. Ideally, the goals and priorities would be the same as those which had been used by the inner cabinet to determine departmental priorities and new policy directions. The throne speech, which includes a summary of the legislative program discussed earlier, is drafted by the PMO or PCO and, like any important document, is discussed in cabinet. Unfortunately, the utility of this link is diminished by the weakness already present in the relation between goals and legislative proposals.

In 1968 the British practice of attaching a list of all the legislative proposals was included in the Canadian speech from the throne. In this fashion the government informed the House of its entire program and thereby encouraged both public servants and parliamentarians to focus on the relationship among the policies and bills. Despite this, and the fact that the cabinet considers it a significant political document, the government was reluctant to have the public judge its accomplishments against the promises in the throne speech. In fact, governments often depart from the original list of legislative items and sometimes introduce trial-balloon bills merely to ascertain the reactions of parliament and the public. In light of this, the government must be prepared to accept that a degree of cynicism will accompany the introduction of any legislation.

Once the throne speech has been delivered, the government deposits with parliament its bills, estimates, regulations, white papers, the reports of royal commissions and advisory committees, and those departmental and agency reports required by statute. The avalanche of documents is accompanied by ministerial answers to thousands of written and oral questions both on the floor of the House of Commons and in its committees. Such activities are organized for the government by the prime minister, the government House leader, and their advisors. Negotiation on substantive issues is required with government followers in the House and on the scheduling of government business with the leaders of other parliamentary parties. The four parliamentary House leaders meet at the beginning of each week to plan the sequence of parliamentary activities.

The task of linking the executive to parliament falls most heavily on the caucus of the governing party. The government caucus is composed of all party members who support the government. An elected chairman presides over meetings and maintains continuous contact with backbenchers and the House leader. Cabinet ministers attend caucus and provide information about pending government policy which serves as a foundation for caucus debate. Much of this information is given before caucus committees whose terms of reference parallel, to some extent, cabinet's subject-matter committees and the standing committees of the House of Commons.

This open forum affords opportunities to discuss and reconcile divergent opinions. Backbenchers occasionally use caucus to demonstrate to the prime minister that divisions exist in the cabinet, and individual ministers may employ it to illustrate that support exists for their pet projects. Caucus is able to amend, stall, and even stop legislation when it is cohesive and has the support of at least some provinces or some interest groups. In recent sessions of parliament the Liberal caucus has, for example, succeeded in delaying parliamentary consideration of the Young Offenders bill and in halting a minor amendment to the British North American Act which would have increased the size of parliament. Most of the time, however, the government can obtain, at minimum, acquiescence in its policies and in its schedule of business for the House. The preeminence of the prime minister and cabinet exerts unarticulated psychological pressures on caucus members, even within their own jurisdiction. In addition, some organizational advantages are available to the prime minister, particularly his traditional prerogative to review the substance of the entire meeting immediately before adjournment. When Prime Minister Trudeau was openly criticized by an outspoken member of caucus over the government's foreign-ownership bill, he used this prerogative to reply that all viewpoints had been heard, compromises made, and that no new major amendments could be entertained. Frequently, outspoken caucus members encounter opprobrium from their colleagues and feel conscious of the need to refrain from such open confrontations. In this case one Liberal backbencher found that none of his colleagues would speak with him.

Every party in parliament can claim a direct link with the executive through the consultation among House leaders which takes place each week in the office of the government House leader. While each minister conducts a defence of his department in the House, it is the government House leader who represents the interests of the entire cabinet in its parliamentary interface. He is in charge of his party's whip and manages the flow of business and the innumerable personal matters which are so important to individual members of parliament. The House leaders' meeting has become the forum where all parties are told of the manner in which the government intends to use parliamentary resources and the place for negotiation over the scheduling of parliamentary and committee activities. The amount of time devoted to a legislative item and the procedures to be adopted during its passage exert considerable influence on the likelihood of its success. Since Prime Minister Trudeau came to office in 1968 — and especially during the 1972 minority government — the responsibility for negotiating solutions to parliamentary problems has rested heavily on the four House leaders because of their sensitivity to the mood and the sometimes cumbersome mechanisms of the House of Commons.

If we juxtapose the personal influence which the government House leader exercises over the parliamentary timetable with the fragmentation of responsibility in the preparliamentary part of the legislative system, it can be appreciated that a certain incoherence in policy formation and legislative action may occasionally emerge. It is somewhat incongruous that the government should erect a complex set of institutions for the development of legislation without considering how it might strengthen all the linkages in the legislative system. When the government introduced its monumental tax bill in the fall of 1971, parliamentary advisors soon realized that the bill had been drafted with so few clauses and so many sections that a united opposition could have stalled the bill by forcing a debate on what sections required a vote, or by debating and voting on almost every sentence. This and other procedural questions required renewed cabinet deliberation and set in motion a series of private meetings between representatives from the departments of Finance and Revenue, the PCO, the PMO, and the Office of the President of the Privy Council. The issue was finally resolved, with the aid of an all-night parliamentary sitting, but if more foresight and concern for parliamentary procedures had been demonstrated at the drafting stage, some of the obstacles could have been avoided.

Both parliamentarians and public servants have generally been unwilling to accept that they share a responsibility for the entire legislative system. The first requirement in the reform of the Canadian legislative system is to improve these inchoate links between the executive and parliament. If the inner circle is to supply the guns and ammunition for what Trudeau has called Canada's parliamentary

"Coney Island shooting gallery," then actors in the inner circle will be obliged to become more aware of the procedures, activities, and functions of parliament.

NOTES

1. The powers and responsibilities of cabinet are discussed in R. M. Dawson and Norman Ward, *The Government of Canada*, 4th ed. (Toronto: University of Toronto Press, 1971); J. R. Mallory, *The Structure of Canadian Government* (Toronto: Macmillan of Canada, 1971); Thomas Hockin (ed.), *The Apex of Power*, 2nd ed. (Scarborough, Ont.: Prentice-Hall of Canada, 1977); and G. Bruce Doern and Peter Aucoin (ed.), *The Structures of Policy-Making in Canada* (Toronto: Macmillan of Canada, 1971). Detailed comments on cabinet organization and the role of ministers may be found in A. D. P. Heeney, "Mackenzie King and the Cabinet Secretariat," *Canadian Public Administration*, 10 (September 1967), pp. 366-75; Gordon Robertson, "The Changing Role of the Privy Council Office," *Canadian Public Administration*, 14 (Spring 1971), pp. 487-508; Marc Lalonde, "The Changing Role of the Prime Minister's Office," *Canadian Public Administration*, 14 (Spring 1971), pp. 509-37; Michael Pitfield, "The Shape of Government in the 1980s: Techniques and Instruments for Policy Formulation at the Federal Level," *Canadian Public Administration*, 19 (1976), pp. 8-14; Thomas d'Aquino, "Prime Minister's Office: Catalyst or Cabal? Aspects of the Development of the Office in Canada and Some Thoughts about Its Future," *Canadian Public Administration*, 17 (1974), pp. 55-79, with comment by Denis Smith, pp. 80-84; and G. Bruce Doern, "Horizontal and Vertical Portfolios in Government," in G. Bruce Doern and V. Seymour Wilson (ed.), *Issues in Canadian Public Policy* (Toronto: Macmillan of Canada, 1974), pp. 310-36. General works on the prime minister and cabinet include R. M. Punnett, *The Prime Minister in Canadian Government and Politics* (Toronto: Macmillan of Canada, 1977) and W. A. Matheson, *The Prime Minister and the Cabinet* (Toronto: Methuen, 1976). On the role of the public service and senior public servants, see Colin Campbell and George J. Szablowski, *The Superbureaucrats* (Toronto: Macmillan of Canada, 1979) and J. E. Hodgetts, *The Canadian Public Service* (Toronto: University of Toronto Press, 1973).
2. Denis Smith, "President and Parliament: The Transformation of Parliamentary Government in Canada," in T. Hockin (ed.), *Apex of Power*, 2nd. ed., pp. 308-25, and F. F. Schindeler, "The Prime Minister and the Cabinet: History and Development," in *ibid.*, pp. 22-47.
3. See Walter Stewart, *Shrug: Trudeau in Power* (Toronto: New Press, 1971); For a more balanced journalistic treatment, see George Radwanski, *Trudeau* (Toronto: Macmillan of Canada, 1978).
4. Robert Dahl, *Modern Political Analysis*, 2nd ed. (Englewood Cliffs, N.J.: Prentice-Hall, 1970).

5. Carl Friedrich, *Man and His Government* (New York: McGraw-Hill, 1963), Chapter 11.

6. Punnett, *The Prime Minister in Canadian Government and Politics*, p. 86.

7. For a comprehensive treatment see Richard D. French, "The Privy Council Office: Support for Cabinet Decision Making," in Richard Schultz *et al.*, *The Canadian Political Process*, 3rd ed. (Toronto: Holt, Rinehart and Winston, 1979), pp. 363-94.

8. Blair Williams, "The Para-Political Bureaucracy in Ottawa," a paper prepared for the Legislative Studies in Canada Conference, Simon Fraser University (February 1979), p. 18.

9. *Ibid.*, p. 19.

10. Szablowski and Campbell, *Superbureaucrats*.

11. Mitchell Sharp, "Decision-Making in the Federal Cabinet," in Hockin, *Apex of Power*, 2nd ed., p. 67.

12. The Study of Parliament Group, *Seminar on the Budgetary Process*, 1 (1977), p. 10.

13. Detailed and sensitive discussions of the budgetary process and the main actors can be found in Douglas Hartle, *The Expenditure Process in the Government of Canada* (Toronto: The Canadian Tax Foundation, 1978) and H. V. Kroeker, *Accountability and Control: The Government Expenditure Process* (Montreal: C. D. Howe Institute, 1978). For a dated but excellent account of the functions of the Treasury Board, see A.W. Johnson, "The Treasury Board and the Machinery of Government in the 1970s," *Canadian Journal of Political Science*, 4 (September 1971), pp. 346-66.

14. Hartle, *The Expenditure Process*, p.7.

15. Harry Rogers, the first Comptroller General, has outlined the role of the office and the obstacles to program evaluation in "Program Evaluation in the Federal Government," in G. Bruce Doern and Allan M. Maslove (ed.), *The Public Evaluation of Government Spending* (Montreal: Institute for Research on Public Policy, 1979), pp. 79-89.

16. Richard W. Phidd and G. Bruce Doern, *The Politics and Management of Canadian Economic Policy* (Toronto: Macmillan of Canada, 1978), p. 102.

17. M. J. L. Kirby, H. V. Kroeker, and W. R. Teschke, "The Impact of Public Policy-Making Structures and Processes in Canada," *Canadian Public Administration*, 21 (Fall 1978), pp. 413-14.

18. A. W. Johnson, "Public Policy: Creativity and Bureaucracy," *Canadian Public Administration*, 21 (Spring 1978), pp. 1-15.

19. For an important discussion of the relation between drafting and policy, see William H. R. Charles, "Public Policy and Legislative Drafting," in William A. W. Neilson and James C. MacPherson (ed.), *The Legislative Process in Canada* (Montreal: Institute for Research on Public Policy, 1978), pp. 267-91, with comments by Douglas Lambert and Richard F. Dole, pp. 295-99.

20. Kenneth Kernaghan, "Power, Parliament and Public Servants in Canada: Ministerial Responsibility Re-examined," a paper prepared for the

Legislative Studies in Canada Conference, Simon Fraser University (February 1979), p. 11.

21. Kenneth Kernaghan, "Changing Concepts of Power and Responsibility in the Canadian Public Service," *Canadian Public Administration*, 21 (Fall 1978), p. 395.

22. J. R. Mallory, "Responsive and Responsible Governments," Presidential Address, Section II, *Transactions of the Royal Society of Canada*, 12 (1974). For a discussion of the evolution of the doctrine of ministerial responsibility, see T. M. Denton, "Ministerial Responsibility: A Contemporary Perspective," in Schultz *et al.*, *The Canadian Political Process*, pp. 344-62.

23. Canada, Royal Commission on Financial Management and Accountability, *Final Report* (Ottawa: Supply and Services, 1979), p. 485.

24. Kroeker, *Accountability and Control*, pp. 66-69.

25. Canada, Royal Commission on Financial Management and Accountability, *Final Report*, p. 374. According to Douglas Hartle, the Commission "went badly off the rails" in proposing the direct accountability of deputy ministers to parliamentary committees. See his "The Report of the Royal Commission on Financial Management and Accountability: A Review," *Canadian Public Policy*, V (Summer 1979), pp. 377-78.

26. John Courtney, *The Selection of National Party Leaders in Canada* (Toronto: Macmillan of Canada, 1973), p. 157.

27. Punnett, *The Prime Minister in Canadian Government and Politics*, p. 15.

5. The House of Commons and the Senate

On November 15, 1976, electors in the province of Quebec returned a majority Parti Québécois government. The next day in the House of Commons, opposition members tried to elicit from the government some response to the election of a party devoted to achieving a measure of political sovereignty for the province of Quebec. Cabinet ministers refused to provide anything beyond the anticipated platitudes; it was not until January that Prime Minister Trudeau offered a considered response. His forum was the United States House of Representatives and his remarks were carried on both Canadian and American television networks.

In this dramatic series of events, parliament played a minor role. There was no formal discussion of Quebec separatism on the floor of the House of Commons until February, long after Claude Ryan, Liberal leader in Quebec, had criticized parliament for failing to address the issue. By the time the debate occurred, all of Canada's major newspapers and magazines had responded to the situation and several television programs had been devoted to the topic. Parliament appeared paralyzed when confronted with a major change in the political atmosphere. In the mobilization of public opinion, parliament does not have the resources to compete with other structures in society. It remains, for purposes of textbook description, the symbol of legitimate authority in the regime, but this event illustrates parliament's failure, and perhaps its inability, to keep pace with other institutions in terms of skills and resources.

The purpose of this chapter is to examine parliament's capacity to act as an arena for the clash of major societal forces. This includes a consideration of the constitutional context in which parliament operates, the procedural features of parliamentary organization, the clash between government and opposition forces, and the status of parliament as a symbol and legitimizing agency.

THE CONSTITUTIONAL CONTEXT

The major written portion of the Canadian constitution is the British North America Act. While no reference to cabinet is made, the Fathers of Confederation embraced the ruling constitutional principles of the United Kingdom with their emphasis on representation and parliamentary supremacy. The document contains two major sections with direct relevance to parliament: one on its composition, the other on the extent of its authority.

Part IV of the BNA Act, entitled "Legislative Power," specifies that Canada is to have one parliament consisting of a queen, a House of Commons, and a upper house called the Senate. In the bicameral legislature, membership in the lower house is determined through the electoral system. While membership is adjusted occasionally, as dictated by the requirements of electoral law, the House of Commons in 1980 had 282 members elected from individual constituencies in the provinces and territories. The Senate, by contrast, is a totally appointed body whose membership is set at 102 (with provision for the addition of either four or eight members), although it is unusual that the maximum membership is ever attained. On the advice of the prime minister, the governor general appoints senators from five regions in Canada: 24 from the Maritimes, 24 from Quebec, 24 from Ontario, 24 from the western provinces, and 6 from Newfoundland. The obvious provincial inequities are the subject of controversy, as is the relatively minor role accorded the Senate in the legislative system.

Provision for the authority of the Canadian parliament is located in the preamble of the BNA Act: it stipulates that Canada is to have a constitution like that of the United Kingdom. The doctrine of parliamentary supremacy was thereby transplanted in Canada, albeit with some adjustments owing to the adoption of a federal system and to the fact that Canada could not amend the BNA Act without referral to the British parliament. Briefly, parliamentary supremacy is a constitutional principle which requires the executive to be responsible at all times to the legislature, while the legislature is neither controlled by the executive nor interfered with by the courts. In both Canada and the United Kingdom the executive is chosen from members of the legislature and must resign if and when the legislature determines that the executive no longer enjoys its support. Constitutionally, the British parliament may enact legislation on any subject whatsoever. In principle it could even abrogate liberties or abolish the courts. In neither country, however, may the doctrine of parliamentary supremacy be used to restrain a future parliament from exercising its own prerogatives.

In view of the growth of government activities, the responsibilities assumed by modern executives and the competition of other sectors of society, a constitutional principle like parliamentary supremacy may seem to have little relevance in contemporary political life. Even the BNA Act restricts parliamentary supremacy by specifying those areas of jurisdiction which are the exclusive reserve of the provinces, and demarcating those subjects in the act whose amendment is beyond the authority of parliament. Nonetheless, this principle still pervades theories about interaction between the executive and the legislature and provides the theoretical foundation for notions such as ministerial responsibility, parliament's final authority in the collection and appropriation of public monies, and motions of nonconfidence in the government.

In most countries, executives and legislatures are separate institutions tied to one another by a shared responsibility for lawmaking. The manner in which powers are shared has evolved over time, however, and continues to change under the pressures of environmental forces. The British parliament slowly acquired the rights and privileges now referred to as the supremacy of parliament. In the initial stages of its development, parliament was primarily a consultative body established at the initiative of barons who had a direct interest in maintaining control of the English king. Although the king did not always act on the advice proffered, he was required at least to consult his barons. Parliament slowly enhanced its status, first by restricting the king's choice of advisors, then by controlling taxation. Except for brief periods of extreme conflict, relations between the crown and parliament were mutually beneficial. Parliament forced kings to consult on major policy questions, while monarchs like Henry VIII employed parliament's claim to supremacy to sanction laws unpopular with some sections of the population. Until the British parliament was reformed in the nineteenth century, it was composed of representatives of traditional elements such as the aristocracy and the church. Because of its composition, parliament often found itself in sympathy with the crown on contentious issues and many monarchs behaved as if parliament's role was to help secure their control over the people. Thus, parliamentary supremacy and executive control evolved in tandem as ideas around which the parliamentary process was organized.

By the time Canadians had drafted their major constitutional document, limitations had already been placed on the supremacy of parliament. Only during the period 1867 to 1906 did the Canadian legislature display the major characteristics of the nineteenth-century British parliament. By 1913 the procedures which characterize the present relationship between the executive and the legislature in Canada were evolving. The government was beginning to construct a legislative program and to claim for itself the parliamentary time required to realize its objectives.

The principle of parliamentary supremacy allows parliament to participate in the performance of two major functions, lawmaking and surveillance. As indicated in Chapter 4, those institutions which make the most significant contribution to the initial development of legislation are in the inner circle. Nonetheless, parliament is quite correctly viewed as that part of the legislative system which transforms bills into statutes by moving them through various stages during which they are exposed to the public, subject to partisan attack, and refined into acts of parliament. Much parliamentary time is also consumed in scrutinizing government expenditure, overseeing administration, and interpellating cabinet ministers. This surveillance function results in some of the most publicized parliamentary activities.

In passing laws and in supervising executive actions, parliament acquires the ability to perform other functions for the legislative system. The fact that all functions have intangible aspects and are interrelated makes it extremely difficult to distinguish among them or to measure their performance, as we shall see in Chapter 8. In the case of legitimation, parliament may be said to perform this function in a manifest way when it votes on and approves legislation. It performs the same function in a latent manner simply by holding regular meetings and debating government actions. When parliament meets in an emergency sitting to discuss a crisis situation, lawmaking may be the operation carried out, but usually a conflict-management function is performed as a consequence. In the following section we will describe how both the House of Commons and the Senate participate in the making of laws and in the surveillance of the executive. In each case it is important to understand that these operations may contribute to or detract from the performance of other functions.

THE LEGISLATIVE PROCESS IN THE HOUSE OF COMMONS

To most outsiders and to some participants, parliament consists of a mystery of relics, dignitaries, and ceremonial debates. Many of the rituals originated in Britain with the struggle between parliament and the crown and, while their practical significance may be obscure, they are important symbolic outputs of the legislative system. The procedures of parliament have also been influenced by our British heritage. The most important rules for the conduct of parliamentary business in Canada are entitled "standing orders." They are written in conformity with the constitution and represent the agreed-on procedures by which parliament normally conducts its affairs. It is through the amendment of standing orders that the House alters its procedures.

The standing orders should be viewed both as a series of impartial routines designed to facilitate the debate and transaction of parliamentary business and as a political weapon which aids the executive in governing the country. When ministers answer questions during Question Period the rules are intended primarily to permit the open criticism of government activities. On the other hand, the restrictions placed on the use of parliamentary time by private members illustrate how the rules have been progressively manipulated since 1913 to allow the government to manoeuvre its legislative program through parliament. Despite the tensions that exist between the two objectives of parliamentary rules, participants have normally achieved a consensus on procedure which has helped to maintain the viability of the institution. Occasionally this consensus breaks down, as it did in 1969 when the government had to use closure to terminate debate on new procedures.

The control and the allocation of available parliamentary time is determined generally by constitutional requirements and specifically by procedural rules. Parliaments are summoned and dissolved by the governor general on the advice of the prime minister. Since there is no fixed date for elections, their occurrence is, in practical terms, determined when the governor general agrees to a prime minister's request for the dissolution of parliament. This occurs when the prime minister, for whatever reason, chooses to dissolve parliament or when he clearly loses the confidence of the House of Commons. Constitutionally, an election must be held every five years and, regardless of their length, parliaments must meet in at least one session every year. The beginning of each session is marked by a speech from the throne and the termination by the ceremony of prorogation. Following the Second

World War, sessions normally began in the fall and ended in the spring. Recently, partially due to the prevalence of minority governments, the scheduling of sessions has been less consistent and planning has been made more difficult. Members of the House of Commons have often been required to sit for more days during the year, and the traditional summer recess has been placed in jeopardy.

The standing orders state the daily time dimensions within which parliament has chosen to operate. Except for rare emergency sittings, parliament sits every weekday, and each sitting follows a normal pattern. After opening ceremonies members usually rise in their place to ask the unanimous consent of the House to make motions without notice (S.O. 43). Such consent is rarely granted and the House normally moves promptly to the 40-minute oral Question Period. This is the best-attended event in the parliamentary day and at least one prime minister, John Diefenbaker, has regarded it as the most important. Oral Question Period usually ends before 3:00 PM and is followed by matters of privilege and Routine Proceedings. During Routine Proceedings, members of the government use this period to table official documents in the House and to announce government policy to parliament. Both the government and private members employ Routine Proceedings to make motions about the business of the House of Commons and its committees. The Parliamentary Secretary to the President of the Privy Council may then read ministerial answers to written questions placed on the order paper by members of the House and announce the government's attitude toward specific notices of motion for the production of papers. Occasionally, if members have provided written notice to the speaker in advance, they may take this opportunity to move, under Standing Order 26, that the House adjourn to discuss "a definite matter of urgent public importance."

Orders of the day, a period during which government business or opposition resolutions are considered, occupies the attention of the House until 5:00 p.m. It is attended by at least one minister and by scattered representatives from each of the parties. Before dinner, time is set aside for the bills and the resolutions of private members. When the House meets in the evening it is usually between 8:00 p.m. and 10 p.m. to consider government business. On three days of the week this is followed immediately by a debate on the motion to adjourn. This 30-minute debate, known to parliamentarians as the "late show," consists of three short debating periods monopolized by backbenchers and parliamentary secretaries.

The time allotted to some activities is specified in the standing orders, while the time assigned to others requires negotiation among the parties. In general, the rules limit speeches to 40 minutes. While members must rise in their place and be recognized, the choice of speakers is determined by a list of members drawn up by the party whips. The traditional right of privy councillors to be recognized before others is usually respected by the speaker. When the rules do not specify the scheduling of events in the House, negotiations between the House leaders, and occasionally the whips, are used to resolve disputes. In the unusual event that the House leaders are unable to agree on the scheduling of parliamentary business, time allocations, closure, or a filibuster of debate may occur.

The orderly conduct of the legislative process rests in the hands of the speaker and a permanent staff of the House of Commons. Obstacles to the creation of a ''permanent speakership'' have not been overcome and the speaker continues to be an ordinary member of parliament — agreeable to both government and opposition — formally elected by his colleagues at the beginning of each parliament. He is responsible for the procedures of the House of Commons and its administration, a responsibility he shares with the Board of Internal Economy composed of the speaker and four cabinet ministers. The House of Commons' staff, headed by the Clerk of the House of Commons, hold permanent positions but are not linked to the public service. Their responsibilities include procedure, finances, and the administration of the research and library facilities.

A. Lawmaking: Types of Bills

In Chapter 4 the creation of a legislative program and the development of a single legislative item in the preparliamentary stages were treated in some detail. It was clear from that description that the preparliamentary stages are used to develop policy proposals and draft legislation, but that formal lawmaking only begins when the draft legislation is introduced in parliament in the form of a bill. Neither committees of the House nor the House itself actually legislates, except in the formal sense that legislation is ''read'' by parliament. The power to initiate legislation was lost to the British parliament in the first half of the nineteenth century and, by the turn of the twentieth century in Canada, the government-sponsored public bill had become the chief vehicle for accomplishing changes to the law. The government is the main initiator of legislation and pilots the bills through the

House and committees on the strength of its majority. A bill, when it is passed by parliament, is called an act, and only after royal assent and proclamation does it become law.

The passage of bills through parliament bears some similarity to their movement in the inner circle: debate is often protracted, progress sporadic, and precise scheduling difficult. At each of the preparliamentary stages, policy proposals are infused with new qualities—priority labels, detailed amendments, and legal form. To some degree parliamentary consideration represents a continuation of this process, but two new dimensions are added. Parliamentary examination is more formal and more open. Formal action and consent is required at virtually every stage and, while this sphere of lawmaking is more public than any other, paradoxically, the ritual occasionally serves to conceal the process more effectively than ministerial oaths of secrecy. In the preparliamentary stages, legislative items are differentiated primarily on the basis of availability, urgency, and compatibility with political goals. Parliament distinguishes among bills on constitutional and legal grounds in two major ways. First, legislation may be divided into private and public bills. Private bills apply to specific individuals or groups of people and are usually designed to accomplish a particular and narrow purpose. They are required to incorporate companies, for example, and, until 1964, were used to grant divorces for residents of the provinces of Quebec and Newfoundland. Public bills are of two types: bills sponsored by the cabinet and private members' bills which are introduced by individual members of parliament. In each session since 1867, parliament has enacted many more government bills than private members' bills, but this trend became particularly pronounced after 1896. Except for changes in the name of a constituency it is not uncommon for parliament to pass no private members' bills during a session.

Public bills are also divided into financial and nonfinancial varieties. Most public bills have financial implications, but money bills—those which authorize taxation and expenditure—are special in a variety of ways. Their passage through parliament resembles the passage of ordinary legislation, but only ministers of the crown are permitted to introduce money bills. While parliament initiates neither expenditure nor taxation, parliament's particular interest in financial legislation rests on its traditional right to demand that the crown hear grievances before the Commons grants supply—that is, the funds necessary to conduct the king's affairs. The consideration of financial measures is intended to be a time when the cabinet accounts for its management of the economy, listens to the complaints brought forward by private members of parliament, and (usually) weathers an opposition motion to the effect that in one or more ways cabinet has failed in its responsibilities. To accentuate the importance of financial questions, many of the procedures employed in the consideration of money bills differ from those employed in the examination of ordinary legislation. These differences are outlined below.

It is necessary to make two further points before proceeding to a consideration of the legislative process in parliament. First, financial bills, as implied above, may be either tax bills — designed to raise revenue — or appropriation bills which authorize expenditures. In private households and private business it is standard practice to establish a budget based on a simultaneous consideration of revenues and expenditures. In parliament, however, taxing and spending procedures are separate and have been since the British parliament created a Consolidated Fund in 1787 and began to draw on it without concern for the precise source of revenues. This original division between taxing and spending is a peculiar feature of the British parliamentary experience and, in Canada, has led to the creation of two separate streams of financial legislation. Consequently, the budget speech, normally presented in the spring by the minister of finance, contains a summary of the government's tax changes. Specific tax legislation follows. Government spending, on the other hand, is presented to parliament in February in the form of estimates which comprise the government's "expenditure budget." Appropriation bills authorizing these expenditures are introduced subsequently. Parliament is never given the opportunity to consider taxes and spending simultaneously.

The second point concerns the nature of expenditure legislation. Bills which authorize expenditures may be divided into those which merely appropriate funds requested by the cabinet to meet annual expenditures, and those which authorize expenditures for particular purposes such as pensions, subsidies, and allowances. The former type of expenditure is accomplished by appropriation bills. The latter is included in the statutes which establish programs. The government must ensure that appropriation bills are passed annually, but once particular payments are authorized by statutes they remain authorized indefinitely. These "statutory appropriations" are obligations which no government can avoid without amending the original statute. Statutory appropriations usually comprise approximately 50 per cent of the annual sums approved by parliament; annual appropriation bills account for the remainder.[1] Much of the rigidity which observers detect in government budgeting can be traced to statutory obligations such as the Canada Pension Plan, family allowances, and equalization payments to the provinces.[2]

B. Lawmaking: Stages of Deliberation

The movement through parliament of all the types of legislation discussed above may be divided into seven stages. At each step, decisions on timing contribute significantly to the eventual success or failure of the proposals. After receiving final cabinet approval, the draft legislation is initialled by the prime minister and deposited with the clerk of the appropriate House. The initial motion is for leave to introduce the bill in the House and subsequently a first reading motion is introduced, usually by the sponsoring minister. Its acceptance, which is normally a matter of course, allows the bill to be printed, given a number (a "C" prefix if it originates in the Commons, an "S" prefix if it originates in the Senate), and distributed to members of parliament. If the bill is a money bill which would authorize a statutory appropriation, the Parliamentary Council drafts a document called a royal recommendation which states, as specifically as possible, the purposes for which money is being appropriated. It is subsequently used as a frame of reference to determined the validity of proposed amendments.

The bill is now on the order paper, which is the schedule of pending parliamentary business. It has been brought to parliament's attention and, if it is a government bill, it can be called by the government House leader to form the basis for debate during the period set aside for government business.

The next stage of the process is the second of three readings. Out of courtesy and political considerations, the government announces the general schedule of parliamentary business one week in advance, but no notification is required once a bill is in the House. During second reading the speaker enforces strict rules of relevancy and permits no amendments, because this stage is designed to focus attention on the principles of the bill. Sponsoring ministers almost always appear to defend their bill; the government and opposition front benches monopolize debate. This stage usually takes one or two days, though there is no requirement that they be consecutive.

Like many procedures in the House of Commons, there are disagreements over what is implied in adopting a second reading motion. Governments, regardless of political stripe, are attracted to the view that approval at second reading implies that the House has accepted the bill in principle and that subsequent delays, or amendments that address anything but the details of the bill, contradict the spirit of second-reading approval. In 1968 the Special Committee on Procedure attacked this view, arguing that the importance of second reading has been exaggerated to the detriment of private members who have amendments to pose.[3] The committee was reluctant, however, to indicate the scope of amendments which could justifiably be entertained later in the proceedings, especially at the committee stage. As a result, governments persist in their narrow construction of this motion and opposition members continue their futile efforts to have bills referred to standing committees before the second reading stage is finished.

When debate at second reading is completed, Standing Orders 74(1) and 74(2) stipulate that "unless otherwise ordered" a bill must be sent directly to a standing, special, or joint (Senate and House) committee where the detailed consideration of bills is commenced. Committee of the Whole House, which is the House sitting as a committee with rules relaxed and the deputy speaker presiding, has lost much of its routine importance except for the detailed examination of money bills. Clause-by-clause consideration of bills is now almost always the task of the committee system. In this third stage of legislation, the several standing committees are able to meet and consider bills simultaneously. Debates may take place and amendments be moved on every clause of the bill. While most amendments originate with the opposition, the government itself may take this opportunity to amend the legislation.

For committee members the overriding problem at this stage is to decide what committees are to do with bills. Some members believe that committees should be concerned only with shaping the details of bills, making refinements, and preventing administrative oversights. But others believe that the examination of bills by committees should provide an opportunity to investigate the general policy behind the bill. Studies of committee amendments fail to provide conclusive support for either of these general interpretations. In a study of the Broadcasting Act, 1968, Tom Hockin drew attention to the number of amendments adopted in committee and subsequently accepted by the minister. He optimistically concluded that committees could force changes to legislation.[4] In this case, however, most of the 22 successful amendments were technical in nature and were proposed, not by the opposition, but by the minister's parliamentary secretary. Nonetheless, some substantive amendments were accepted — small victories that have been repeated on other occasions. A special joint committee made almost 50 substantive amendments to the Public Service Staff Relations Bill introduced in the 27th Parliament (1966-68).[5] In the 28th Parliament (1968-72) the language bill and breathalizer legislation both had amendments put which were accepted by the government. In the minority situation of the 29th Parliament (1972-74) more amendments were directed to the essentials of bills. Major changes in legislation took place, for example, on the election expenses and wiretapping bills. During the 30th Parliament (1974-79) the Justice Committee successfully urged the Minister of Justice to accept a new definition of obscenity and changes to government-sponsored criminal-code legislation.

These examples notwithstanding, it requires a combination of fortuitous circumstances to afford backbenchers much scope in amending government legislation. As we have argued in previous chapters, governments are more inclined to agree to amendments when there is outside pressure from influential groups or the provinces. Moreover, governments are less protective of bills of intermediate or minor importance, but tend to insist that their intentions be respected and that party discipline be imposed on major legislative items.[6] Other imponderables — including minority government and the personalities of ministers — combine to make the consideration of legislation in committees a highly variable process.

The amendment of appropriation bills is restricted even further by the text of a royal recommendation which is transmitted by the governor general, accompanies the bill, and sets forth — often in detail — the terms for which money will be granted. Unless a proposed new expenditure can be interpreted as consistent with the royal recommendation it is constitutionally invalid. Not even a minister is permitted to make amendments: he must withdraw the bill and introduce a new royal recommendation. The only remedy open to the private member and the committee is to reduce or vote against the amount of money recommended. Distinguishing between valid and invalid amendments can be an exceedingly difficult task. While it is obvious that a major increase is beyond the scope of the royal recommendation, an amendment to the Small Business Loans Act which sought to add the Alberta Treasury Board to the list of lending agencies was not an obvious violation. However, like almost all of these backbench initiatives, it was ruled out of order.

The fourth step in the parliamentary process is the report stage, so called because it refers to the reporting of the amended bill back to the House. Debate ranges over both the principles and the details of the bill. Amendments defeated in committees may be reintroduced in the House, a practice which consumes valuable time and tends to negate the purpose of committee consideration. Nonetheless, opposition members may use this opportunity to publicly advocate their proposals while the government uses report stage to "correct" committee amendments or to launch new ones. During the 28th and 29th Parliaments, report stage consumed between 10 and 25 per cent of the time devoted to legislation in the House of Commons.[7]

By comparison with the first four stages of parliamentary consideration, the final proceedings may seem somewhat perfunctory. At least 24 hours must elapse before the fifth stage (third reading) can be embarked on, although the House may waive this time restriction by unanimous agreement. Debate during third reading is not impossible or unknown, but it is usually commenced only at the opposition's insistence. At this stage it is still possible to halt proceedings on the bill by moving that the bill be considered six months hence ("the hoist") or by moving a "reasoned amendment" which outlines why the measure should not be acted on at this time. These efforts, while seldom successful, can be employed to underline hostility toward the purpose of the bill. As usual, the problem is to convey the significance of these procedures beyond the tiny audience which understands them.

The sixth stage in the process covers Senate consideration (unless the bill was introduced in the Senate) which is often brief and normally attracts little public attention. Procedures resemble those of the House of Commons and most of the refining of legislation is confined to the committee system. When the Senate does react, it is frequently to challenge provisions considered harmful to business. The Banking, Trade and Commerce committee is by far the most active standing committee. Its members propose most of the legislative amendments and, on the strength of their business contacts, some senators can influence a bill's consideration in the House of Commons.[8] The best recent example of this phenomenon concerns the Senate's consideration of the Bank Act. Although introduced into the Commons during the 30th Parliament by the minister of finance, detailed consideration of the bill occurred in the Senate. Following the now established "Haydon formula" (after Senator Saltar Haydon, its author), the Senate automatically began consideration of the subject matter of the bill even though it was formally on the Commons' agenda. In March 1979 the Banking committee tabled its report and the finance minister, Mr. Chretien, promptly announced his intention to withdraw the bill pending an evaluation of the Senate's recommendations. In a most subtle and unobtrusive fashion the Senate, or more precisely a tiny portion of the Senate's membership, had left its mark on the banking community for the succeeding ten years.

On rare occasions the Senate may obstruct the House. In December 1973 the Senate amended the wire-tapping bill, C-176. This action deleted a clause which had been opposed by the minority Liberal government but sponsored by a majority of the members of the House of Commons. Such action would not be tolerated if it occurred repeatedly. In this particular case the House repassed the bill with the amendment intact and the Senate capitulated.

In the final stage of legislation the executive, in the garb of the governor general, returns to seal the process by royal assent which is given in the Senate, usually to several bills at once. This does not mean that the bill is automatically law on that day. With greater frequency in recent years, statutes require proclamation, a decision usually entrusted to the departments involved but requiring the approval of cabinet through a special committee of council. Delays in proclamation are by no means unusual and are designed, ostensibly, to provide departments with time to change forms and manuals and alert staff to the new rules. The secretary of state, for example, delayed by several months proclamation of an act which would grant females equal status with males in the sponsoring of spouses who wished to assume Canadian citizenship.

Money bills, as outlined earlier, follow the same general, seven-stage process but are unique for two reasons: first, they have a longer gestation period; second, they are not considered in standing committees but in Committee of the Whole House. The longer gestation period derives from the fact that the bills themselves are not the only, or even the most important, basis for debate. In the case of tax bills, much of the debate centres on the budget speech, delivered by the minister of finance, which outlines the government's economic strategy and summarizes changes that will subsequently be proposed in the form of tax legislation. In the case of appropriation bills, virtually all the debate occurs in standing committees on the estimates themselves: the appropriation bills are introduced later and merely give legislative effect to the government's spending proposals. Billions of dollars of expenditure, in the form of an appropriation bill, are approved in a matter of minutes, a procedure which must give pause to the gallery observer who does not know that this is the culmination of an excruciatingly long process.

There are few objections to the process of *legislating* appropriations: criticisms focus instead on standing committees' consideration of the estimates themselves, a matter taken up in the following section of this chapter. Tax specialists and economists, however, have become increasingly critical of the tax-legislation process. In a recent submission to the minister of finance, the Canadian Tax Foundation has argued that tax changes announced in the budget are founded on inadequate consultation with experts and affected groups and on a misplaced compulsion to maintain secrecy. This general problem, they maintain, is aggravated by the consideration of tax bills in Committee of the Whole rather than in the Standing Committee on Finance, Trade and Economic Affairs where witnesses could appear and argue their case. The present process precludes this by restricting tax legislation — including major overhauls like the 1971 tax bill — to the floor of the House.[9] This is not a minor point because, unlike the appropriation process which is an annual affair, tax changes, once approved, remain in place indefinitely. Moreover, even less information is provided to parliament regarding the purpose and likely impact of tax changes than is provided regarding the estimates. Ken Woodside has concluded that governments which are interested in avoiding intense scrutiny of their programs of assistance to business will be more attracted to tax incentives rather than subsidies. In addition to other advantages, the tax option simply poses fewer legislative obstacles: "lack of expertise and opportunity for detailed analysis result in relatively superficial consideration of proposed tax changes."[10]

The entire legislation process is complex and variable. Although governments, especially those which command majority support in the House of Commons, have procedural weapons and the votes to invoke them, there is nothing certain or preordained about the process. Many opportunities remain for parties or factions to thwart the conversion of bills into statutes. Moreover, few governments are naturally adept at managing their legislative program in the House to the point of avoiding all opposition criticism. In a speech commenting on the Trudeau government's record, Walter Baker summed up a great deal of opposition sentiment when he maintained that, "the government has refused week after week to give us an idea of what it wants to deal with. It changes its mind all the time."[11] A classic case of inadequate planning occurred in the final hours of the 4th Session of the 28th Parliament when the government requested unanimous consent to proceed with the third reading of the Family Income Security Plan bill. One member denied permission and this single action stopped proceedings on the legislation. Since FISP was never reintroduced, this action effectively killed the bill. Many bills in the government's program are left on the order paper and must be reintroduced in the next session, regardless of their previous progress. Some bills are promised but take years to appear. A Canadian Development Corporation was promised by Liberal governments in virtually every throne speech from 1963 to 1970. Legislation authorizing its creation was finally passed on June 30, 1971.

In the parliamentary theatre many performances occur simultaneously and efficient government direction is required to ensure that its priority items survive without endless compromise. In a majority-government situation, the opposition may be unable to prevent the passage of a single bill, but, despite its advantages, the government rarely succeeds in achieving its whole legislative program, a subject we return to in Chapter 8.

THE SURVEILLANCE PROCESS IN THE HOUSE OF COMMONS

The importance of accountability in a democracy lies in the need for the governed to be protected in some manner from the arbitrary use of power on the part of the governors. Somehow, those we trust with the instruments of power must be made to explain and justify their actions. In response to this need the Canadian parliament engages in another set of activities that can be described generally as surveillance of the executive. Between elections the legislature finds techniques to hold the executive responsible and such surveillance can take many forms. In fact, if the term is defined very generally, almost every parliamentary activity, including legislative amendment, could be considered an aspect of surveillance. In this book the concept will refer more specifically to the means by which parliament demands information and justification from the executive for the general direction of policy and for the detailed activities of government, expressed, for example, in the estimates and subordinate legislation. An adversary style of question and debate often accompanies the performance of the surveillance function.

A. *Overseeing Finances*

Theoretically, the opportunity for parliamentary scrutiny of government policy is best afforded by consideration of departmental estimates. The estimates represent the government's projected spending pattern. They are prepared by the Treasury Board Secretariat for the forthcoming fiscal year, April 1 to March 31, and are tabled in parliament in the form of the Blue Book, an imposing compilation of spending proposals. As mentioned earlier, only ministers of the crown (in effect the cabinet) may propose expenditures. Parliament's responsibility is to formally extend or withhold approval; while parliament may reduce an expenditure, it is prohibited, by the constitution, from increasing a government's financial commitment. Although parliament is the final arbiter of government appropriations in Canada, the executive actually does the spending. The executive is restricted in one important respect: it cannot spend money for purposes which have not been specifically approved by parliament.

Before the final estimates reach the parliamentary stage, their precise composition has been the subject of extensive deliberation among departmental officials and budgeting and cost accounting experts. The introduction of PPB and the strengthening of budgetary control in the hands of the Treasury Board Secretariat and the Treasury Board itself have enhanced the process of centralized control over expenditure in the departments. With the possible exception of the postaudit process,[12] which is the responsibility of the auditor general who reports directly to the House of Commons, parliament has nothing to compare with the techniques of control the government imposes on itself. Parliament has barely managed to remain stationary in the evolution of appropriations control, and by comparison with the executive it has experienced a relative decline.

Prior to the procedural reforms introduced in 1968, the main government estimates were considered in Committee of Supply, which was actually the House meeting under another name with the rules relaxed and the speaker replaced in the Chair by another member.[13] The motion to enter Committee of Supply gave members an opportunity to launch into a wide-ranging debate not necessarily on financial matters. In 1913, 1955, and 1965, time restrictions were placed on the business of Supply; in 1968 the whole procedure was replaced by the referral of main estimates to the Commons' standing committees. The main estimates are usually referred to parliament during the final week of February and to committees of the House on or before March 1. This is accomplished by the passage of a government motion on which there can be neither debate nor amendment. Once the main estimates are referred, the standing committees are required to report them back not later than May 31.[14] If they have not been reported by that date, Standing Order 58(14) provides that they "shall be deemed to have been reported." Thus, there is no requirement that the committees formally approve the estimates.

The new procedure which refers estimates to standing committees has not been accompanied by a new consensus on how to approach them. Members of parliament devote their committee time primarily to the policies and administrative practices of the department whose estimates are being considered. This tendency has been enhanced by the committees' ability to summon and question officials. In the old Committee of Supply, department officials occupied seats in the aisle on the floor of the House of Commons, advised their ministers on questions, and escaped direct interrogation. Literally hundreds of officials now attend hundreds of committee meetings: once the minister has made his initial statement to the committee and departed, these senior public servants remain to answer questions.

With officials available in the new system the consideration of estimates has become primarily a device for gathering information. Committee members pose few questions which concern the cost of government programs, rarely admonish ministers, and even less frequently reduce specific expenditure items.[15] In a study conducted in 1972, Paul Thomas found few MPs who were motivated by the idea of searching for economies and efficiencies in departmental operations.[16] Opposition members are more concerned with gathering information and extracting statements that may be potentially embarrassing to the government, while MPs from all parties use this opportunity to convey the complaints of constituents to the bureaucrats responsible. Examination of the estimates of the CBC, for example, invariably includes questions about programming decisions, including the advisability of scheduling World Series or CFL football games. This lack of cost consciousness is neither a new nor uniquely Canadian phenomenon. As early as 1902 the Committee of Supply in the United Kingdom was regarded as a political forum and the opinion developed that simply controlling costs was of little purpose unless it was also possible to examine the policies and administration of government departments.

Getting members to set their sights that high is not particularly easy. The order of reference, which instructs a committee to consider the estimates in its area, is at least partially responsible for this state of affairs. It is so wide that it implies that every item in the Blue Book should be considered while not commanding an in-depth investigation of any department. Estimates reports in Canada are exceptionally brief and, since the government is not required to take action, both the government and the House generally ignore appended recommendations. No committee has produced a substantive report on the estimates since 1973 when the parliamentary secretary to the government House leader wrote to committee chairmen telling them to decrease or eliminate, but not to recommend on, estimate items.[17] Some committees persist in the belief that every estimate should be considered and voted on separately as in the old Committee of Supply and, in deference to this notion, considerable committee time is devoted to the formal passage of votes. It is not surprising that meetings on estimates are the worst attended of all types of committee meetings and that most are conducted in the absence of a quorum. It is by no means unusual for committees to approve votes at the outset of a meeting — when a quorum is present — and then proceed to question witnesses on the millions of dollars that have just been approved.

Numerous suggestions have been made which are intended to relieve the present malaise. Most prominent among them is the proposal that MPs be provided with more intelligible information regarding spending proposals. It was expected that the introduction of PPB with a budget format based on objectives would provide parliament with a new opportunity to offer a more fundamental critique of government spending.[18] Nothing of the sort has transpired. In fact, critics of the present estimates format argue that the PPB presentation hides details such as salaries and contracts under broad headings and remains unhelpful to MPs interested in transcending the votes and subheadings to ask about the purposes and progress of specific programs.[19] MPs still operate without the program information on which the government bases much of its planning. Consequently, members remain concerned primarily with the programs that have been added or eliminated, not with the strategic aspects of control which the PPB format was designed to emphasize.

In response to critics of the estimates procedure, including the auditor general,[20] the Trudeau government promised, in the speech from the throne opening the 4th Session of the 30th Parliament, that parliamentarians would be given access to program evaluations conducted internally by the government. This type of innovation represents the foundation on which a deliberate and effective estimates procedure could be built. However, because no committee considers the totality of departmental estimates, no institution is made responsible for a comparative study of the expenditure patterns of all departments. It should be possible for parliament to compare the estimates of one department with those of another and to improve its capacity to analyze the operations of ongoing government programs when requests are made for refunding.

Organizational reform aside, there remains the problem of enticing members of parliament to participate actively in the estimates process. The Lambert Commission has suggested that the Commons' rules be changed to make it easier for MPs to reduce items of expenditure in the estimates.[21] It is by no means clear, however, that members have any interest in making spending reductions. Specific expenditures, particularly when they relate to constituency problems, remain the focus of individual members' interests. Beyond the organizational and procedural disincentives outlined above, there are no rewards for MPs to emphasize concerns broader than constituency or partisan issues. For all of these reasons it can be safely concluded that parliament presently lacks the institutional resources and incentives for members to exercise a proper surveillance of government spending.

B. Subordinate Legislation

It has long been accepted that for practical reasons parliament must delegate much of its legislative authority to the executive.[22] Parliament does not have the time to debate the detailed rules that must be used to implement policy, nor does it have the technical expertise. Thus, in many cases, parliament provides only a framework for the rulemaking that will take place in the bureaucracy. Until recently, the Canadian parliament has expressed little interest in examining how this delegated authority is exercised. Yet these rules often have an enormous impact on the lives of individual Canadians. When the Ministry of Transport decided that the foliage around airports needed control it passed a regulation, pursuant to the Aeronautics Act, which empowered officials, much to the consternation of landowners, to enter private property and destroy the offending trees. Examples such as this one can be multiplied hundreds of times. Without knowing it, Canadians are subject to a myriad of regulations, prompting some to argue that this constitutes a devolution of power to the executive which, without proper safeguards, might easily deteriorate into a "new despotism."

For many years Canada lagged behind other parliamentary systems in providing for the publication of rules and regulations and their tabling in parliament.[23] The Regulations Act of 1950 imposed these requirements on most subordinate legislation (most regulations are now published in the *Canada Gazette*), but parliament still lacked opportunities to systematically review the exercise of delegated legislation. In Britain, by contrast, some pieces of legislation stipulate that parliament must pass a resolution affirming the exercise of delegated authority and others provide for the annulment of rules and regulations. Few Canadian laws contain such requirements. The Canadian parliament has permitted the extensive delegation and redelegation of its authority and has agreed to bills with sweeping enabling clauses that provide a great scope for the formulation of regulations. But it has not developed special techniques to review delegated legislation and relies instead on other surveillance devices.

In 1969 the House of Commons Special Committee on Statutory Instruments made several recommendations to improve the surveillance of delegated legislation.[24] The committee was concerned with imprecision in the formulation of regulations, the lack of public debate and consultation, and the inadequacy of parliamentary control. The Statutory Instruments Act, 1971, incorporated many of the committee's recommendations, including the establishment of a parliamentary committee — much like the Scrutiny Committee in the United Kingdom — that would have the authority to review delegated legislation. It was intended that this committee report to parliament on what it considers to be the unusual or unwarranted use of delegated powers.[25]

The Standing Joint (Senate and Commons) Committee on Regulations and other Statutory Instruments was formed in 1973 and began its work in late 1974. It did so in something of a vacuum since the committee was given no clear mandate and no real powers to correct abuse.[26] The committee began by retaining two counsel (one lawyer trained in civil law, the other a common-law lawyer) and by establishing 15 criteria to be employed in assessing statutory instruments.[27] Only one of these grounds for objection concerns the issue of whether a regulation is or is not in conformity with the terms of the enabling act. Although the other 14 criteria include such concerns as the rights and liberties of subjects and the rule of law, the government is interested almost exclusively in the *vires* question, not in the merits of a statutory instrument. Instead of drawing the Department of Justice into every transgression detected, the committee objects directly to the department involved, draws attention to its criteria, and requests that the offending instrument be amended or revoked. From its origin in 1973 to July 1976 the committee considered 1348 statutory instruments, of which 689 were objected to or queried.

The committee continues to labour under some severe constraints. For example, there is no clear definition of what constitutes a statutory instrument. The Committee is forced to use as its frame of reference those regulations published in the *Canada Gazette*. This is far from being a technical problem or an inconvenience. Not only does this exempt matters of national security from the committee's orbit, but also the rules which govern the granting of licences and permits, for example, since strictly speaking they do not conform to the Privy Council Office's definition of a statutory instrument. Thus, the National Energy Board has devised guidelines to govern the granting of export licences, but these are outside the committee's purview, as is the Unemployment Insurance Commission's definition of an effective "job search." What the committee sees is the tip of the iceberg. A second problem is that most of the committee's work is *post hoc*. Since only about a dozen Canadian statutes require that statutory instruments receive an affirmative resolution before coming into effect, the committee concentrates entirely on correcting abuses that have already occurred. This problem is exacerbated by the absence of any means of forcing departments to comply with recommendations or even to respond to queries. One of the committee's counsel has written that, while some departments are accommodating, "others have been reluctant and still others might even be considered intransigent."[28]

The committee has several adversaries, particularly the Department of Justice. Of several areas of friction or disagreement, one is the wording of general grants of power contained in many Canadian statutes. In the first place, there is a tendency in Canada—that is not duplicated elsewhere — to delegate subordinate legislative authority to the Governor-in-Council instead of to individual ministers. More important, perhaps, is the tendency to grant this power "in relation to" some subject matter. This very general statutory authority imposes virtually no limits on the executive and, in the words of the Committee's Second Report, "sets up the delegate as the equivalent of and with the same power as parliament itself." Statutes in Britain and Australia contain much more detailed descriptions of what delegates are empowered to do.

Most debates over delegated legislation are couched in the language of administrative law, which tends to obscure the fact that they also pose fundamental constitutional problems and can have a profound effect on the lives of individuals. In Canada only a handful of parliamentarians are diligent participants in parliament's review of the exercise of the power that has been delegated. Once again, part of the problem is that MPs cannot be induced to participate in a venture that is plagued by frustrations. Until more subordinate legislation is subject to disallowance or positive affirmation, MPs and the cabinet will continue to ignore the Committee in spite of its excellent leadership and legal staff.

C. Oral Question Period

Oral Question Period is the most celebrated forum for continuous, open criticism of government policy. As a surveillance device it has the attractive feature of being an uninterrupted 40-minute period which the executive cannot avoid. Question Period is unconnected to the routine processing of legislation and it stands out as a time when the opposition assumes its most militant posture. To strengthen the inquisitorial nature of the proceeding, cabinet ministers seldom receive advance notice of the content of questions. The types of questions and their order are an important part of the tactics of parliamentary leadership. Under Joe Clark the Conservative party assumed a much more disciplined approach to the organization of Question Period and other opposition activities in the House.[29] A member of the shadow cabinet, for example, was assigned responsibility for providing leadership in the organization of the daily Question Period. A list of questioners is prepared for the Speaker who generally follows the suggested order, occasionally disrupting it to recognize a backbencher with a constituency problem. Questions are selected for their potential political benefit and discussion often centres on the opening question of the day, the symbolic core of opposition grievance.

In addition to the structural qualities which make the Oral Question Period a potent weapon, it is also the event which daily attracts the greatest attention from observers of the Canadian parliament. The constant badinage during Question Period provides political journalists with a continuous source of material.[30] In addition, it brings party leaders together and thus holds the promise of newsworthy surprises. Largely in response to the attention of the media, and partly because of possibilities for direct participation, members of parliament also turn out for Question Period in greater numbers and with greater regularity than for any other occurrence in the parliamentary day. Its importance as a public forum was enhanced even further in April 1975 when Oral Question Period was assigned a fixed time immediately before Routine Proceedings. This has ensured Question Period greater prominence, since neither ministers nor members of the Press Gallery are obliged to guess precisely when questions will be asked.

Even with these inherent advantages, Question Period has become an object of criticism. It is clear, for example, that it is no longer of sufficient length to accommodate most of the questions which members wish to raise, and opposition members object to questions emanating from the government backbenches. Cabinet ministers criticize what they maintain are purely partisan questions, backbenchers claim that cabinet denigrates Question Period by refusing to supply direct answers, and academics profess that too many oral questions are trivial, information-gathering devices. Moreover, academics and backbenchers combine in their criticisms of the present restrictive disclosure policy and the procedural rules which permit ministers to refuse to answer a question without providing a justification.

These criticisms stem from a belief that Question Period can be improved from a procedural point of view; while this position is undoubtedly valid, a more fundamental weakness exists. Most parliamentarians are unable to structure debate in Question Period around competing party policies or philosophies. Many of the questions are orchestrated for the sole purpose of embarrassing the government. Thus, questions appear desultory and, apart from the facts around which questions are organized, there is little to link one question to another or one Question Period to the next. One MP, Bob Rae, has put the problem this way: "You've got Otto Lang on the ropes and someone else stands up and asks a question to the Minister of State for Small Business. You're left with a feeling of frustration. . . . There are so many loose ends at the end of Question Period.''[31] Effective parliamentary surveillance requires new procedures for Question Period and the existence in parliament of a few fundamental ideas about governing which clearly distinguish one party or faction from another.

D. *Special Debates*

In their search for new modes of surveillance, members of parliament sometimes succeed in detracting from the major opportunities that already exist. At the outset of the parliamentary day, private members, primarily from the opposition, often attempt to obtain unanimous consent to present a motion without notice for a ''pressing and urgent necessity.'' Ostensibly Standing Order 43 provides an opportunity for postponing regular business for an emergency debate. Unfortunately, members often use ''43s'' simply to raise controversial questions in the knowledge that they will attract the attention of the media and they are unlikely to receive the unanimous consent required to proceed with debate. The abuse of this rule restricts the time parliament has at its disposal and, because they directly precede the Oral Question Period, such motions may detract attention from the main questions of the day.

A substantial proportion of the House time devoted to surveillance is consumed by the budget and throne speech debates and by what are referred to as ''opposition days.'' Parliamentarians are permitted six days to debate the Address in Reply to the Speech from the Throne. This procedure provides parliament with a relatively lengthy period for the criticism of only vaguely worded policy announcements. The lack of depth in the policy debate is implicitly acknowledged by the relaxation of rules regarding relevancy — a tradition which encourages backbench speeches on local issues. The Budget Debate consists of six days of discussion of the government's taxation proposals and general financial policy. The debate, which follows the speech by the minister of finance, is similar to the Throne Speech debate in that rules of relevancy are not strictly enforced. Unlike the Throne Speech, however, the days set aside for debate are not required to be consecutive and this prevents a prolonged hiatus in the passing of legislation. On the other hand, this procedure wastes parliamentary time because those debates which do not take place directly after the Budget Speech receive almost no attention from the press or the public.

The opposition parties now have at their disposal a definite amount of parliamentary time to be used for the purpose of general surveillance and criticism. When the Committee of Supply was erased from the parliamentary timetable in 1968 the opposition parties were accorded a total of 25 days (plus three days for supplementary estimates) divided unequally among three supply periods during which opposition motions could be debated. These ''opposition days'' were designed to compensate for the lack of debate on supply under the new rules and it was originally assumed that motions would refer to financial matters. In practice the parties merely divide the opposition days among themselves and use the opportunity to force debates on topical motions which deplore the government's behaviour or urge a particular course of action. On six occasions during the parliamentary year, opposition day motions may contain a nonconfidence provision. Because two nonconfidence motions are assigned to each supply period, motions of nonconfidence occur with some regularity and it is now impossible for governments, especially minority governments, to relax for long periods simply because supply has been granted. However, most opposition motions, including nonconfidence motions, make little reference to government spending. Committee reports on estimates have rarely been used as a foundation for debate. Between October 1977 and October 1978, for example, only two of the 25 opposition motions dealt directly with governmental spending.

The government retains the ultimate responsibility for deciding the precise days to be allotted for opposition motions. Unlike the procedure in Question Period, 24-hour notice of the content of the opposition resolution must be given. This period provides government officials with an opportunity to prepare detailed briefs on which ministers may base their replies. In these debates, as in the Budget and the Throne Speech debates, the opposition is handicapped by its lack of technical knowledge. In placing an opposition motion before the House on February 28, 1978, Joe Clark defended the broad wording of the motion by saying that the Conservatives wished to avoid the impression that they were endorsing any specific proposals. The government, on the other hand, is buttressed not only by its public service but also by interest groups which continuously attempt to inform the government of the technical requirements of policy.

Conclusion

Parliament's surveillance devices are adequate for ensuring the opposition a fixed amount of time during which they can command the attention of the government. However, all of them share the quality of diffuseness. It is a rare occasion on which opposition members are able to spar on equal terms with ministers, or when parliamentarians have acquired formidable expertise in a specific policy area. Instead, surveillance opportunities are exploited primarily for their theatrical potential, a trend which has been encourged by the advent of television in the House of Commons.

THE SPECIAL ROLE OF THE SENATE IN THE LEGISLATIVE SYSTEM

Few changes have been made in the Senate's composition or activities since the Fathers of Confederation made provision for it in the British North America Act. Apart from a 1965 amendment to the act, which requires senators to resign at the age of 75, the Senate persists in much the same form as the Fathers envisaged. Although the colonies had experimented with elected and appointed upper houses and dissatisfaction had been expressed with both, there was a consensus on the necessity for an upper house in the new federation. The provision of an assembly of unelected senators would effectively balance the principle of popular representation which governed the composition of the lower house. The Fathers of Confederation harboured a deep suspicion of the virtues of unqualified democracy and were eager to establish what Georges-Etienne Cartier called "a power of resistance to oppose the democratic element."[32] The Senate would also be used to represent property. Contrary to the British tradition, there would be no hereditary titles and senators would not represent a special class in society, but a prospective senator would be obliged to own property valued at $4000 in the province represented. The Senate's composition was also designed to allay concern that the provinces would lack direct representation in the new parliament. The powers of the central government appeared awesome, but when the provinces were granted representation in an assembly whose announced purpose was to exert a conservative, protective influence, Confederation became a more palatable prospect.

Agreement on the composition of the Senate was instrumental in securing Confederation, but there was no explicit agreement on the specific role the Senate was to exercise in the legislative system. It was clear that there was to be no equality between the two chambers and that the cabinet should be responsible to the Commons and not to the upper house. According to John A. Macdonald, the second assembly would "never set itself in opposition against the deliberate and understood wishes of the people."[33] Yet the Senate was not denied a role in the legislative process. No constraints were placed on the Senate's formal authority because, as Macdonald declared, the Senate "would be of no value whatever were it a mere chamber for registering the decrees of the Lower House."[34] A balance of powers was intended, but a dilemma has emerged. As R. A. McKay has observed, "if it (the Senate) rejects or drastically amends a bill for social or moral reform, it is condemned by impatient reformers as reactionary, autocratic and perhaps immoral. If it is quiescent, it is assumed to be a fifth wheel on the government coach."[35]

The Senate has been restrained in its formal lawmaking and surveillance activities. The Senate amendment of government legislation has declined to about 10 per cent of the bills introduced and normally the House of Commons agrees to the amended version. The tendency of the Senate to amend government bills increases appreciably when the majority of senators do not belong to the government's party in the House of Commons. The actual rejection of important government legislation is very unusual (although amendment may be tantamount to rejection, as it was in 1961 on the government's customs-tariff legislation). Money bills cannot even be introduced in the Senate and there has been continual dispute between House and Senate officials over the latter's right to amend money bills. The Senate has amended such bills, but in practice it has never exercised any formal financial control. In all these facets of lawmaking the Senate is subordinate to the House of Commons.

However, the Senate could be considered an active legislative refinery. Senators have demonstrated assiduity in the consideration of certain types of legislation, and when unanticipated changes are required in government bills the Senate is a convenient place to make amendments. Particularly in the area of private bills the Senate has departed from its relatively passive lawmaking role. Private bills, as discussed earlier, are extremely limited in their scope. They apply to individuals, corporate "persons," or charitable organizations, many of which require legislation to obtain authority or avoid responsibility. Before 1964 the bulk of this legislation consisted of divorce bills from Quebec and Newfoundland whose provincial courts, up until that time, were not empowered to hear divorce cases. Most private bills are introduced in the Senate where the fee is lower and where enough time exists to guarantee thorough treatment. Procedure on private bills is designed to protect the rights of third parties. For example, interested persons must be informed of the bills' intentions by publication and neither house will examine private bills in Committee of the Whole.

The formal limits on the power of the Senate sometimes create the misleading impression that the Senate is entirely excluded from important legislative matters. On the contrary, a small portion of the Senate's membership is actively engaged in challenging, delaying, and amending any government legislation which may be detrimental to major business and financial concerns. In a critical analysis of the Senate, Colin Campbell has argued that these "business reviewers" enjoy the indulgence and encouragement of the government and the advantage of a specific mission in their work.[36] Employing the "Haydon formula" and the Senate's Banking, Trade and Commerce Committee, this group has anticipated changes in government policy by studying bills introduced in the Commons and launching the equivalent of preemptive strikes. Their narrow constituency and the absence of publicity accompanying their work has given business reviewers a formidable role in the legislative system.

It is difficult for the Senate to participate actively in the performance of a surveillance function because the executive has never considered itself responsible to the upper house. Cabinet ministers, with the exception of the government leader in the Senate, have rarely been drawn from Senate ranks, since the House of Commons demands the opportunity to confront the entire executive. Nonetheless, the Senate may be used on occasion as a source of cabinet material. When the electorate denies a governing party representatives from major regions or languages groups, the prime minister may be forced to look elsewhere. In 1979 Joe Clark had to appoint to the cabinet the only two Tory MPs elected in the province of Quebec. To buttress his party's lack of success in French-speaking areas of the country, Clark was forced to recruit three cabinet ministers from the Senate. The difficulties inherent in such appointments are extensive. Senatorial ministers may be accused of lacking a popular mandate and of being unable to answer questions and defend policy in the Commons' chamber.

Surveillance activities in the Senate have been most effective when prominent Senators have launched highly publicized studies of particular social issues. Senators who comprise the small band of "social investigators" have produced excellent reports on such subjects as the mass media, science policy, and aging in Canada. The lack of an electoral mandate, however, has severely decreased their impact and even attentive publics remain sceptical about how much the Senate can contribute to the legislative system.

The fact that the Senate has occasionally clashed with the popularly elected lower house in the areas of lawmaking and surveillance does not make it an anomalous, outmoded institution. In a federal system an upper house, with representatives from the various sections of the nation, is often considered a necessary institutional device for representation and integration. In a multicultural and bilingual country it can also be argued that national viability is enhanced if the upper house can aid in the performance of a legitimation function. It is the centre of parliamentary ritual, where the speech from the throne is read and royal assent accorded. Despite these possibilities the image of the Senate is such that none of the functions of integration, representation, and legitimation are performed with success. The obvious loyalty and regard shown by Canadians toward the crown and the sarcastic barbs that are aimed at the Senate constitute a strange anomaly in the Canadian political system. Senate inactivity (and, on occasion, obstruction) is the source of some of the discontent. The work of the Senate is assumed by a few diligent senators and the House of Commons usually provides the Senate with little legislation until the end-of-session avalanche descends. The fact that the Senate is obliged to perform a major patronage function has not enhanced its prestige. Appointment to the Senate is considered a reward for those members of a political party who have served it loyally over the years. For many appointees the Senate is a convenient and well-paid exit from the political system. For others it is an advantageous site from which to manage election campaigns and raise party funds. The fact that senators have no direct responsibility to an electorate is a serious liability, and the use of the Senate to reward the devoted constitutes an added weakness.

FORCES IN PARLIAMENT: GOVERNMENT AND OPPOSITION

If our knowledge of parliament were confined to the formal precedures which govern lawmaking and surveillance in both houses, there would be a tendency to assume a mechanical view of this part of the legislative system. In reality, parliament does not react automatically and in a predetermined fashion to environmental pressures or even to the initiatives of the inner circle. Members of parliament have individual goals which are often distinct from those held by interest groups or the bureaucracy. Some goals, such as the termination of a rail strike, involve conditions to be imposed on the environment; others, such as the restructuring of the parliamentary committee system, impose change on the House of Commons itself.

The most important goals are those espoused by the parliamentary parties. Loyalty to a particular leadership means that on most occasions individual goals must be compromised so that group goals will have a possibility of success. The existence of cohesive parliamentary parties in Canada permits the government of the day to introduce and remain responsible for a legislative and financial program. It also makes individual behaviour relatively predictable, thus facilitating the establishment of norms which strengthen the parliamentary organization as a whole. In Chapter 3 we discussed how the organization of national parties has made them important participants in the political system. In parliament their cohesion is attributable in part to the existence and regular functioning of caucus. As well as being a forum for the suggestion of policy changes, caucus is also a platform for the development of party strategy and an assembly where frustrations with the leadership may be aired. House leaders and party whips are also instrumental in the maintenance of party cohesion. They insure the party's voting strength at divisions (formal votes), decide on the order of parliamentary speakers, and are responsible for dispensing minor organizational rewards and meting out criticism.[37] In the face of pressures for party conformity, individual members of parliament retain their personal goals and often construct informal coalitions to secure the recognition of demands. But the overriding fact of parliamentary life is the existence of persistent and powerful political parties, and members of parliament are encouraged to regard party cohesion as more important than freedom of action in the House.

Canadian parliamentary procedures are predicated on the existence of cohesive political parties, but the rules also recognize two other aspects of parliamentary government: first, the existence of responsible government, which implies cabinet control over policy direction; and, second, the opportunity for opposition criticism of the government in parliament.[38] These ideas command a high degree of support in parliament: leaders and followers on both sides of the House are prepared to acknowledge their value and necessity.

Opposition to the policies of British monarchs was originally provided by the British parliament as a whole. By the end of the eighteenth century a government had developed which was responsible to parliament and it was possible for an opposition to exist without any overtones of treason. Instead of simply criticizing a king who could not be replaced, the opposition could now offer itself as the alternative government and political parties could be used to communicate parliamentary criticism to the public. The opposition thus became an institution of the British parliament and in 1905 Canada became the first nation to officially recognize the position of Leader of Her Majesty's Loyal Opposition.

In Canada, like Britain, the style of opposition which has emerged may be characterized as one of confrontation. Unlike presidential systems in which the executive and legislative branches rarely confront one another publicly, communication between the government and the opposition in parliament is always direct. Criticism is a continuous and unavoidable aspect of a government's parliamentary experience and while the government must produce and defend a series of politics with at least implied goals, the opposition can content itself with one overriding goal — replacing the government. The confrontation style of opposition puts a premium on electoral success via parliamentary criticism, not on the changing of policy to suit party programs.

The confrontation style of opposition depends on the development of certain behavioural norms. On a general level, opposition members recognize the government's responsibility to carry on the business of governing and will often lend their support to that end, while at the same time retaining for themselves the right to adequately criticize government policy. The government recognizes the opposition's right to criticize but denies it the right to obstruct. All governments attempt to anticipate opposition criticism and to formulate their strategy and tactics on the basis of this evaluation. Other norms have emerged to complement this arrangement. It is tacitly agreed, for example, that the government should refrain from introducing substantive amendments to legislation which has reached the committee stage of the parliamentary process. In June 1973, when Solicitor General Warren Allmand attempted to introduce an amendment to a government bill on capital punishment during committee deliberations, his move was greeted with loud objections. When, on other occasions, the government considers there has been an excess of opposition obstruction, it applies the rules of the House to terminate debate. An overly pugnacious opposition or an intransigent government may violate the norms of government-opposition interaction and hinder the resolution of other issues on which the government and the opposition initially agree. As both the government and the opposition recognize, it is more satisfactory to use the House leaders' meeting or informal discussions among party whips to negotiate the disposal of parliamentary time rather than force the issue to a division in the House of Commons where the government will normally emerge victorious.

The relationship between government and opposition in Canada is further complicated by frequent minority governments and by the different issues which emerge from the political environment. If a government is defined as an administration which assumes office after a general election or after a change in the prime minister, and a minority government as a situation in which the administration is controlled by a single party which lacks a majority of votes in the House of Commons, then Canada has experienced more minority than majority governments since the end of the Second World War. Given the present party system and what appear to be stabilized levels of party support, minority situations will be a frequent outcome of federal elections in the future. When a minority government is in office, the clearcut distinction between the government and the opposition disappears, as at least one opposition party is periodically called upon to lend its voting support to the government. Support is not offered for an indefinite period of time and under the threat of withdrawal governments have been led to stipulate that a defeat in the House will not be followed automatically by the government's resignation. John A. Macdonald was frequently defeated without resigning, and this traditional British practice was revived by the Pearson minority government in 1968. It suffered a defeat but tested the will of the House the following day on a formal nonconfidence motion. The fear of losing support has also led some Canadian prime ministers to seek the dissolution of parliament before an election was constitutionally required. In 1926 Mackenzie King requested (and was denied) dissolution when it appeared his minority government was about to be defeated. Lester Pearson sought a majority with a premature election in 1965, as did Pierre Trudeau in 1968. Some prime ministers — Arthur Meighen in 1926, John Diefenbaker in 1963, Trudeau in 1974, and Clark in 1979 — were forced to seek dissolution when support in the House of Commons was withdrawn.

Canadian governments are inclined to be impatient in minority situations. Research in other countries indicates that parties which are able to secure between 45 and 50 per cent of the legislative seats (a condition in which minority governments in Canada have often found themselves), have an excellent chance of commanding the continual support of smaller parties.[39] Nonetheless, Canadian minority governments have often resorted to elections in their search for majority status. Apart from wartime arrangements, Canadian political parties have not experimented with coalitions which would, in effect, manufacture majorities. This mistrust of coalitions, inherited from Britain, contributes to a condition in which the membership of the smaller political parties is constantly denied the type of governmental experience that may generate voter confidence. However, the reluctance of opposition parties to enter coalition governments is not surprising. In Canada the dominant opposition style has emphasized that the goal of opposition parties is to establish themselves as viable alternatives, not as contributors, to government policy.

It has been argued that the discomfort which accompanies minority status encourages a more responsive attitude in governments. Unfortunately, it is difficult to determine the validity of this argument, although statistical indication of the impact of minority governments on legislative output is offered in Chapter 8. Certainly there seems little dispute that the relationship between the opposition and the government becomes more complex and the government's ability to insist on its policy diminishes. Factors which were certainties for a majority government become imponderables. And the opposition, without sharing in the advantages of governing, also faces new intractable problems of internal cohesion and electoral strategy. After the 1972 election the New Democratic Party faced these difficulties when its caucus decided to extend its consistent support to the minority Liberal government. In 1979 the Social Credit party, led by Fabien Roy, was forced to weigh the advantages of providing continuous support to the minority Clark government against the hostile attitude shown by that government to the Social Credit request for party status in the House of Commons.

Different issues force the opposition to adopt different styles.[40] Although the basic style is one of party confrontation, in Canada many new issues defy categorization on the basis of traditional ideological divisions among parties. None of the political parties, for example, may call on their philosophies for distinct policies in the fields of consumer protection, pollution, or telecommunications satellites. Parties are forced to adopt positions on such issues, but the absence of historical precedents and ideological cues may provoke a splintered opposition and internal party dissension. During the 1973 debate on the Trudeau government's resolution on bilingualism in the public service, it was clear that agreement existed between the Prime Minister and the Leader of the Opposition on the basic content of the policy. However, the traditional Conservative response to the question of bilingualism had been ambiguous and Robert Stanfield's commitment caused a break within the parliamentary party when the vote was taken. In this case a factional style of opposition replaced one of confrontation.

On occasion, individual MPs assume almost total responsibility for an issue area in which they are specializing. During the 29th and 30th Parliaments, Elmer McKay launched a singlehanded attack on the Liberal government's relations with the RCMP and Ged Baldwin led a spirited criticism of the government's policy on the release of information. The appearance of both individualized and factional opposition may increase if more opportunities are provided for members to acquire policy expertise and for groups within the party to develop policy views when there are no firm party commitments.

The Canadian parliamentary opposition faces persistent problems, regardless of the pattern of opposition that dominates at any one time. There seems to be a consensus among politicians (warranted or not) that a necessary condition of electoral success is a creditable performance in the House of Commons. It might be argued, therefore, that the primary problem faced by the opposition is the government's domination of both parts of the legislative system and in particular its ultimate control over the parliamentary timetable. The opposition has lost the right to "talk out" government bills (closure, 1913), to filibuster (a limit on individual debate, 1927), to extend indefinitely major debates (1955), and to appeal the rulings of the speaker (1965). But procedural changes have been slow and methodical and there is agreement, even among members of the opposition, that tactics that may once have been considered legitimate modes of criticism are now undeniably instruments of obstruction. Even the complaint that the opposition lacks the research facilities to conduct a criticial campaign in the House has been partly blunted. In 1978, parliament allocated $832,000 for research units designed to offer partisan assistance to each of the four parties.[41]

Furthermore, the opposition as a whole is granted, on a continual basis, large blocks of time during which it assumes responsibility for the initiation of debate in the House. It is the government backbencher, not the opposition, who has lost the battle for parliamentary time.

If the government is unable to secure the passage of legislation in a suitable period, the House rules provide two opportunities to circumvent parliamentary opposition by the termination of debate. These rules are not only difficult to apply, but also their persistent use violates the norms of government-opposition relations. The most notorious procedure is closure. Introduced in 1913, it is a weapon which governments impose only reluctantly because of the adverse political ramifications. In addition, various procedural conditions must be met before it can be employed. Closure must be moved at each stage of a bill's consideration, not on the entire bill at once. Notice of the intention to move closure must be given at a previous sitting, followed by a one-day debate on the closure motion itself. Closure is a particularly unwieldy weapon at committee stage. Before closure can be moved on a bill, debate on each clause must have been adjourned or consideration of it "postponed." To be postponed, a clause must have been discussed. During the pipeline debate of 1956, C. D. Howe was forced to introduce the first clause of the bill, speak to it briefly to satisfy procedural requirements, and then move that it be postponed, a tactic which attracted violent objections from the opposition. Not surprisingly, the use of closure is a rare parliamentary event. John Stewart maintains that closure "resembles so much a death sentence and a public execution that ministers shrink from using it; and when they do, the opposition, regardless of their true sentiments, feels obliged to lament the end of a thousand years of freedom and democracy."[42]

In 1969 the government introduced — and had to to use closure to pass — a complicated standing order which provided a formal basis for the negotiated settlement of time disputes in the House. The rules provide that if all of the parties (in the case of Standing Order 75A), or a majority of the parties (in the case of 75B), or two — but possibly one — of the parties (in the case of 75C), can agree, a particular amount of time will be allotted to the consideration of a particular stage of a bill. Unfortunately, this set of rules can become an unwieldy and unpredictable procedure. The rules have often been considered a continuum with the parties obliged to seek agreement under 75A first, then 75B, and finally 75C, but there is some doubt that 75B is a necessary step. Since the imposition of 75A implies unanimous party approval, the requirements for its introduction are not particularly stringent. No notice of motion is needed, the allocation for more than one stage may be moved at once, and no amendment or debate is allowed. The moving of 75B requires no notice, but debate can take place for a maximum of two hours. More stringent rules apply to 75C, including a notice of motion, a debate on the motion, a provision for amendments, separate motions for each stage, and at least one day's debate at each stage before the motion can be presented to the House. Since invoking time allocation may require as much time as the normal process of debate, the government must be committed to a fixed deadline, as it was on the 1971 tax bill.

In the 30th Parliament, time allocation was used 15 times, occasionally twice on the same bill. The parties were able to achieve agreement under 75A four times and on the remaining occasions the government imposed its own time allocation under 75C. Standing Order 75B was never employed. Time allocation is becoming more acceptable to governments that wish to avoid major delays in their legislative program. Opposition spokesmen continue to insist, however, that the use of 75C indicates government mismanagement of priorities and a sinister willingness to railroad unpopular legislation, such as the Medical Care Act amendment of 1976 and the Income Tax amendment of 1978.

Our contention is that opposition criticism has not been stifled in the House by procedural innovations, but that opposition difficulties are traceable to more fundamental problems which in some cases apply to parliamentary oppositions in other countries. One of the problems is that much of the most articulate and publicized criticism of government policy does not originate with the opposition in parliament but with other structures in the political environment. Interest groups, in particular, too often provide the major reactions and criticisms to government proposals. The government has also established quasi-independent agencies such as the Economic Council of Canada and provided them with resources and experts that outweigh those of the opposition in the House of Commons. Such bodies represent a highly competitive source of ideas and criticism, and are often accorded more attention by the press than specific opposition criticisms in parliament. The familiar argument that the Canadian provinces provide the effective political opposition also deserves serious consideration in this context. Voters may not choose provincial governments on these grounds, but there is little doubt that the clashes between the provinces and the federal government at intergovernmental conferences detract attention from the federal parliamentary opposition on some of the most important issues in Canadian politics. Increased opportunities for parliamentary surveillance of all federal-provincial conferences would strengthen the role of federal politicians, particularly the opposition, in the legislative system.

It is often difficult for oppositions to offer major policy alternatives. By lending support to the regime and the accepted norms of government, the Canadian parliamentary opposition is unable to reflect certain forms of dissent in society. The opposition endorses only legitimate means of political expression. This is not the case in France and Italy, for example, where the parliamentary opposition reflects an array of ideologies aimed at reconstituting the regime and/or the social structure. Moreover, not all issues evoke automatic responses from opposition parties. With the achievement of the welfare state and a mixed economy, ideological disputes in North America seem to have given way to a search for policy consensus. Parliamentary oppositions are encouraged to criticize the specifics of government policy rather than develop comprehensive policy alternatives. The opposition usually represents an alternative source of leadership, not ideas.

In the Canadian legislative system, opposition activities ought to contribute to the system's capacity to perform its diverse functions. In a country where there are alternating governments, the parliamentary opposition may perform a vital recruitment function by providing an experienced political elite equipped to assume political office. The dominance of a single political party in Canada has diminished the opposition's capacity to aid in the performance of this function. In a political system dominated by linguistic, cultural, and regional cleavages, the existence of a legitimate and representative parliamentary opposition might help to integrate the political system. However, the reasonably high level of fragmentation in the Canadian political culture makes it difficult for opposition parties to span all the important political cleavages. The fact that the opposition freely participates in parliamentary rituals and demonstrates a commitment to legal procedures should enhance parliament's ability to perform a legitimation function. When criticism is publicized it creates the impression that there is little need for an extraparliamentary opposition. In Canada this function is performed reasonably well, but institutional change could enhance the salience of the opposition and thereby improve the status of parliament as a whole.

THE PRESTIGE OF PARLIAMENT

Since the turn of the century the executive has developed policies and legislation largely independent of systematic parliamentary influence, and it has introduced almost all of the legislation that parliament eventually adopted. The constitution stipulates that it is the government alone which can initiate the expenditure of public monies, while parliament must simply react to executive requests. Cabinet's ability to prevail on legislative and financial matters has been perfected by the existence of cohesive and disciplined parliamentary parties which support cabinet actions in the House of Commons. Cabinets' dominance of the lawmaking function has not been matched by the development of a strong tradition of parliamentary surveillance. Although it remains a force in parliament, the opposition does not have the capacity to offer comprehensive critiques and detailed amendments of government policy. These circumstances and the expansion of government activity in the economy have occasioned the view that parliament, whether or not it has declined, is an institution irrelevant to the mainstream of policymaking.

One of the responses to this conclusion has been to argue that regardless of its weakness in lawmaking and surveillance, parliament is or should be the foremost national arena for the debate and the communication of political issues. Parliament, in this schema, need not take any decisions or possess any independent capacity to influence decisionmaking. It is crucial, however, that parliament both reflect public opinion as well as take the lead in its formation; that it be the scene of a continual confrontation among different versions of the most appropriate manner in which to govern the country. This "communications theory" of parliament has been summed up best in Bernard Crick's description of parliament as, ideally, a "permanent election campaign."[43] A parliament which functions well in this role is assumed to contribute to the support of the regime, or the existing rules of the game. But to make such a contribution, parliamentarians must enjoy respect themselves and, above all, must be listened to, at least by those attentive publics responsible for the formation of public opinion. In Canada there is some reason to doubt that either of these requirements has been fully satisfied.

In 1964 a nationwide public-opinion poll, conducted by the Canadian Institute of Public Opinion, found that 45 per cent of their respondents believed that parliament was doing a "poor job," while only 16 per cent felt it was doing a "good job." On the whole, the results of CIPO polls since 1969 have not been particularly encouraging for parliament or parliamentarians. Although the responses to some questions are undoubtedly contaminated by partisanship, other, more specific questions have also elicited scepticism and cynicism. In June 1970, for example, 77 per cent of those interviewed disapproved of a proposed increase in the salaries of MPs to $24,000. Salaries are naturally a sensitive topic for taxpayers, but in 1963 a smaller proportion (59 per cent) disapproved of a salary increase.[44] CIPO pollers in December 1974 asked respondents to compare the respect they had for parliament with their respect for the Supreme Court and the churches of Canada. Only 17 per cent of respondents volunteered that they had "a great deal of respect" for parliament, but 25 per cent had a great deal of respect for the court and 35 per cent offered this positive judgment of Canadian churches.[45] Surveys also indicate that consistently large proportions of the Canadian public consider political corruption and conflict of interest to be serious problems among federal politicians. Moreover, a large minority of the electorate remains sceptical that MPs would even read a letter that was sent to them, let alone draft a reply.[46]

What are the underpinnings of this mistrust and suspicion? A partial answer is to be found in the knowledge Canadians have of their MPs and their parliamentary system. American studies have shown that positive attitudes toward legislative institutions vary directly with interest and knowledge.[47] In Canada, party discipline effectively obscures the work of private members, so citizens have difficulty recalling the name of their MP. In 1978 a survey conducted by McMaster students found that only 58 per cent of respondents, drawn from both working- and middle-class areas in Hamilton, could identify their member of parliament.[48] In response to a CIPO poll conducted in January 1974 that asked which MP they most admired, 41 per cent of those interviewed were unable to name anyone they admired and an additional 11 per cent stated that they admired no one.[49] Party discipline extends outside the House to the point that MPs are unable to transcend the anonymity that being a party supporter imposes on them. Congressmen may run successfully against the evils of Congress, but MPs owe their livelihood to the party machines which operate and dominate the House of Commons. They are unable to "run against parliament."

This situation has been aggravated by the arrival of what has been called "judgmental journalism."[50] For members of the electronic and print media, straight reporting is no longer sufficient. It is necessary to infuse the news with dramatic quality. This requires, among other things, that the forces of good and the forces of evil be identified and that whenever possible political stories be given a human-interest dimension. The daily proceedings of parliament cannot provide much nourishment for journalists committed to this recipe. Consequently, ordinary MPs receive very little attention from the media. Kornberg and Wolfe concluded their preliminary content analysis of newspaper coverage of parliament by saying, "Parliament emerges from the pages of the newspapers of this period (1958-1973) as an institution dominated by a single person, the Prime Minister." References to backbenchers, when they occur, are generally positive, but, on the whole, "the press...devotes remarkably little attention to the country's single most important and visible political institution."[51]

Those who work in the news media have accepted a cavalier attitude toward parliament partially because many have come to consider themselves the major source of informed criticism of government activities. According to the Canadian Radio-television and Telecommunications Commission, journalists "tend to regard themselves as forming a much more effective form of opposition to a government than any political party with the second largest vote can ever exert."[52] Instead of reporting on the ongoing debate between the government and the opposition, members of the media insert themselves into the process. The opinions and attitudes Canadians hold about their political system are at least partially determined by the exchange of information and the political discussions which occur between members of the cabinet and representatives of the media. Although Question Period remains a dramatic and newsworthy event, it is no longer sufficient for reporters to cover debates in the House of Commons. Press conferences which pit the prime minister and other politicians against journalists supplement traditional forums for political discourse. Here journalists, unfettered by partisan allegiances and the constraints imposed by the necessity of being reelected, can ask the questions which politicians are either unable or unwilling to ask in the House of Commons. Moreover, it is no longer sufficient for reporters to relate the content of these exchanges. Instead, they must dissect, analyze, and interpret.[53]

Whatever advantages may accrue from this adversarial style of journalism, it has done nothing to promote the prestige and influence of the House of Commons. On the contrary, both government and opposition members make a practice of basing questions, both in the House and in committees, on stories in local and national newspapers. It has frequently been argued that *The Globe and Mail* writes the agenda for parliament and that anyone wishing a preview of the questions to be aired on a given day in the House of Commons need only consult the paper's front page.[54]

Partly in an attempt to arrest the erosion of institutional prestige and partly to adopt a style of open government, the Liberal cabinet agreed to broadcasting Commons' debates. Televising began on a very limited scale in October 1977. This represented the culmination of a long process characterized chiefly by hesitancy and indecision. Several private members' motions to broadcast House proceedings had been debated throughout the 1960s. In 1970, under increasing pressure to take some action, the government referred the matter to the Standing Committee on Procedure and Organization. On June 30, 1972, this committee presented a report to parliament which recommended an experiment in closed-circuit television. Although the government mentioned the subject in the 1973 speech from the throne, opposition to televised debates persisted. Members on both sides of the House worried that some of their colleagues would seek to monopolize debate in order to grandstand and advertise their diligence, that too much of the debate would be conducted in English (thus offending a francophone audience), and that negative reaction to rows of empty seats would compel attendance at debates. It was not until 1975, when Mitchell Sharp became government House leader, that televising debates had a successful champion. In January 1977, the House passed a government-sponsored motion which approved broadcasting in principle and instructed a special committee to examine the costs and ramifications.

After two years of operation, coverage of House of Commons proceedings is neither full, live, nor national in distribution. About one-third of the total cable subscribers in the country have access to all or part of the House proceedings, although virtually the entire viewing audience have the opportunity to watch parliamentary clips on newscasts.[55] No one, however, can watch committee proceedings since they are not televised at all.

For the most part of the original apprehensions of MPs have largely disappeared. Television producers, however, are not thoroughly satisfied that the product which emerges is a faithful reproduction of the atmosphere and action on the floor of the House.[56] This is primarily because the speaker controls proceedings and the directors are instructed to pay exclusive attention to the MP who has been recognized and to studiously avoid other action. This directive was extended to the point that the cameras failed to capture one of the more dramatic moments of the 30th Parliament when Ralph Stewart crossed the floor of the House to sit with the Conservatives.

Most of the reaction to televised debates has come from the principal participants. In one of the few studies conducted on viewer responses, a Carleton University survey found that the largest proportion of respondents, 41 per cent, claimed that after having watched the debates on televison, their opinion of parliament was unchanged. Somewhat more distressing for advocates of broadcasting was the finding that 33 per cent had a lower opinion of parliament after having been exposed to it on television, while only 26 per cent volunteered that they had a higher opinion.[57] Although these are rather raw and undigested results, they are confirmed by a CIPO poll conducted on January 21, 1978. Of those who had watched televised debates, 32 per cent had negative reactions compared to 11 per cent with positive reactions. A more complete picture will be provided when researchers control for the extent and type of exposure viewers have had to debates.[58] It seems safe to conclude, in the meantime, that those who believed that televising parliament would produce a stronger, more credible legislature will have to reconsider their position. Preliminary results of a panel study, conducted by Harold Clarke and Richard Price, suggest that freshmen MPs, at least, have lower expectations than some of the more enthusiastic reformers of the early 1970s. The largest proportion of members interviewed, 39 per cent, felt that television would have only negative effects, while an additional 39 per cent either anticipated both positive and negative results, or saw no effect whatsoever.[59]

Parliament's status and related prestige as an arena for the debate of contemporary issues are important for two reasons. First, if parliament is to break out of its present shadowy existence, its deliberations must be held in high regard by attentive publics. Until that happens the various media can ignore, with impunity, parliamentary debates other than Question Period. And if parliament cannot command the attention of the media, it will have difficulty commanding the attention of the government.

Second, and perhaps more important, legislatures are expected to legitimate the activities of executives and others in the political system, a function discussed in Chapter 2. Inasmuch as ordinary MPs enjoy a direct link with the electorate, parliament can claim to be expression of the exercise of popular sovereignty. This claim is buttressed by such traditional notions as parliamentary supremacy and the rule of law. Actions sanctioned by parliament acquire not only a legal status, but also the quality of moral rightness. If parliament's status in this regard is intact, it is assumed that support for parliament can spread to other elements in the regime. The absence of support, on the other hand, undermines parliament's capacity to legitimate the activities of the whole legislative system. The study of legitimation and the measurement of support are complex undertakings and the research findings outlined above touch only marginally on them. But if parliament's prestige is as tenuous as some of these findings suggest, parliamentary approval may be a convenient but basically unnecessary ingredient in the making of authoritative decisions which are binding on society.

NOTES

1.　John Stewart, *The Canadian House of Commons: Procedure and Reform* (Montreal: McGill-Queen's University Press, 1977), p. 111.
2.　Richard Simeon, "Studying Public Policy," *Canadian Journal of Political Science*, 9 (December 1976), p. 555.
3.　Canada, House of Commons, Special Committee on Procedure, *Third Report* (December 6, 1968), p. 433. See also Stewart, *The Canadian House of Commons*, p. 84.
4.　T. A. Hockin, "The Advance of Standing Committees in Canada's House of Commons: 1965 to 1970," *Canadian Public Administration*, 13 (Summer 1970), pp. 185-202.
5.　James R. Mallory and B. A. Smith, "The Legislative Role of Parliamentary Committees in Canada: The Case of the Joint Committee on the Public Service Bills," *Canadian Public Administration*, 15 (1972), pp. 1-23.
6.　Paul G. Thomas, "The Influence of Standing Committees of Parliament on Government Legislation," *Legislative Studies Quarterly*, 3 (November 1978), pp. 699-701.
7.　Calculated from Stewart, *The Canadian House of Commons*, Table 15, pp. 268-69.
8.　Colin Campbell, *The Canadian Senate: A Lobby from Within* (Toronto: Macmillan of Canada, 1978).
9.　The Tax Legislative Process Committee, The Canadian Tax Foundation, "The Tax Legislative Process," *Canadian Public Administration*, 21 (Fall 1978), pp. 324-57.
10.　Kenneth Woodside, "Tax Incentives vs. Subsidies," *Canadian Public Policy* (Spring 1979), p. 251. Woodside also notes, pp. 253-55, some of the advantages to subsidies, including visibility.
11.　*Debates*, March 29, 1977, p. 4440.
12.　For a study of the Public Accounts Committee, see Norman Ward, *The Public Purse* (Toronto: University of Toronto Press, 1962).
13.　Between 1955 and 1962 Canada experimented unsuccessfully with an Estimates Committee comprised of 60 members of the House. See Norman Ward, "The Committee on Estimates," *Canadian Public Administration*, 6 (March 1963), pp. 35-42.
14.　The procedures for supplementary estimates are different. These may be referred to standing committees at any time, since Standing Order 58 (15)

provides only that "supplementary estimates shall be referred to a standing committee...immediately [when] they are presented in the House." However, the standing committees are required to report the estimates back to the House not later than three sitting days before the final sitting or the last allotted day in the supply period in which they are referred. If the committees do not comply, the estimates will be deemed to have been reported by that date. Consequently, standing committees could theoretically be given as little as one day to report supplementary estimates.

15. Peter Dobell, "Impotent," *The Globe and Mail* (February 4, 1978), p. 10.
16. Paul G. Thomas, "Parliament and the Purse Strings," a paper prepared for the Legislative Studies in Canada Conference, Simon Fraser University (February 1979), pp. 8, 11.
17. *Debates*, April 10, 1974, p. 1319.
18. See the statement by the Hon. E. Benson reported in *The Parliamentarian*, 49 (1968), p. 36.
19. Thomas, "Parliament and the Purse Strings," p. 9.
20. *Supplement to the Annual Report of the Auditor General of Canada* (Ottawa: Supply and Services, 1975), p. 39. See also the remarks of the Auditor General, Mr. Macdonell, in Study of Parliament Group, *Seminar on the Budgetary Process* (Ottawa: Queen's Printer, 1977), pp. 36-37.
21. Royal Commission on Financial Management and Accountability, *Final Report* (Ottawa: Supply and Services, 1979), pp. 404-05.
22. Of course, not all executive power is delegated by parliament. For a discussion of prerogative powers, see J. R. Mallory, *The Structure of Canadian Government* (Toronto: Macmillan of Canada, 1971), pp. 137-46.
23. John Kersell, *Parliamentary Supervision of Delegated Legislation* (London: Stevens and Sons, 1960).
24. Canada, House of Commons, Special Committee on Statutory Instruments, *Third Report* (Ottawa: Queen's Printer, 1969).
25. James R. Mallory, "Parliamentary Scrutiny of Delegated Legislation in Canada: A Large Step Forward and a Small Step Back," *Public Law* (1972), pp. 30-42.
26. Graham Eglington, "Scrutiny of Delegated Legislation in the Parliament of Canada," *The Parliamentarian*, 59 (October 1978), pp. 271-75.
27. Senate and House of Commons, Standing Joint Committee on Regulations and Other Statutory Instruments, *Second Report* (Ottawa: Supply and Services, 1977), pp. 2-12.
28. Eglington, "Scrutiny of Delegated Legislation," p. 272.
29. For a discussion of the pre-Clark period and the conclusion that "weak and underdeveloped in-House opposition organization has contributed to poor performance," see Gary Michael Caplan, "The Dynamics of Opposition," in Jean-Pierre Gaboury and James Ross Hurley (ed.), *Regards sur la chambre des Communes* (Ottawa: Editions de l'Université d'Ottawa, 1979), pp. 239-56.

30. Ralph Bertram, "Question Period," in *ibid.*, pp. 13-15.
31. Cited in *The Globe and Mail* (November 14, 1978), p. 8.
32. *Confederation Debates*, 1865, p. 571.
33. *Ibid.*, p. 36.
34. *Ibid.*
35. R. A. MacKay, *The Unreformed Senate of Canada*, revised ed. (Toronto: McClelland and Stewart, 1963), p. 9.
36. Campbell, *The Canadian Senate*, especially Chapters 1 and 4.
37. On the whip's office, see Michael Juneau, "Le Whip," in Gaboury and Hurley, *Regards sur la Chambre des Communes*, pp. 273-92.
38. For an overview, see T. A. Hockin, "Adversary Politics and Some Functions of the House of Commons," in Richard Schultz *et al.* (ed.), *The Canadian Political Process*, 3rd ed. (Toronto: Holt, Rinehart and Winston), pp. 314-29.
39. Valentine Herman and John Pope, "Minority Governments in Western Democracies,"*British Journal of Political Science*, 3 (April 1973), pp. 191-212.
40. For an extended discussion, see Andrew J. Milnor and Mark N. Franklin, "Patterns of Opposition Behaviour in Modern Legislatures," in Allan Kornberg (ed.), *Legislatures in Comparative Perspective* (New York: David McKay, 1973), pp. 421-46.
41. Alistair Fraser, "Legislators and Their Staffs," a paper prepared for the Legislative Studies in Canada Conference, Simon Fraser University (February 1979), p. 12.
42. Stewart, *The Canadian House of Commons*, p. 244.
43. Bernard Crick, *The Reform of Parliament* (New York: Anchor Books, 1965), p. 201. For a critical perspective on the "communications theory," see S. A. Walkland, "The Politics of Parliamentary Reform," *Parliamentary Affairs*, 29 (Spring 1976), pp. 190-200.
44. Allan Kornberg and Judith Wolfe, "Legislators and 'Others': The Canadian Case," a paper prepared for the Legislative Studies in Canada Conference, Simon Fraser University (February 1979), p. 4.
45. *Ibid.*, p. 5.
46. Allan Kornberg, Harold D. Clarke, and Lawrence LeDuc, "Some Correlates of Regime Support in Canada," *British Journal of Political Science*, 8 (April 1978), pp. 199-216.
47. See, for example, S. C. Patterson, R. D. Hedlund, and G. R. Boynton, *Representatives and Represented: Bases of Public Support for the American Legislatures* (New York: John Wiley and Sons, 1975).
48. The study was conducted by students in Political Science 3U6 under the direction of Professor William Coleman. We gratefully acknowledge his permission to use the data.
49. Kornberg and Wolfe, "Legislators and 'Others'," p. 5.
50. Carmen Cumming, "The Coming Battle Over Media Power," *Carleton Journalism Review* (Spring 1977).
51. Kornberg and Wolfe, "Legislators and 'Others'," pp. 19-22.
52. Canadian Radio-television and Telecommunications Commission, *Report of the Committee of Inquiry into the National Broadcasting Service* (Ottawa: 1977).

53. Anthony Westell, "The Press: Adversary or Channel of Communication?", a paper prepared for the Legislative Studies in Canada Conference, Simon Fraser University (February 1979), p. 6.

54. Westell argues that this reduces considerably the scope for variety in political comment. *Ibid.*, p. 3.

55. Gordon Cullingham, "Broadcasting the House of Commons," a paper prepared for the Legislative Studies in Canada Conference, Simon Fraser University (February 1979), pp. 21-24.

56. *Ibid.*, p. 18. "The product that emerges from such a highly charged and delicate political situation looks wooden. You will have noticed that there are no pan shots, few long shots, no split screens, no reaction shots, indeed no *action* shots. . . ."

57. Carleton Journalism Poll conducted by A. Frizell and A. Westell.

58. Information on the size of audiences varies considerably depending on how viewer exposure is measured. The Carleton Journalism Poll found that 63 per cent of respondents had seen or heard a broadcast of parliament; 44 per cent of those surveyed in the McMaster study had watched TV debates; and CIPO pollers found that, after four months of televising, 55 per cent had watched some of it.

59. Cited in Kornberg and Wolfe, "Legislators and 'Others'," p. 27.

6.   The Committee System

Many of those who have expressed discontent with parliament's present role in the legislative system have urged that more power and responsibility be given to committees. Members of Special Committees on Procedure pioneered committee reforms in the 1960s in the expectation that debate in committees would be "well-informed and pertinent, and their members [would] become influential in the areas of their specialized expertise."[1] These reformers calculated that, if private members were given the opportunity to acquire knowledge in a particular area of policy, they would be more inclined to speak out in caucus and in parliament. The result would be a more cautious and responsive executive because private members, informed by participation in specialized committee work, would "find out and publicize the real choices open to the Government at any particular time."[2] This is a reasonable and important hypothesis which has yet to be tested in the Canadian parliament.

Committees of the House of Commons have been employed for a variety of purposes and their structure is the confused product of a series of compromises among several points of view about their role in the system. In Canada there is no generally accepted model for committee activity. In order to share the workload, the House divides into standing committees which are relatively permanent, *ad hoc* special committees, and special joint committees which include members of the Senate. No consensus has emerged in any of these committees on questions of independence and partisanship in internal committee proceedings. There are three main obstacles to transforming the committee system into an arena for the exposure of options and the effective criticism of government policy.

First, the government in power has little or no reason to promote the criticism of its policies in a strengthened committee system. For the government the standing committees are convenient forums for the time-consuming chores of clause-by-clause consideration of bills and the review of spending estimates. As we pointed out in Chapter 5, unless ministers are prepared to agree, important changes are rarely made during either of these proceedings. In 1968, Donald Macdonald, President of the Privy Council, made it clear that the goal of efficiency in the conduct of parliamentary business was central to the government's interest in reform.[3] Changes to the committee system at that time would be evaluated primarily in terms of how they contributed to this goal. The persistence of this view from one government to another suggests that cabinets will always cling to a desire for efficiency even if it impedes effectiveness.

The second obstacle is the widely held belief that more independence for standing committees constitutes a dangerous step toward a congressional form of government. Defenders of this position cherish the party battle which is engaged in daily on the floor of the House of Commons.[4] They fear that the weakening of party discipline, implied in the development of specialized knowledge among backbenchers, will inevitably spread from the committees to the Commons and eventually erode the principle of party cohesion on which parliamentary government is established. A weaker version of this argument holds simply that the real forum for debate ought to be the floor of the House of Commons and any attempt to increase the role of committees will be at the expense of the House. While government backbenchers are among the least likely to subscribe to this argument, according to Professor John Stewart, a former Liberal MP, the Conservative opposition in recent years has alternately rejected and supported this point of view.[5]

What seems to guide this argument is the erroneous impression that the increased activity and independence of committees can only lead away from a parliamentary form of government and toward some variation on the American congressional system. This, however, represents only one of a multitude of possibilities. Committee autonomy or dependence is always a matter of degree, as all committee systems are controlled by their legislatures to a certain extent. In the American House of Representatives, where committees enjoy considerable independence, a majority of members, by signing a discharge petition, can still force bills and other matters out of committee. Moreover, the power to draft and redraft bills is not confined to committees in Congressional systems. Although committees in Canada and Britain are used merely to ''tidy up'' bills, in the Italian parliament, for example, they are employed in the actual drafting of legislation. Similarly, a professional research staff, often regarded as the hallmark of a congressional committee system, is to be found operating under a variety of conditions in several countries. Just as research staff and facilities are not confined to congressional committee systems, constitutional forms in general are not the sole determinants of committee activity.[6]

The final obstacle to the transformation of parliamentary committees is the system of rules and norms that limit their autonomy. Most of the institutional devices which would permit committees to have a more authoritative voice in the consideration of alternatives have been underused. Committee reports seldom come to the attention of the House and even in minority situations committees have been reluctant to insist on legislative changes or make demands of government departments. Membership turnover continues at the unprecedented pace and committee chairmen remain eager to solicit the favour of cabinet ministers.

Most important, the basic organizing principle on which the committee system is premised — namely, that standing committees should be multifunctional — has failed to produce a large contingent of informed critics. According to this principle, most committees should perform a variety of functions — legislative, surveillance, and investigative — in a single policy field. Committee members would then be exposed to government initiatives, ongoing programs, and problem areas within this field, thus broadening their appreciation of government "policy." Unfortunately, this argument overestimates the policy interests of most members of parliament and underestimates the obstacles to the system's successful operation.

DISCONTINUITIES IN THE DEVELOPMENT OF THE COMMITTEE SYSTEM

At Confederation, Canada adopted a weak standing-committee system. The committees were designed to parallel government departments and, in much the same way the government has reorganized its departmental structure, committees have changed to keep pace with changes in specialization. But until recently they remained generalist committees. They were often inactive and performed whatever task the House assigned to them during the course of a session.

Since Confederation there has been some pressure to increase the number of committees. In 1867 there were ten committees; in 1945, 15 committees; and, by 1965, 21 standing committees were in operation. In the nineteenth century the size of the committees fluctuated, but since the session of 1910-11 there has been a general decrease. In 1907 one committee had nearly 200 members and two had 125, but from 1927 to 1964 the largest committee had 60 members, while most had 35 or fewer.

Large or small, the work of these committees depended almost entirely on the needs of the government of the day. For most of the nineteenth century these needs amounted to the careful, but expeditious, study of dozens of private bills. Some committees undertook special studies, albeit without instructions from the House, while others, such as the Committee on Banking and Commerce, were kept busy with public bills.[7] No committee, however, could be certain of a role in the conduct of parliamentary business. It was not until after the Second World War that any committee was assigned the responsibility of reviewing the government's spending estimates, and these were invariably *ad hoc* or special arrangements. With few exceptions the work of standing committees from 1867 to 1965 was incidental to the task of governing. Yet their multifunctional structure remains the guiding principal on which the present committee system has been erected.

Academic critics of this system condemned the unwieldy size of committees, the lack of truly specialist committees with expert members, and the practice of electing excessively partisan chairmen. Some of these criticisms were heeded, but until the early 1960s reform of the committee system remained a topic incidental to reform of procedures in parliament itself. The old committee system was based on the premise that the floor of the House was the centre of significant parliamentary activity.

This premise began to be questioned in the early 1960s. Committee work expanded considerably, first to occupy the large contingent of Diefenbaker supporters and later to relieve the crushing burden of legislation that Liberal governments began to heap upon the House. As early as the 26th Parliament (1963-1965) some committees were beginning to assert themselves. The Defense Committee, in particular, broke new ground both by travelling abroad and by questioning the minister and a large number of defence experts. By 1965 a spirit of reform had overtaken the entire committee system. A Special Committee on Procedure tabled its fifteenth report in December 1964: it recommended, among other things, that committees be given a much expanded role in the consideration of estimates, that the list of committees be revised, and that committees have sufficient powers that they need not depend on the good will of the government.

Through the work of the Special Committee the old list of standing committees was drastically revised and the membership on an average committee was substantially reduced. The House also agreed in 1965 to make greater use of standing committees for the detailed examination of legislation and public spending. Throughout the 27th Parliament, more departmental estimates were referred to standing committees and, as never before, public servants and MPs were brought into direct and continuous contact. At the same time several frontbench politicians on both sides of the House expressed scepticism about the Special Committee's desire for a thoroughly specialized standing committee system; Paul Thomas has concluded that the Pearson government endorsed proposals that would enhance the procedural rights of the government but ignored others, such as staffing increases, that would have strengthened standing committees.[8] In short, the enthusiasm for standing committees prevalent among Special Committee members was not entirely shared by others. Most members were prepared to agree, however, that the transfer of work to the committee system was a logical means of relieving pressure on the floor of the House.

In December 1968 the provisional reforms of 1965 were consolidated and some additional important reforms introduced. While these changes may appear to be the culmination of an unbroken movement for reform in the committee system, this view is not entirely accurate. The Special Committee on Procedure (1967-68) which initiated these final changes was more interested in improving proceedings in the chamber than in the committee system. It decided that the Committee of Supply, the Committee of Ways and Means, and the Committee of the Whole House were too cumbersome and inefficient to handle the increased volume and complexity of legislative and public spending. The operations of the standing committee system were not reviewed extensively and those changes that were made were designed essentially to expedite proceedings in the House.

In the new system all bills were to be referred to the appropriate standing committees for clause-by-clause study after second reading unless the House specified otherwise. Only money bills continued to be referred to the Committee of the Whole. Thus, use of the Committee of the Whole was drastically curtailed and this enhanced the role of standing committees in studying legislation. It was hoped that debate at report stage would not repeat detailed debate in committee.

Departmental estimates were referred to an appropriate standing committee for detailed study. Simultaneously the Committee of Supply was abolished, making the standing committee system the important forum for the scrutiny of government spending. The main estimates were to be tabled normally in February, allowing approximately three months for detailed examination by committees after which they were automatically deemed reported to the House. In addition to the scrutinizing function, it was hoped that standing committees would become familiar with the estimates and through them the operations of the departments and agencies examined. The result was an overall increase in time devoted to estimates and related activities and some relief to the timetable of the House. In order to compensate the opposition for the abolition of the Committee of Supply, 25 days were allotted over three separate "supply periods" during which the opposition could choose the topics for discussion.

At the time of these procedural amendments it would have been worthwhile to have undertaken a complete examination of the committee system itself. However, this option was not chosen and the committee system which had been in operation since 1965 was reconstituted with only minor changes. The new committee system was therefore the product of a tremendous increase in duties and responsibilities, but procedures and functions were not made congruent with the entire legislative process.

Far from resolving disagreements about the direction of committee evolution, the 1968 rule changes have compounded existing tensions. The increase in committee workload, documented below, has made the coordination of committee and House activities much more difficult. Early organizational criticisms of the system centred on the desire of many committee chairmen to meet on the same day and at the same time. The government has taken steps to create a scheduling procedure that would minimize conflicts, but this is still hampered by the unwillingness of many members to meet on Mondays and Fridays when they prefer to be in their constituencies. The smooth organization of committee activity is further impeded by the uneven distribution of work throughout the year and by the natural preference of committee members to conduct on-the-spot investigations far from Ottawa (and the whip's office). Increased committee activity has also created additional responsibilities for senior public servants who now spend a considerable amount of time defending their departments before standing committees. If it is true, as Douglas Hartle has argued, that "to attend a meeting of a parliamentary committee is to be depressed for days,"[9] the costs of this type of arrangement must be calculated in terms of morale as well as of time.

The government has added to these essentially managerial problems by failing to clarify procedural devices which link the House to its committees; namely references, reports, and concurrence. Outstanding points of disagreement remain in each of these areas and, far from being a backwater of interest only to procedural aficionados, their operation determines the status of committee work before the House of Commons. Equally unclear are the roles to be played by committee leaders, especially chairmen and vice-chairmen. After more than ten years of experience in the "new" committee system a consensus on norms of behaviour for committee leaders, other than parliamentary secretaries, has yet to emerge.

These procedural and managerial deficiencies are illustrative of a more profound problem which lies at the heart of the present committee malaise. In spite of the expectations of some committees and the hopes of backbench members of parliament, the committee system lacks the necessary independence to act as a legislative counterweight to the executive. Committees remain totally dependent on outside resources and initiatives. They seldom conduct their own appraisals of social and political problems and even more rarely succeed in commanding an audience for their work. In short, the committee system lacks institutional autonomy. An appreciation of the dimensions of this problem and the reasons for it requires a more detailed examination of committee activities and structure.

HOUSE AND COMMITTEE INTERACTION

Since committees are extensions of the House, they must be subordinate to it for constitutional and practical purposes. Arrangements may be weak and ineffectual, permitting the committees considerable independence, or they may bind the committees very closely to the House and hence the government. By naming the committees in the standing orders and by establishing the procedural devices of references, reports, and motions of concurrence, Canadian committees are linked closely to the House of Commons.

Provision is made in the Standing Orders of the House of Commons for 19 standing committees. Thirteen of these committees — Agriculture; Broadcasting, Film and Assistance to the Arts; External Affairs and National Defence; Finance, Trade and Economic Affairs; Fisheries and Forestry; Health, Welfare and Social Affairs; Indian Affairs and Northern Development; National Resources and Public Works; Justice and Legal Affairs; Labour, Manpower and Immigration; Regional Development; Transport and Communications; and Veterans Affairs—closely parallel one or more government departments. These committees represent the heart of the system and give it a multifunctional nature. The remainder of the committees—Public Accounts Privileges and Elections; Miscellaneous Private Bills and Standing Orders; Miscellaneous Estimates; Procedure and Organization; and Management and Members' Services—have specialized tasks to perform. Unlike the others they may be expected to consider legislation, review estimates, or launch investigations, but they are not expected to do all three.

Committees cannot operate unless their activities are specified in the standing orders or unless they receive a reference instructing them to pursue a particular topic. Orders of reference are debatable and, while most originate with the government, the opposition may also suggest that particular subjects be referred to committee. In 1970 the Biafran crisis was referred to a Commons committee on a motion from the opposition leader, Robert Stanfield. It is rare, however, that the government will permit its control over committee references to be usurped by the opposition. Joe Clark, for example, accused the government of refusing to supply references when issues are too "hot," and other opposition members have complained about the lack of committee authority to launch investigations.[10] Committee chairmen, for that matter, occasionally have to plead for references and the government House leader has been known to refer numerous items to one committee in the expectation that all will be returned quickly to the House. Faced with the necessity of referring an item to committee, the government may use its ultimate weapon, that of creating a special committee to handle the problem and handpicking its membership. Members of the Finance Committee successfully objected to this tactic in connection with the White Paper on Taxation, but constitutional matters, for example, have been considered too delicate for ordinary standing committees.

While committees may consider only those topics which have been referred to them by the House, their members are inclined to ignore the specific terms of their references or to expand them whenever possible. There have been occasional suggestions that committees should be penalized in some way when they expand their references by interpretation. Some members believed, for example, that the External Affairs and National Defence committee should not have received another general reference in the 28th Parliament (1968-72) because its report on Canadian-American relations went beyond the committee's reference. Others argued that in practical terms the general reference of the government's foreign-policy papers allowed the committee to examine any issue on this broad topic. In the case of the penitentiaries subcommittee, formed in October 1976, the opposition lobbied the Solicitor General, Francis Fox, who ultimately agreed that the sub-committee should be empowered to examine not only maximum security institutions, but also "such other institutions as the committee deems advisable."[11]

In spite of the occasional concession extracted by committees, references — especially those which sanction general investigations — are jealously guarded by the government's parliamentary party leadership. They agree to such references only when they are persuaded that it is necessary to create the appearance of concern. Although committees will often request "permanent references" to study perennial issues, in only three special cases has the government agreed.[12] But even when a reference is granted, the government is still able to exercise ultimate control since, for practical purposes, committees are essentially advisory bodies. Neither the House nor observers of the legislative system are entirely clear on the status of various types of committee work.

The standing orders declare that committees have the power "to report from time to time." There are, however, several types of reports. Most common are "housekeeping" reports which usually make requests for the right to travel or engage staff. They consume roughly three lines in Hansard. Also common are reports which inform the House of the results of committee deliberations on bills and estimates. Least common, but most enlightening, are investigative reports such as the report of the penitentiaries subcommittee or that of the Joint Committee on Immigration Policy. This type of report is frequently hundreds of pages in length and contains numerous recommendations.

When housekeeping and investigative reports are tabled in the House, a motion for concurrence is in order. Passage of such a motion implies that the House is prepared to accede to a request or endorse the contents of a report. Unfortunately, there is no agreement on the status of a report once this has been accomplished. As in other House proceedings, it is necessary to determine if a motion for concurrence is an order of the House or a statement of opinion. Orders are binding on the officers and servants of parliament; a second reading motion, for example, is an order to the Table to read the bill a second time.

Resolutions, on the other hand, are opinions; they may have political ramifications, but they do not express the will of the House. As a consequence of this ambiguity a large percentage of investigative reports do not receive concurrence from the House, but the government still implements their contents. On the other hand, some investigative reports receive concurrence but no government action.

The government is reluctant to have concurrence moved in committee reports not only because of the uncertainty associated with this procedure, but also because these motions trigger debates and debates consume the time of the House. The government's enthusiasm for concurrence declined even further on January 22, 1970, when the speaker ruled that any member of a committee may move concurrence in a committee report.[13] In spite of this ruling, the government is still able to limit debate on these motions to one day since, once debate is adjourned, an order for its resumption must be a government order. Stewart has pointed out that, while this practice gives the government the right to shelve a committee report, perhaps prematurely, without this power in someone's hands the prospect is one of an endless series of motions for concurrence and subsequent debate.[14]

A report is the only instrument which will force the House to recognize the collective views of the committee membership. Some members have attempted to use the reports of committees to give expression to personal opinions. However, minority reports are not considered procedurally valid. In rejecting the tabling of a minority report to the main report of the Special Joint Committee on the Constitution on March 16, 1972, the speaker declared that this practice is "unknown" in Canadian and British experience.[15] On occasion minority ideas have been appended or smuggled into the text of a report. In a report on NATO from the External Affairs and National Defence Committee, the lack of unanimity was suggested in several places. At least one of the authors was quite pleased that his minority ideas had been smuggled into the main body of the study. More common, however, is the tactic of simply drafting press releases and relying on the media to publicize differences of opinion.

There are arguments for and against the inclusion of minority reports in a formalized way. The basic argument in favour is that they allow backbenchers to have an input into the report even when they disagree with the majority opinion in the committee. This technique is desirable from the point of view of participation, since it increases information sent to the House and the public about the views of individual members. On the other hand, there are several disadvantages. The acceptance of minority reports may discourage members from reaching a consensus, and every report might be divided into a majority report which expresses the government's views and a minority report which expresses the views of the opposition. Moreover, if it became the usual practice that members other than the chairmen moved concurrence or that minority reports were acceptable, a majority government might be tempted to deny references to committees or to instruct its majority not to produce a report at all.

The primary objective of a committee report is to influence government policy. The primary problem standing committees face is that of commanding the government's attention. Departments regard committee reports as less significant than those from royal commissions or task forces. In the formative stages of policymaking, influence flows from departments to committees rather than from politicians to bureaucrats. Occasionally, as in the case of the report of the penitentiaries subcommittee, the government will respond to recommendations, but silence is the rule. Generally, the government does not bother to explain why it has been unable to accept committee recommendations, regardless of whether or not they have received concurrence. Stanley Knowles provides some indication of how frustrating such indifference can be:

> What is the point of talking about the committee system and matters being referred to a committee for detailed study if, after all this is done and a thoroughly researched report is tabled, the government takes no action. . . . surely there comes a time when pleading which is consistent, unanimous and responsible ought to have some effect on the cabinet.[16]

In Australia, committee reports continually provide the basis for debates in the House of Representatives. In Canada a procedure to trigger automatic debate of committee reports is required and proposals to stimulate such House and committee interaction will be offered in the final chapter.[17]

INSIDE COMMITTEES

The success of standing committees in the legislative system is influenced by the same dynamics that effect all small groups. If committees are too large for the tasks they are required to undertake, or if they are forced to accomplish too much in too short a time, members feel frustrated and morale suffers. Since 1968, this is what has occurred in the standing committees of the House of Commons. There have been repeated complaints about the organization of the committees and about the timing and scale of committee operations.

The allotment of positions on committees to the various parties is determined by a consideration of party strengths in the House and certain norms about appropriate parliamentary organization. The Striking Committee, which meets at the outset of each parliament and contains the whips and House leaders of all the parties, is the forum for bargaining over the distribution of committee positions. In a majority situation, no government party will accept fewer than 50 per cent of the members of each committee. To date, the weakest party has not been denied representation on any committee and the official opposition is usually granted more positions than a strictly proportional allotment would allow. These anomalies aside, the proportionality rule is normally applied even during minority governments when it compounds the problems facing the governing party. During the 29th Parliament (1972-74), for example, only 19 positions were filled on most 20-member committees: the Liberals were assigned eight positions, the Conservatives eight, the NDP two, and the Social Credit party one.

Unlike the U.S. House of Representatives where certain committee assignments are coveted and seniority is still the governing factor, requests for particular committee positions in the House of Commons can usually be accommodated. Members tend to choose committees whose subject matter accords with their professional training or their constituency interests. On occasion, the parliamentary party leadership will intervene directly in assignments as it did during committee consideration of the Time-Readers' Digest bill when four recalcitrant Liberals were unceremoniously removed from the Standing Committee on Broadcasting, Films and Assistance to the Arts. Such intervention is unusual, however, and costly since it advertises the government's inability to secure its objectives via the normal path of persuasion.

If a member is unable to obtain his preferred assignment at the outset of a session, all is not lost. Turnover in committees is so rapid and attendance often so poor that the persistent MP can usually secure the desired spot within a matter of weeks. The procedure for substituting members is perversely simple. All that is required is a notification to the committee chairman authorized in the office of the chief government whip. This procedure, introduced in 1968, has added a great fluidity to the membership of committees. The rate of membership substitution has been high ever since: substitutions during the first three sessions of the 30th Parliament (1974-79) totalled 4310, 1749, and 1409, respectively.[18] The officials in the whip's office who approve substitutions are extremely sensitive to the demands for quorums and voting majorities. However, many of the substitutions are, strictly speaking, unnecessary and it is not at all uncommon for both "substitutes" and "regular" members to be absent.

In the midst of this flux, a certain degree of stability can still be found. Each committee contains a "core" of committed members who attend meetings regularly and follow the committee's work. This core numbers no more than 12 members for each 20-member committee. The views and interests of these members are of concern to committee chairmen and committee clerks. Core members have earned the right to be consulted and, where possible, accommodated. But the same members frequently belong to the core of several committees and the burden of committee attendance is by no means equally distributed. Both MPs and outside observers agree that only 60 or 70 members of the House can be considered active committee participants. According to John Reid, a former parliamentary secretary to the President of the Privy Council:

> Right now, to make the committee system work we should have approximately 150 members. We actually have about 65 members from both sides of the House who make the committee system operate.[19]

In a study of the second session of the 30th Parliament the Lambert Commission found that "half of the attendance of all committee meetings was accounted for by just 42 MPs."[20]

These figures hide party, committee, and subject-matter differences. According to Kornberg and Mishler, during the 28th Parliament, the Liberals met 68 per cent of their attendance opportunities, the NDP 64 per cent, the Conservatives 55 per cent, while Social Credit members attended an average of 24 per cent of the meetings for which they were eligible.[21] Attendance also varies from committee to committee. In the second session of the 28th Parliament, the average attendance ranged from a low of 8.2 members in the case of Miscellaneous Estimates to a high of 15.5 in the case of Transport and Communications, with an average attendance for all 20-member committees of 11.2 members. As the Kornberg and Mishler research suggests, there is only a very weak relationship between the prestige of committees and the diligence of the members. More important, perhaps, is the subject matter under consideration. The attendance of members at meetings on legislation is usually significantly higher than on either estimates or general investigations. It is reasonable to speculate that legislative work evokes a confrontation style in all parties and the whips endeavour to maintain a high level of attendance among committee members for the sake of party interests.

Table 6-1 SIZE AND MEMBERSHIP OF STANDING COMMITTEES, 1960-1979

Periods	No. of Standing Committees*	Total Membership	Average Membership/ Committee	Number of Committees/ Average Member
1960-1962	14	571	40.8	2.4
1962-1963	13	536	41.2	2.3
1963	13	571	41.2	2.4
1964-1965	14	571	40.8	2.4
1965-1968	21	525	25.0	2.2
1968-1969	18	364	20.2	1.6
1968-1975	18	376	20.9	1.6
1975-1979	19	388	20.4	1.7

*Does not include joint standing committees.
SOURCE: House of Commons, *Journals and Debates*.

Table 6-2 COMMITTEE MEETINGS: 27TH THROUGH 30TH PARLIAMENTS

	Meetings	Sitting Days	Ratio of Meetings to Sitting Days
27th Parliament	714	405	1.76
28th Parliament	2590	684	3.79
29th Parliament	750	256	2.93
30th Parliament*	2302	667	3.45

*Includes only the first three sessions.

Part of the problem in maintaining a reasonable attendance level lies in the number of meetings which members are required to attend. As Table 6-2 illustrates, the average number of committee meetings held during a sitting day more than doubled between the 27th and 28th Parliaments. Committee activity declined during the minority 29th

Parliament, but resumed a high level during the 30th Parliament. Now that bills, estimates, and general investigations are the responsibility of committees, multiple meetings during a normal sitting day are the rule, not the exception. While there are doubtless other reasons for sagging attendance, core members in particular have been plagued by timetable conflicts. In an effort to minimize this problem the government instituted, during the 28th Parliament, a scheduling system that was intended to suit core members. Complaints about conflicting meetings have subsided, but as the Lambert Commission has shown, this has done little to arrest the general erosion of interest in committees.

To complicate the matter further, committees, like most organizations, experience peak periods of operation. Seldom does business flow so smoothly that activity is kept at a constant level. The period of heavy activity begins in February with the referral of estimates to standing committees and ends in May with their return to the House. Unfortunately, this is also the time when many government bills, introduced in the fall, are ready for clause-by-clause consideration. The Finance, Trade and Economic Affairs Committee, for example, met 64 times between October 1974 and September 1975. But almost half of these meetings took place during the months of March, April, and May when the committee busied itself with departmental estimates and Bill C-2, a bill amending the Combines Investigation Act. MPs, on occasion, warn ministers of the consequences of these timetabling arrangements: ''I say to the minister that even if this bill does get to committee, it is not going anywhere. Estimates are the priority until May 31.''[22] Moreover, during a busy period in committee, members are still required on the floor of the House of Commons. Where no special arrangements are made to cope with the burden of work, some items of business may be given less than proper attention.

According to the philosophy of the Special Committees on Procedure, which pioneered the 1968 rule changes, members were to develop more expertise in the subject matter of their committees. The committee system, it was hoped, would provide ''a counter-balancing force to the executive.''[23] Unfortunately, the organization of committee work and the pattern of committee membership have undermined these objectives. Committee workload has increased, but attendance has not kept pace and the ease with which MPs can move from one committee to another effectively thwarts the principle of stable, continuous membership. These problems are aggravated by the uneven flow of business to committees and the tendency of many members to avoid committee deliberations on estimates.

Leadership is one of the most important, but least understood, aspects of committee behaviour. Within the first few months of each session the government whip arranges for each committee to hold an organizational meeting to elect a chairman. Committee chairmen are therefore technically elected by the committee itself. In fact, however, these elections are the products of the consultative process which includes the government House leader, the government whips, and the minister whose bills and estimates will be sent to a particular committee. During the 1970s, and especially during the 30th Parliament, aspirants for chairmanship positions began lobbying fellow committee members and, increasingly, the determination of leadership choices was made by the government caucus on each committee. By 1979, leadership choice was the shared responsibility of the party leadership and the committee, a trend reflected in the increasing importance of committee service as a criterion for leadership selection.[24]

Since 1968, in both majority and minority situations, almost all of the committee chairmen have been drawn from the government side of the House. By convention the chairmanship of the Public Accounts committee, and the chairmanship of the Management and Members' Services committee, and the vice-chairmanship of the Standing Committee on Procedure and Organization have been filled by opposition members. At the outset of the minority 29th Parliament the government House leader, Allan MacEachen, offered half of the chairmanships of the standing committees to the official opposition, but after a lengthy debate in caucus the Conservatives finally rejected the offer and with it the opportunity to inject some nonpartisanship into committee proceedings.

Like any elected official, the chairman is expected to preside over committee meetings, maintain decorum, and decide questions of order subject to appeal. However, the standing orders fail to specify the role and functions of committee chairmen beyond these broad notions and no effort has been made to correct inconsistencies in the practices and rulings of committee chairmen. Since chairmanships are often considered either stepping stones to greater heights or consolation prizes for those not appointed to the cabinet, there are pressures on the chairman to help the government achieve its legislative and policy goals. At the same time the rules imply that chairmen of committees should be as impartial as the speaker. Therefore, under present practice chairmen have two somewhat contradictory roles, one as the instrument of the government and the other as an impartial official. These difficulties have been compounded by the absence of any institutional arrangement whereby chairmen, House leaders, and whips might be drawn together to discuss mutual problems and to schedule committee activities. Moreover, neither chairmen nor vice-chairmen receive extra remuneration for their services and there are no additional staff privileges. Nonetheless their workload is heavier than that of most backbenchers and they do not enjoy the luxury of being able to miss committee meetings. In the judgment of Thomas and other observers of the committee system, very few chairmen can be expected to make the job a permanent parliamentary career.[25]

Since committees are extensions of the House and not the government, the standing orders do not specify the duties of ministers or parliamentary secretaries in committee activities. Since the 28th Parliament it has been clear, however, that parliamentary secretaries are responsible for government leadership on committees. They advocate the government's position on procedural questions, accompany public-service witnesses presenting evidence to committees, and, in the absence of the minister, set forth government policy and defend it before the committee. Parliamentary secretaries are usually regarded by their colleagues as purely partisan committee members whose task is to defend the government's interest on contentious amendments and to act as a liaison between the committees and the caucus. Unfortunately, not all committees have parliamentary secretaries and some committees encompass more than one ministry. When there is no one to do the work of the minister, the chairman is automatically forced to become the arm of the government, thereby compounding the problem of his role in the system.

There is little doubt about who represents the government's position when the minister is in attendance. It is at these times that members feel they are making a useful contribution to the parliamentary system as opposed to merely talking about the problems of the day with public servants and other backbenchers. Unfortunately, ministerial attendance is, at best, spasmodic. As a rule, ministers are present at the introduction of a bill in committee and at the committee's initial meeting on the minister's departmental estimates. Once the opening statement has been read, however, public servants generally discuss the details of the legislation or departmental operations. Ministers attend fewer than 20 per cent of committee meetings, a record which elicits occasional grumbles from opposition members and probably contributes to the lacklustre attendance patterns.

Committee deliberations are expedited by the efforts of several parliamentary organizations. The Committees and Private Legislation Branch of the House provides procedural and administrative support to committees. When the budget of the House of Commons tripled between 1964 and 1972, the Committees Branch accounted for a large proportion of the increase. It includes 20 committee clerks, a data section, plus a chief and a deputy chief. Despite its aggrandizement, it has never been staffed with subject-matter specialists and could not readily change its focus from procedural to substantive matters even if a major organizational change was contemplated. At present the committee clerk is responsible for advising on matters of practice and procedure, preparing agendas, handling finances, and generally facilitating the work of the committee chairman. Some thought could be given, however, to encouraging committee clerks to assume a more activist role in organizing the substance of committee work. The committee clerk, it must be remembered, normally has a longer tenure on the committee than virtually anyone else, including the chairman. In matters such as the selection of witnesses and the strategies to be employed in examining the estimates, committee clerks possess valuable, and certainly scarce, expertise.

Committees rely primarily on three sources for research assistance. The main source is the Research Branch of the Library of Parliament which consists of 45 professional researchers and a support staff of 23. Although the Branch is chiefly occupied with serving the needs of individual MPs, researchers are made available to committees regularly or part-time. The research is conducted in a decidedly nonpartisan spirit, is professional, and is widely valued. Independent of the Research Branch is the Parliamentary Centre for Foreign Affairs and Foreign Trade. This group regularly assists the Standing Committee on External Affairs and National Defence, but has also lent its efforts to the joint committees on Immigration and the Constitution. Finally, all committees may request that the Clerk of the House authorize the hiring of outside consultants to assist them in particular projects. The Finance, Trade and Economic Affairs committee has been one of the most active employers of professional assistance, hiring lawyers and economists to aid in the review of such matters as the White Paper on Taxation, the Competition Bill, and the Bank Act.

It is tempting to endorse the idea that a significant increase in staff assistance will solve many of the problems facing parliamentary committees. But, until committees are given an independent capacity to influence public policy, it is unlikely that the addition of even the most competent of research assistants will do more than contribute to the frustrations of MPs and researchers alike.

THE POTENTIAL OF STANDING COMMITTEES

If standing committees are to become independent sources of criticism and policy advice, they will first have to command the attention and respect of the inner circle and the variety of attentive publics that are aware of committee proceedings. Experience has shown that this respect is not easily earned. When committees are successful, two ingredients are normally present: first, the committee behaves generally in a nonpartisan manner and, second, the committee's contribution is timed to have the maximum impact on government policy. Both of these prerequisites are usually obtained only when the committee has been given the authority to conduct a general investigation.

The increase in the volume of committee deliberations, noted above, is attributable in part to the government's willingness to permit committees to conduct general investigations. In the 28th Parliament particularly, members exhibited a voracious appetite for white papers and annual reports which could be used as the basis for investigative studies.[26] In the second session of the 28th Parliament, approximately 60 per cent of committee meetings were consumed in this type of work in spite of the fact that standing committees had also assumed responsibility for the consideration of estimates and legislation. Enthusiasm, and perhaps the government's generosity, declined during the 29th and 30th Parliaments. In the 29th and the first three sessions of the 30th Parliament, investigatory work accounted for approximately 30 per cent of committee meetings.

Perhaps the most celebrated of committee studies in the 28th Parliament was the review of the White Paper on Tax Reform conducted by the Standing Committee on Finance, Trade and Economic Affairs. The minority 29th Parliament produced no investigations of comparable significance, but during the 30th Parliament a subcommittee of the Standing Committee on Justice and Legal Affairs pursued a reference to examine the penitentiary system in Canada. The investigation and the final report attracted both media and cabinet attention. In the 30th Parliament, the Standing Committee on External Affairs and National Defence maintained its tradition of investigative work by conducting hearings and producing reports on the problem of international development. This committee, during the 28th Parliament, had considered the "Foreign Policy for Canadians" papers and, much to the discomfort of the government, had recommended 51 per cent ownership of Canadian industry. When given the opportunity, committees also respond to specific demands. In May 1972 the question of rail passenger service in Ontario was referred to the Standing Committee on Transportation and Communication. The committee visited several cities in the province, heard 68 witnesses, received 55 briefs in addition to petitions and letters, and finally recommended that all discontinued passenger service be restored.

Ministers are not always anxious to grant committees general investigatory references. Although the reference was finally granted, many ministers and senior officials expressed serious misgivings about sending the Green Paper on Immigration to a parliamentary committee (even a Special Joint Committee) on the grounds that such a committee would only produce extravagant and unworkable recommendations which the government would find it embarrassing to ignore.[27] Moreover, when an investigatory reference is granted, the government frequently has other objectives than merely soliciting the views of parliamentarians. The government may attempt to use the committee system as a forum for public response to proposals, as it did (with unexpected results) in the case of the White Paper on Tax Reform. Committees may also be used to delay consideration of an item, as with the Special Committee on Drug Costs and Prices in the 27th Parliament. Most important, committee investigation is a convenient way of employing the energies of those backbenchers eager for a larger role in policymaking.

In the course of an investigation, committee members occasionally set aside partisan allegiances and give their loyalty first and foremost to the collective enterprise. The experience of the subcommittee on penitentiaries stands out as the best recent example of this phenomenon. After holding more than 70 meetings, hearing over 400 witnesses, and visiting 24 penal institutions, this subcommittee, on June 7, 1977, placed before parliament a 200-page report containing 65 recommendations, which, in the words of the chairman, Mark MacGuigan, "proposed nothing less than the complete revitalization of the prison system."[28] MacGuigan described the unanimous report as "a symbol of inter-party cooperation by members who were prepared to place the importance of the problem before all other considerations."[29] A reading of the transcripts of the initial meeting makes it clear that this spirit of cooperation was not present at the outset. Opposition members disputed the composition of the committee and the order of reference. The feeling of trust which subsequently grew among members of the Justice and Legal Affairs committee contributed to another unanimous report, this time on obscenity. In an understandable burst of enthusiasm MacGuigan has since written that, "there is almost no limit to the Committee's ability to determine government action."[30] A Special Joint Committee on Immigration Policy revealed a similar capacity for nonpartisan work in 1975 when it conducted hearings on the government's Green Paper. As in the case of the penitentiaries subcommittee, debate and discussion were never dictated by party affiliation and the Committee behaved as a cohesive unit in the face of criticism.[31]

When committees achieve this kind of cohesiveness it is often because committee members have shared the experience of hearing and questioning witnesses. Committees hear witnesses both to obtain expert opinions and to acquaint themselves with competing points of view on the issues under consideration. The power to summon and examine witnesses in standing committees derives from the Senate and House of Commons Act and Standing Order 65. On subjects of a technical or private nature the usual practice had been to summon those directly involved. In such cases committee members are usually well informed and can compile an exhaustive list of witnesses. On matters of wider public interest most witnesses request to be heard, so the chairman or a steering committee acts as a screening device. The vast majority of witnesses appear on behalf of groups who either have a special interest in the matter at hand or make it a general policy to keep in touch with committees and present briefs on various occasions.

The new committee system has established stronger lines of communication with interested publics and departmental officials. These lines of communication are enhanced when committees obtain the right to travel. Committee sojourns are frequently described as "junkets" by media observers and they undoubtedly contribute to the problem of maintaining quorum levels in the House and in the remaining committees. However, committees that travel are invariably exposed to a wider range of opinion than those which conduct their work exclusively in Ottawa. In addition to contributing to the political sensitivity of recommendations, committees that travel to hear witnesses also acquire a much needed legitimacy.

An enormous increase in the appearance of witnesses occurred between the 27th and 28th Parliaments and aggravated a serious, unresolved problem respecting the legal rights of witnesses in the face of committee interrogation.[32] The protections afforded to witnesses derive both from general law and from the practices and procedures of parliament. It seems reasonably clear, however, that most witnesses are unaware of their rights or avenues of appeal or that they may claim the protection of the Canada Evidence Act if they feel their testimony might be self-incriminating. Furthermore, witnesses who have been damaged by unfair criticism in a committee report do not have a remedy before the courts by way of a defamation action because of the absolute privilege of members of parliament which applies to things said in the House and in committee. The need to establish some common procedural safeguards is most acute in the case of departmental and agency witnesses who can be criticized, sometimes severely, without having the opportunity to enter a defence. Hearings on the *Bonaventure* refit scandal often assumed the appearance of adversarial proceedings with witnesses being treated as accused and with a verdict on their behaviour included in a committee report. The need to clarify the relationship of parliamentary committees to courts of law will become more pressing if prevailing notions of ministerial responsibility are modified and officials are required to assume a larger public responsibility for their actions.

The growth of trust and respect among committee members contributes to the committee's corporate identity and, ultimately, to its autonomy from governmental and party constraints. But none of this will increase the committee's influence perceptibly unless it is organized to affect government policy and is given the opportunity to do so. This influence requires, in the first place, that the committee act on policy before major commitments and decisions have been taken. Since the most important decisions on legislation are taken long before committees examine bills, deliberations at this stage may serve to educate MPs and permit witnesses to establish parliamentary contacts, but they do little to affect the direction or substance of the legislation. In majority situations very few substantive amendments are made in committee without the prior consent or cooperation of the government. Unless it is the hope of witnesses to influence the details and technical wording of legislation, much of their time is wasted.

As outlined earlier, the power to reverse this sequence rests with the government. Ministers are concerned, however, that general investigatory references encourage bipartisan positions, foment internal party dissent, and interfere with their personal initiatives. A compromise is required. Committees should be permitted to take part in the early stages of policymaking in exchange for curtailing their activity in the later stages. Specifically, committees require a regular flow of general references and annual reports so that they may initiate inquiries into fields *before* the government tables legislation. When bills are tabled, however, committees would be obliged to restrict their investigations and travel.

Committees need to be reorganized to take advantage of the opportunities presented by general investigatory references and departmental estimates. This requires that committees devise strategies which encompass not only the procedures but also the substantive concerns of members. Robert Miller has argued that, in most committee proceedings, members remain isolated from one another, unwilling to agree on a focus for discussion. "The dispersal of energy contrasts sharply with the unity of purpose displayed, for example, by government witnesses and their support staff."[33] As chairman of the Standing Committee on Indian Affairs and Northern Development, Ian Watson demonstrated that a committee organized to pursue a particular topic — in this case native education — could produce a detailed and critical report even if it had to rely on the estimates procedure to do it. The recent work of the External Affairs and National Defence Subcommittee on International Development also reflected a conscious effort on the part of all parties to agree on the substantive issues to be pursued before meetings commenced. Unfortunately, this type of preparation is unusual. More often than not committees permit themselves to be hamstrung by such conventions as the "ten-minute rule" which limits the length of individual questioning and encourages the view that it is "every man for himself."

A lack of preparedness is particularly harmful when it affects the number and type of witnesses being heard. On subjects of general interest, such as those being handled at the level of a white paper, the assumption that all views have been heard may be unfounded. The Special Joint Committee on Immigration was scrupulous in its efforts to canvass a wide range of opinion, but it is by no means certain that the same could be said of the Standing Committee on Finance and Economic Affairs when it selected the groups and individuals it would hear from among the more than one thousand who wished to comment on the White Paper on Tax Reform. During the 30th Parliament members of all parties complained that committee hearings on a consumer-protection bill were dominated by banks and other lenders and that insufficient attention had been paid to consumer groups. At best, the present system is haphazard, relying as it does on newspaper advertising of committee hearings and the collective intuition of committee members. An important role for committee staff in a revitalized system would be to make certain that a representative cross-section of opinion — including people other than the representatives of institutionalized interest groups — are heard on matters of importance.

It is likely that the future reform of parliament will focus on the committee system and the improvement of its support facilities. The committees provide an excellent forum for change because their expressed purpose is to enhance both the effectiveness and efficiency of the House. As the demands for increased committee support are met, the bond between committees and the House will have to be adjusted. Many Canadian parliamentarians on both sides of the House are prepared to advocate such an evolution. But the aggrandizement of committees means increased pressure on party cohesion. This dilemma will not be resolved until the fundamental obstacles to reform have been removed and there is agreement on a model for committee activity in the Canadian legislative system in which the realities of party politics are accommodated.

NOTES

1. Canada, House of Commons, Special Committee on Procedure, *Third Report*, 1968.
2. John P. MacKintosh, "Reform of the House of Commons: The Case for Specialization," in Gerhard Lowenberg (ed.), *Modern Parliaments: Change or Decline* (Chicago: Aldine-Atherton, 1971).
3. Donald S. Macdonald, "Change in the House of Commons: New Rules," *Canadian Public Administration*, 13 (Spring 1970), pp. 30-39.
4. Gordon Churchill, "Parliamentary Reform," unpublished manuscript, (September 17, 1968).
5. John B. Stewart, *The Canadian House of Commons: Procedure and Reform* (Montreal: McGill-Queen's University Press, 1977), pp. 169-70. For another view, see Allan Kornberg and William Mishler, *Influence in Parliament: Canada* (Durham: N.C.: Duke University Press, 1977), p. 307.
6. John D. Lees and Malcolm Shaw (ed.), *Committees in Legislatures: A Comparative Analysis* (Durham, N.C.: Duke University Press, 1979).
7. Stewart, *The Canadian House of Commons*, Chapter 6.
8. Paul G. Thomas, "The Role of Committees in the Canadian House of Commons, 1960-72," Ph.D. dissertation (University of Toronto, 1975), pp. 48-52.

9. Douglas Hartle, "Canada's Watchdog Growing Too Strong?" *The Globe and Mail* (January 10, 1979), p. 7.

10. Joe Clark, *Debates*, December 9, 1976, p. 1828; Paul Yewchuk, *Debates*, December 9, 1976, p. 1831.

11. House of Commons, Standing Committee on Justice and Legal Affairs, *Minutes and Proceedings*, Issue 1 (October 26, 1976), p. 4.

12. Permanent references are held by: Public Accounts, Regulations and Other Statutory Instruments, and Management and Members' Services.

13. *Debates*, January 19, 1970, pp. 2513-23; January 20, 1970, pp. 2575-76; January 21, 1970, pp. 2681-2727.

14. Stewart, *The Canadian House of Commons*, pp. 194-95.

15. *Debates*, March 16, 1972.

16. *Debates*, December 11, 1975, pp. 9930-33, The report in question, from the Veteran's Affairs committee, had been tabled six months previously.

17. For a discussion along these lines, see Douglas Rowland, *Debates*, November 19, 1971, p. 9738.

18. From Peter Dobell, "Committee Staff — What Else is Needed?" a paper prepared for the Legislative Studies in Canada Conference, Simon Fraser University (February 1979), p. 14.

19. *Debates*, June 2, 1975, pp. 6362.

20. Royal Commission on Financial Management and Accountability, *Final Report*, 1979, p. 298.

21. Kornberg and Mishler, *Influence in Parliament*, p. 160.

22. Marcel Lambert, *Debates*, March 29, 1977, pp. 4442.

23. C.E.S. Franks, "The Dilemma of the Standing Committees of the Canadian House of Commons," *Canadian Journal of Political Science*, 4 (December 1971), p. 462.

24. Michael M. Atkinson and Kim Richard Nossal, "Executive Power and Committee Autonomy in the House of Commons: Leadership Selection, 1968-1979," *Canadian Journal of Political Science* (June 1980).

25. Thomas, "The Role of Committees," p. 89; Atkinson and Nossal, "Executive Power."

26. Stewart, *The Canadian House of Commons*, p. 184.

27. Peter Dobell and Susan d'Aquino, "The Special Joint Committee on Immigration," *Behind the Headlines* (Toronto: Canadian Institute for International Affairs, 1976), p. 3.

28. Mark MacGuigan, "The Role of the Standing Committee on Justice and Legal Affairs," unpublished manuscript, 1978, p. 35.

29. House of Commons, Sub-committee on Penitentiaries, *Minutes and Proceedings*, Issue 45 (May 26, 1977), p. 5.

30. MacGuigan, "The Role of the Standing Committee," p. 40.

31. Dobell and d'Aquino, "The Special Joint Committee on Immigration," pp. 13, 16.

32. See Table 2, "Comparison of Committee Activities," in *The Canadian Legislative System*, 1st ed., 1974, p. 125.

33. Robert Miller, "Reflections of a Staffer," a paper prepared for the Legislative Studies in Canada Conference, Simon Fraser University (February 1979), p. 12.

7.   Representation and the Member of Parliament

The institutions described in the preceding chapters form the legislative structure of representative government in Canada. Representative government is supposed to be an institutionalized arrangement whereby the elected are held accountable for their actions by periodic elections and the governors are restrained by the collective vigilance of the elected assembly. Electors are considered to be involved in the legislative system in the sense that members of parliament are responsive to their views and initiate policy on their behalf. Distinguishing between representative and other forms of government requires, therefore, an assessment of the government's capacity for responsiveness and of the role of representatives in the entire legislative system.

In the Canadian political system there is some doubt about the degree to which representatives are and can be responsive to their electors. Representatives establish relationships with sectors of the political environment other than their own electoral districts. They must reconcile the demands of organized interests, the constraints of party loyalty, and the dictates of individual conscience. Even within their own constituencies the scope of representation has increased dramatically. In 1896 each MP represented just over 6000 voters; by 1979 each constituency contained about 50,000 to 55,000 voters. The lack of voter knowledge on specific political issues prevents politicians from effectively embodying the attitudes and opinions of the electorate. Furthermore, electoral research indicates that the policy positions of individual candidates have little effect on their personal electoral success. Finally, in the Canadian legislative system the opportunity for initiatives by individual members of parliament is severely restricted by the dominance of the inner circle in all facets of government. It is within these constraints that Canadian legislators must solve the intricate problems of representation.

REPRESENTATIVES AND THE REPRESENTED

Some scholars believe that the puzzle of representation will be solved if the representative assembly mirrors the basic attributes of the population. Proponents of proportional representation, for example, allege that if the social divisions in society are reproduced in parliament, they will have an impact on the content of legislative output. It is assumed that such representatives will act to defend the interests of their constituents. In Canada it is well known that an accurate resemblance of the representatives to the represented is approximated only in a few select characteristics. Canadian legislators, by and large, constitute an elite which is easily distinguishable from the remainder of the population.

The data available on the attributes of Canadian legislators are fragmentary, but enough individual studies have been completed to suggest a consistent pattern of over- and underrepresentation. Aggregate data comparisons show that there are marked differences between elected representatives and the general public on the basis of age, education, and occupation. MPs have generally been older than their constituents, a fact not particularly surprising since a large proportion of the Canadian population is under 21. According to the 1971 census, 42.2 per cent of Canadians were under the age of 21, while the median age of parliamentarians in the 29th Parliament (1972-74) was 47 years, and in the 30th Parliament (1974-79) 56 per cent of the membership was 50 years of age or older.[1]

The educational status of members is also unrepresentative of the population. The 1971 census indicates that only 7.9 per cent of the labour force had acquired some college education, while almost 60 per cent of MPs who served between 1974 and 1979 had been to university. Occupational differences constitute a further division between representatives and the represented. In the 30th Parliament 25 per cent of the membership were lawyers, another 25 per cent had other professional occupations, while 15 per cent held executive, administrative, or managerial posts. In the population, however, lawyers account for only one-quarter of one per cent of the labour force, while the entire professional group comprises less than 10 per cent of Canadian workers.[2] The vast overrepresenation of lawyers is not uncommon in liberal democracies, but the Canadian House of Commons still ranks well ahead of the British Parliament (17 per cent lawyers in 1974) and the German Bundestag (5 per cent in 1972).[3]

All legislatures have experienced some long-term changes in membership composition, but in Canada the pattern of over- and underrepresentation has remained relatively stable. Using the Blishen occupational scale to rank the population, Caroline Andrew found that almost 75 per cent of parliamentarians in the 26th Parliament (1963-1965) were in the top two groups on the scale, while only 12 per cent of the population was similarly situated.[4] The virtual absence of manual workers has persisted in spite of the presence of the New Democratic party in parliament. In their study of the 28th Parliament (1968-72) Allan Kornberg and William Mishler conclude that the Liberals tend to have the most "elite" social origins, the Créditiste members the most "proletarian," while Conservative and NDP members fall somewhere in between.[5] The authors argue that New Democrats and Social Credit members have succeeded in closing the socioeconomic gap which separated them from the other parties in earlier parliaments.

With a few important exceptions, differences between representatives and the represented are less pronounced in the areas of religion and ethnicity. In both the 25th and 26th Parliaments (1962-63 and 1963-65) British and French descendants were slightly overrepresented. Those constituents of other European origins were slightly underrepresented, while indigenous Canadians — Inuit, Indians, and Métis — were hardly represented at all. Minority religious affiliations, like minority ethnic groups, also tend to have fewer members in the House of Commons. On the other hand, an approximate balance has been maintained between the proportion of Catholic representatives and Catholics in the population. Protestant denominations, particularly the United Church of Canada, have been consistently overrepresented. The greatest distortion of all occurs in the representation of women. In 1979, under 4 per cent of the members of the House of Commons were females.[6]

If elected representatives comprise an identifiable elite on the basis of the factors discussed above, cabinet ministers constitute an even more select circle. In Canada, cabinet ministers are chosen partially on the basis of criteria which give expression to the federal principle. According to this principle every province, where possible, must receive a ministerial appointment and ethnic representation must be delicately balanced. In spite of these apparent constraints on cabinet choice, Canadian prime ministers have managed to appoint persons with background characteristics which separate them to some extent from other members of parliament.

Table 7-1 OCCUPATIONAL AND EDUCATIONAL BACKGROUNDS:
MINISTERS AND MEMBERS OF PARLIAMENT

	Members of Parliament* 1978	Trudeau Cabinet 1974-1979	Clark Cabinet 1979
Occupations			
Legal	25.4%	35.5%	50.0%
Other Professional	24.6%	14.3%	16.7%
Executive, Managerial	15.3%	14.3%	16.7%
Other	34.7%	36.9%	16.6%
	100%	100%	100%
	n = 248	n = 42	n = 30
Education			
Graduate	44.4%	52.4%	60.0%
Undergraduate	14.8%	16.7%	16.7%
Other Post secondary	17.6%	14.3%	10.0%
Other	23.2%	16.7%	13.3%
	100%	100.1%	100%
	n = 250	n = 42	n = 30

*Excludes vacant ridings in 1978.
SOURCE: *Parliamentary Guide*, personal inquiries where necessary.

Cabinet ministers have an overwhelming tendency to be native born and of British or French descent. Educational standards for cabinet are slightly higher than those for the House. As Table 7-1 indicates, cabinet ministers are more likely to have attended university and to have acquired at least some graduate training. Lawyers are even more heavily represented among the elected members of the inner circle than they are in the House of Commons. During the period from Confederation to the Second World War, 60 per cent of federal cabinet ministers were trained in the legal profession and, in 1979, half of Joe Clark's cabinet was comprised of lawyers. If the House of Commons is not representative of the population, the cabinet is even less so. John Porter has aptly summarized the situation: "The extension of democracy has brought about not a widening, but a further narrowing in the occupational background of the political directorate."[7]

When the ideal of representation is taken to be a direct and accurate reflection of the interests of the represented, it is assumed that the personal characteristics of representatives will ensure that they act to defend the interests they mirror. Studies of all Canadian members of parliament have revealed that distortions exist between representatives and the represented, especially in age, sex, education, and occupational patterns. A perfect reproduction of basic societal attributes in a legislature is probably impossible and discrepancies of this kind exist in all liberal democracies. No one in Canada, however, has demonstrated how differences between representatives and the represented affect the pattern of legislative behaviour or the pattern of public policy. Numerous, conflicting environmental factors exert pressure on MPs to act in particular ways and this necessarily compromises the mirror-image notion of representation. Indeed, this idea of representation needs to be modified considerably to allow for the fact that representation implies action and that it is the nature of that action, not merely the background characteristics of MPs, that determines the quality of representation.

REPRESENTATION AND LEGISLATIVE BEHAVIOUR

Even if it were possible to achieve a basic similarity between representatives and the represented on such dimensions as social and economic backgrounds, there would remain an inevitable status difference. The very fact of having been chosen distinguishes the representative, regardless of other characteristics he or she may share with the represented.[8] It is important to appreciate that, textbook treatments aside, there is very little evidence to support the view that citizens in democracies are an important source of policy. Wahlke has argued that, because citizens lack the knowledge or the desire to issue policy directives, it is reasonable to treat representation as a much more diffuse and intricate process than the "simple demand input model" suggests.[9]

At its heart, representation implies some form of responsiveness on the part of the representative. In deciding on an appropriate course of action the representative must take into account the interests of the represented. This does not necessarily mean that representatives and represented must agree on policy matters before representation can occur. Representation is more than a congruence of attitudes and representatives have responsibilities to their constituents which go well beyond matters of broad public policy.[10] It does require that representatives be prepared to respond to constituents when they have something to say and be willing to explain and justify their personal behaviour.

Voting on the floor of the House is one aspect of legislative behaviour. In these public and usually symbolic displays, party discipline demands uniformity. In other facets of policy participation, however, there is considerable scope for individual differences. The party does not require all of its members to have the same policy interests or to hold the same opinions. All members of parliament, moreover, are expected to pay considerable attention to the immediate welfare of constituents. This generally unpublicized facet of legislative behaviour can consume an enormous amount of time. Members lobby constantly for public works and the programs that will bring employment to their constituents. Even more important are the constant requests from constituents that the MP intervene personally with the bureaucracy to correct some injustice or secure some benefit. Members rarely resent this constituency case work,[11] some of which they invite by establishing constituency offices and advertising their services.

It is not only possible but necessary that members respond to constituents in a variety of ways, serving both their wants and their needs, to the degree that it is possible to do either. In doing so members will be forced to make choices. How much time and what financial resources should be devoted to constituency work? Should the floor of the House be the main forum for expression, or is it more important to concentrate on committee work and develop policy expertise? Under what circumstances, if any, is it justifiable to openly break with the party to defend constituency interests or personal views? Is it more effective to be obstinate and threatening or deferential and unassuming? In offering their different answers to questions like these, members of parliament create a complex pattern of legislative behaviour.

In attempting to unravel this complexity and account for the rich diversity of legislative behaviour, researchers have employed two general models. According to the outside model of legislative behaviour those factors which influence the attitudes and behaviour of parliamentarians prior to their election have a continued influence on their behaviour from beyond the institutional boundary of the legislature. The inside model assumes the opposite: that factors such as institutional norms, the hierarchy of offices, and organizational resources have the greatest impact on behaviour.[12]

Of primary importance for the hypothesis that the behaviour of MPs may be explained by the outside model are the social-background variables discussed above. It is often assumed that a group of individuals who share characteristics such as educational achievement or occupational background are likely to behave in the same way. French-Canadian MPs, for example, are expected to defend the use of the French language in the control of air traffic over the province of Quebec. Not all issues evoke a strong response based on social or demographic characteristics, but more general patterns of behaviour can also be traced to these factors. Hoffman and Ward succeeded in showing that regional and linguistic factors influence the pattern of communication members maintain with their constituents.[13] French-speaking members spent more time in their constituencies than their English-speaking counterparts and were less likely to move their families to Ottawa.

In a more recent study Kornberg and Mishler, after surveying their social-background variables, concluded that "no other set of variables in this study predicts parliamentary participation as well."[14] They found, for example, that members were significantly more inclined to participate in debate if they possessed a university degree, but significantly less inclined if they were of French or French-Canadian ancestry. Age proved to be an important variable in a study undertaken by Peter A. Hall and R. Peter Washburn. After establishing that MPs tend to overestimate the well-being of Canadians, they showed that older members were much more likely to do so than their younger colleagues.[15]

In spite of their importance to political attitudes and legislative behaviour, social-background factors operate at a considerable distance. It seems reasonable to assume that members' attitudes and behaviour will also be influenced by their previous political experiences. However, many legislators in Canada are without the advantage—or the disadvantage—of exposure to partisan politics. While once a common attribute of federal politicans, one-quarter to one-third of MPs in recent parliaments have had no prior political experience, even at the level of officeholding within the party. Moreover, relating these experiences to legislative behaviour has proven difficult. In his study of the 25th Parliament (1962-63) Kornberg was unable to link members' prior political experiences to their propensity to choose particular legislative goals.[16] In their later work Kornberg and Mishler were forced to conclude that "the data provide little support for the proposition that early life socialization and recruitment experiences substantially affect later life elite political behaviour."[17]

One might expect that the type of constituency a member represents would influence the judgments he is required to make in the legislature. American research has demonstrated that a candidate's district, its geographic location or its economic base, has an influence on roll-call voting in Congress.[18] This is not surprising in an undisciplined party system where representatives must weigh heavily factors other than their party affiliation. However, there is little evidence that constituency characteristics have a strong influence on the behaviour of Canadian members of parliament. There is some evidence to the contrary. Lovink advises that in the opinion of members of the 28th Parliament the level of competititiveness in a constituency was an inconsequential factor in the allocation of political benefits.[19] Of course, the degree of constituency competitiveness does affect the nature of representative government. In Canada, where the level of electoral competition is extraordinarily high, the level of political experience is correspondingly low, with the result that legislative institutions are frequently staffed by novices.

When an individual is elected to parliament, he is inducted into its norms and standards of behaviour. Like all freshmen, he is constrained by the formal structures as well as the informal patterns of influence. Many of these inside variables were alluded to in the earlier treatment of parliamentary and preparliamentary structures and suggestions were made regarding their impact on legislative behaviour. On the floor of the House, formal rules limit the length of speeches and demand that their contents be relevant to the discussion at hand. In committees the rule which permits frequent membership changes impedes the development of individual expertise and committee autonomy. In other words, the formal requirements in a legislative system set the parameters of legislative behaviour and frequently become the source of informal patterns of influence.

Norms or folkways or rules of the game help sustain the continuity of the legislature and ensure that individual legislators are aware of what other MPs consider requirements for effective action. Norms exist in all groups and the nature of the situation determines the norm in effect. According to those who rely on the inside model, these unwritten rules can be accurate predictors of legislative behaviour. However, a system of norms may be more or less accepted, and in any particular case competing norms may apply. The heavy turnover in Canadian legislative membership undermines the continuity of the learning process and keeps the behavioural standards in a state of flux. In the 1979 election, only 65.5 per cent of incumbents were returned to the legislature. In such circumstances it is to be expected that parties, which are part of both the inside and outside models, will be the main agents in the socialization process.

Substructures in parliament offer perhaps the best opportunity for studying the impact of norms on individual behaviour. Small groups, such as committees, allow frequent and close interaction and the occasional relaxation of party discipline. The norms which develop may influence the level of partisanship in different committee proceedings. When committees undertake general investigations, partisanship is often less pronounced than in the consideration of legislation. Furthermore, most committees will not convene a meeting unless a member of the opposition is present, while some will not proceed in the examination of witnesses unless this condition is fulfilled. Some committees have minimum levels of attendance for hearing witnesses; others do not. None of these rules are specified by the standing orders, but they are recognized as established customs in particular committees. More stringent rules govern the behaviour of government backbenchers. Parliamentary secretaries, for example, act as the source of informal cues regarding speeches, questions, and ultimately votes in committees.

In his research on the Canadian House of Commons Kornberg has emphasized the significance of established conventions.[20] Among those norms cited by MPs in the 25th Parliament were requirements to minimize personal conflict, avoid conduct which reflects poorly on parliament, reinforce existing party divisions, and establish expertise in some subject matter. In their subsequent research on the 28th Parliament, Kornberg and Mishler found members even more inclined to endorse disciplined party action and the development of an expertise. Many MPs learn these rules only after their election, but few MPs experience any difficulty.[21] Informal rules of this type are an intrinsic part of most social situations and freshmen MPs are neither ignorant nor bewildered when they first encounter them in the legislative system. Of course, errors may be committed by even the most highly placed parliamentarians. In the 28th Parliament Prime Minister Trudeau stumbled into the gravest type when he suggested that once MPs were off Parliament Hill, they were "nobodies."

Paradoxically, the investigation of legislative customs may be impeded by the fact that norms exist with regard to answering questions about norms. Members may feel they are required to emphasize collegiality, withhold "trade secrets," appear conversant with the rules, and cite standing orders. Some MPs are unwilling to express their personal view and simply ask their assistants to fill in question-naires for them. In view of these facts, consideration has even been given to screening social-science research on the Hill to prevent what some parliamentarians call a distorted image of parliament.

One of the most important inside variables is the structure of parliamentary offices and the opportunities that exist for advance-ment. Members of parliament who are ambitious for a cabinet post anticipate promotion by preparing for cabinet positions long before they assume them. This process can have a considerable impact on their behaviour as backbenchers as members struggle to adopt attitudes and behavioural patterns congruent with membership in the cabinet.[22] The impact of political ambition may be sharply reduced, however, if there is no established hierarchy of offices or no widely accepted strategies members can employ to reach the cabinet.

Cabinet ministers in Canada, especially during periods of Liberal government, have seldom been recruited through a series of legislative offices. The positions of committee chairman and parliamentary secretary have not become stepping stones in the parliamentary career.[23] Moreover, there is no indication that a strong parliamentary performance is a certain route to the cabinet. During the Pearson and Trudeau eras in particular, greater stress was laid on policymaking and administrative skills rather than on parliamentary experience.[24] Nonetheless, Kornberg and Mishler found that "the ambition to become a cabinet minister is the single most important determinant of participation in debate."[25] Ambitious members may behave in a distinctive fashion, but in Canada this is no guarantee of advancement.

The most important variable of all in a parliamentary system is party affiliation. Cohesive political parties, as we have emphasized, are essential to the operation of the legislative system and individual behaviour cannot be assessed without a consideration of this variable. This is especially the case with respect to a particular aspect of behaviour in the House — voting. In the American Congress and in the state legislatures party affiliation is by no means a reliable predictor of voting behaviour. In Canada, on the other hand, its predictive capacity outweighs that of all the other inside and outside variables put together. An individual's vote almost always indicates a personal commitment to the parliamentary party, not to one or another side of a political issue. Even so-called free votes are the subject of partisan pressures, since most politicians find the challenge of creating alterna-tive organizational mechanisms simply too taxing.[26]

The influence of party affiliation extends beyond the act of voting.

The party acts as a source of behavioural cues for its members and the meetings of caucus foster cohesion.[27] Since Canadian MPs, like their British counterparts, only conceive of politics in terms of parties, they are probably sceptical of the idea that sanctions can be used to manufacture party loyalty. The notion of party is imbedded so deeply in the perceptions of Canadian parliamentarians that little consideration is given to the consequences of independent action.

In the Canadian parliamentary system there are few indicators of individual behaviour whose meaning is undisputed.[28] To get behind the division lists and examine aspects of behaviour other than party voting is a formidable task and one that does not yield easily to the collection of data. To accept only "inside" views of caucus deliberation is clearly unsatisfactory. There are, of course, public activities a member may undertake in his constituency, as we have mentioned earlier, and behaviour in committees and in parliamentary debates may be examined. But in each case researchers must develop valid indicators of the concept they are considering. If they are examining the sources of rebellious or parochial behaviour, convincing arguments must be made that the activities they are studying represent valid examples. Few Canadian political scientists have attempted this type of research.

LEGISLATIVE BEHAVIOUR: ROLE THEORY

Many social scientists have suggested that the concept of *role* may provide a means of understanding legislative behaviour. The term refers to the expectations associated with a particular position in a social system and individuals usually hold many roles. Political roles are fashioned by two forces: first, the individual's own perceptions and expectations of the formal position and, second, the perceptions and expectations of others in related positions. The analysis of legislative roles changes the research emphasis from the actual behaviour of MPs to their personal attitudes and from particular actions to general dispositions. Role is an attractive concept primarily because it effectively summarizes all of the attitudes that are likely to be evoked in any particular circumstance. It is a means of encompassing the entire legislature at the individual level of analysis and it emphasizes that behaviour always takes place in an atmosphere of expectations.

Legislators usually agree on the general norms that govern behaviour in a legislative system, but often find it necessary to choose from among divergent norms in particular circumstances. Competing norms give rise to competing role orientations. Canadian MPs disagree on the types of relationships they should establish with their clientele, party, and the citizens they represent. For our purposes, representational roles are the most illuminating. In their research on American legislators, Eulau and his colleagues offered a threefold classification of representational roles: the trustee, the delegate, and the politico.[29] Representatives who adopt the trustee role consider themselves free agents who act on their own judgment after appraising each situation. The delegate, on the other hand, feels at least partially committed to follow the instructions of his constituents. For some this simply means consultation and possibly some type of constraint, but it may also be considered a mandatory instruction. The politico is a mixture of these pure types. A legislator who is a politico may assume the roles serially (first the trustee, then the delegate) or he may attempt to reconcile them, in which case he is made particularly sensitive to role conflict.

Canadian students of role orientations have made some adjustments to these concepts. Hoffman and Ward, for example, introduce the term "party delegate" to refer to those who receive instructions from the party and the term "constituency delegate" to refer to those instructed by their constituents. This is a clear response to the problem of determining the focus of representation — to whom delegates, trustees, and politicos consider themselves responsive.

Kornberg found that of the legislators interviewed in his study of the 25th Parliament, 15 per cent were trustees, 36 per cent were politicos, and 49 per cent were delegate-servants.[30] In the 26th Parliament, Hoffman and Ward uncovered a greater number of trustees (33 per cent), but precisely the same proportion of politicos. Of the remaining delegates, 18 per cent were party delegates and 12 per cent were constituency delegates.[31] While some discrepancy exists in these figures they suggest that Canadian MPs are inclined to accept some type of instruction. But MPs are also inclined to follow their own conscience. Of the members of the 28th Parliament interviewed by Kornberg and Mishler, the largest proportion (44 per cent) claimed to be accountable, first and foremost, to their own consciences.[32] Members seem to feel that constituency demands can be reconciled with the demands of personal judgment to the point that few conflicts need arise.

Role orientation is usually considered a product of the same variables discussed with the inside and outside models of legislative behaviour. At the level of the political system it may be presumed that the political culture has an initial and lasting impact on the selection of role orientations because it is the culture which effectively structures the MPs' alternatives. Selected correlations from the major studies illustrate the possible sources of particular role orientations in the Canadian context. Kornberg found that education and occupation were related to the propensity to choose one role orientation over another. Those who were college graduates, businessmen, and professionals tended to assume the trustee role more frequently.[33] In the Hoffman and Ward study, MPs with a background in municipal politics were slightly more inclined to a constituent-delegate role, MPs over 60 years of age tended toward a party-delegate orientation, and those with little prior political experience were inclined to adopt a trustee role.[34]

Scholars have experienced difficulty, however, in using role orientations to predict behaviour. In the first place the strength with which roles are held may affect attempts at role enactment. Some individuals hold a particular role with great determination, while others give it little consideration. Legislators may also find that the decisions they are called on to make are so complicated that their personal role orientation is of little help in directing their behaviour. Or they may change their attitude when confronted with an actual policy choice.

According to Eulau and Wahlke, "a role concept can only be used to estimate probabilities of behaviour germane to a particular relationship."[35] Rather than being a predictive tool, it is primarily a means of understanding how people give meaning to their behaviour. Thus, members may exhibit very little independence of party in their voting, for example, yet vary considerably in the interpretation they place on this and other behaviour. Knowing the meanings members give to their behaviour is one means of characterizing the entire legislative system and tracing its development.

THE STATUS OF PRIVATE MEMBERS

In parliamentary systems where cohesive political parties are the main actors it is not hard to lose sight of the private member. The government is the master of the parliamentary timetable, government and opposition front benches dominate debate, and backbenchers by their own testimony obtain their greatest satisfaction from running errands for constituents. Taxing as this might be, it does not require a highly professional staff or the perks of office which American Congressmen have come to expect.

Yet the status of the private member of parliament has improved considerably during the last decade.[36] When sessions were no more than a few weeks in length, members did not require permanent assistance and, until the early 1960s, two members shared a secretary who was employed only when the House was sitting. Since 1965, staff have been employed full-time and, in 1969 and again in 1972, additional part-time assistants were added to the staff complement. In 1974, provision was made for members to establish constituency offices manned by a full-time staff member. By 1979, 230 MPs had taken advantage of the new provisions.

The increase in support personnel brought with it the inevitable political problems involved in distributing limited resources. In 1975 a Standing Committee on Management and Members' Services was created and it quickly set about the task of establishing a new classification and pay system. The new system was introduced on September 1, 1978. It set spending limits, yet gave members some flexibility in allocations to allow for differences in, among other things, constituency demands. Members were limited to $46,000 for their Ottawa parliamentary staff and most MPs employ three persons in their Ottawa office. In addition, all MPs enjoy such fringe benefits as free mailings, telephone calls, inexpensive meals, and an air pass entitling them to 52 round trips annually to their constituencies.

Alistair Fraser, former Clerk of the House of Commons, has estimated that, while members are reasonably well staffed for the performance of their constituency service role, it is unlikely that many MPs are "overserviced" in terms of their legislative work.[37] The caucus research bureaus have not been organized to produce the type of research material backbench members can readily use and, though the Research Branch of the Library of Parliament compensates to some degree, it is not prepared to engage in speech writing and openly partisan endeavours regardless of how appreciative MPs might be.[38] Yet many members structure their general aspirations in terms of policymaking. Hoffman and Ward found that 51 per cent of their English-speaking respondents and 65 per cent of French-speaking respondents mentioned "lawmaker" goals as something they hoped to achieve in their position.[39] Moreover, 60 per cent of those interviewed in the Kornberg-Mishler study discussed their accomplishments in terms of public policy.[40] Before they become incumbents, MPs are aware that there is little room for personal policy initiatives,[41] but the impulse to work toward broad policy goals does not disappear.

An opportunity to satisfy this particular orientation is afforded by the private members' bill. A private members' bill is a public bill which is sponsored by a private member, does not form part of the government's legislative program and, theoretically, does not require the allocation of public funds. At the beginning of each session a lottery is held and 40 private members' bills are drawn in the order they will be called for debate. This is one of the few occasions in which the preparliamentary stages of the legislative system are not involved in the ultimate parliamentary process.

For several reasons the private members' bill is a decidedly unsatisfactory vehicle for satisfying a lawmaker orientation. In the first place, the time available for private members' business is limited to 40 periods each session of one hour apiece on Mondays and Tuesdays and an unspecified number of such periods on Thursdays and Fridays. Not all of this time is spent on bills. For the private member the notice of motion is an attractive means of advocating general plans of action or moral positions. Unlike the private members' bill it avoids the necessity for legal jargon and is considered a device which expresses sentiments without being encumbered by legal, and sometimes practical, considerations. Moreover, it is usually possible to construct such motions without contradicting party policy.

Second, and most important, very few private members' bills are ever passed and most do not come to a vote. Once the one-hour period for second reading debate has been exhausted, bills simply drop to the bottom of the order paper and never reemerge. Of the over 200 private members' bills routinely introduced each session, only one or two will be successful, and these will normally rename electoral districts. The beaver became national symbol via a private member's bill, but most members know that they have very little chance of duplicating such a success, even on matters which are purely symbolic.

Despite the dismal fate that awaits most private members' bills, parliamentarians continue to introduce them in ever greater quantities. In the 24th Parliament (1958-62) an average of 46 private members' bills were introduced per session, but by the 26th Parliament (1963-65) this had increased to 102, and by the 28th Parliament (1968-72) it was an average of 195 per session. In the 30th Parliament (1974-79) this already high figure had climbed to 254, an average of almost one bill per member of parliament in each session. Those MPs who introduce this type of legislation seem content to offer a concrete expression of opinion and seldom aspire to have the bills they bring before the House enacted.[42] On occasion the subject matter obtains consideration in a standing committee even when the bill is not acceptable. An example was the private member's bill which pro-

Table 7-2 RATIO OF PRIVATE MEMBERS' BILLS TO PARTY
REPRESENTATION: 29TH AND 30TH PARLIAMENTS

	Liberals	P.C.	N.D.P.	S.C.
29th Parliament (1972-74)				
1st Session	0.22	0.68	3.06	0.33
2nd Session	0.19	0.69	2.71	0.20
30th Parliament (1974-79)				
1st Session	0.51	1.15	2.25	0.64
2nd Session	0.55	1.15	2.06	0.73
3rd Session	0.57	1.18	2.25	0.56
4th Session	0.66	1.46	2.44	0.33

posed the elimination of advertisements on children's television programs. Simply making their views public is often sufficient incentive
for most members, although some undoubtedly use these bills to
demonstrate their diligence to constituents.

The willingness to introduce private members' bills and debatable
resolutions is by no means evenly distributed among parliamentarians.
As Table 7-2 shows, the members of opposition parties in the 29th and
30th Parliaments were more inclined to introduce private members'
bills than the Liberals. This was particularly true of New Democrats,
although all of the other parties demonstrated more interest in this
vehicle in the 30th Parliament. Kornberg and Mishler showed, in their
study of the 28th Parliament, that members representing urban ridings
and those concerned with policy accomplishments were also more
likely to introduce bills and resolutions.[43]

These members do not expect to have their bills passed or their
resolutions acted upon. They hope merely to prod the government and
air their ideas. Unfortunately for them, there is very little government
feedback. Members may believe they influence government policy
and there is no justification for denying the possibility. However, the
government seldom credits private members' bills with any policy
influence. From the government's point of view, their own backbenchers can use caucus to influence pending policy. Opposition MPs,
on the other hand, are not considered to be involved in government
policymaking. Thus, in addition to technical and administrative difficulties, political dilemmas are involved in openly entertaining the
ideas contained in private members' bills.

Beyond the cabinet's unreceptive attitude toward private members' bills, it is by no means certain that government departments are aware of or react to these initiatives. MPs are seldom—if ever—informed of the difficulties with their suggestions. A glaring general deficiency in many of the private members' bills is legislative drafting. This factor alone has prevented departments from giving some of these bills serious consideration although the addition of staff to assist the legislative counsel should alleviate the problem. Some initiatives have been considered potentially useful additions to departmental policy, but no effort has been made to acknowledge backbench initiative. The government ought to develop an apparatus to evaluate private members' bills systematically and to communicate their conclusions to parliament as a whole. Efforts should be made to create a forum where parliamentarians and bureaucrats can discuss MPs' ideas.

It is doubtful that norms or roles are so thoroughly ossified in the Canadian legislative system that new perceptions of the member of parliament could not be encouraged. In this chapter we have stressed the barriers to role enactment, but there remain opportunities to create legislative institutions which give expression to the personal initiatives of members and permit them to respond to constituents in other capacities than the constituency servant.

NOTES

1. Unless otherwise noted, data on members of parliament are derived from the *Parliamentary Guide*.
2. Statistics Canada, 1971 Census of Canada, *Occupations: Occupations by Sex for Canada and the Provinces* (Catalogue 94-717); Canada Year Book, 1974, p. 324.
3. Gerhard Lowenberg and Samuel C. Patterson, *Comparing Legislatures* (Boston: Little, Brown, 1979), p. 71.
4. Caroline Andrew, "The Political Background of Members of the Twenty-sixth House of Commons," unpublished Honours B.A. thesis (University of British Columbia, 1964), p. 18.
5. Allan Kornberg and William Mishler, *Influence in Parliament: Canada* (Durham, N.C.: Duke University Press, 1976), p. 66.
6. The degree of distortion depends, to some extent, on the recruitment process. On the propensity of Canadian political parties to select high-status "attractive" candidates, see William Mishler, "Nominating Attractive Candidates for Parliament: Recruitment to the Canadian House of Commons," *Legislative Studies Quarterly*, 3 (November 1978), pp. 581-600.
7. John Porter, *The Vertical Mosaic* (Toronto: University of Toronto Press, 1965), p. 392.

8. Heinz Eulau, "Changing Views of Representation," in Heinz Eulau and John C. Wahlke (ed.), *The Politics of Representation* (Beverly Hills: Sage Publications, 1978), pp. 51-52.

9. John C. Wahlke, "Policy Demands and System Support: The Role of the Represented," *British Journal of Political Science*, 1 (1971), pp. 271-90.

10. Heinz Eulau and Paul D. Karps, "The Puzzle of Representation: Specifying Components of Responsiveness," *Legislative Studies Quarterly*, 2 (August 1977), pp. 233-54.

11. See, for example, the findings reported in Richard G. Price, Harold D. Clarke, and Robert M. Krause, "The Socialization of Freshman Legislators: The Case of Canadian MPs," in Jon H. Pammett and Michael S. Whittington (ed.), *Foundations of Political Culture: Political Socialization in Canada* (Toronto: Macmillan of Canada, 1976), pp. 213-15.

12. For a classification of legislatures premised on the relative importance of external and internal influences, see Nelson Polsby, "Legislatures," in F. Greenstein and N. Polsby (ed.), *The Handbook of Political Science*, Vol. 5 (Reading, Mass.: Addison-Wesley, 1975), pp. 257-319.

13. David Hoffman and Norman Ward, *Bilingualism and Biculturalism in the Canadian House of Commons*, Document No. 3 of the Royal Commission on Bilingualism and Biculturalism (Ottawa: Queen's Printer, 1970), Chapter V.

14. Kornberg and Mishler, *Influence in Parliament: Canada*, p. 248.

15. Peter A. Hall and R. Peter Washburn, "Elites and Representation: A Study of the Attitudes and Perceptions of MPs," in Jean-Pierre Gaboury and James Ross Hurley (ed.), *The Canadian House of Commons Observed* (Ottawa: University of Ottawa Press, 1979), p. 311.

16. Allan Kornberg, *Canadian Legislative Behaviour* (Toronto: Holt, Rinehart and Winston, 1967), p. 90.

17. Kornberg and Mishler, *Influence in Parliament: Canada*, p. 244.

18. For example, Morris P. Fiorina, *Representatives, Roll Calls and Constituencies* (Lexington, Mass.: Heath, 1974).

19. J. A. A. Lovink, "Is Canadian Politics Too Competitive?", *Canadian Journal of Political Science*, 4 (September 1973), p. 372.

20. Allan Kornberg, "Rules of the Game in the Canadian House of Commons," *Journal of Politics*, 26 (1964), pp. 258-80.

21. Kornberg and Mishler, *Influence in Parliament: Canada*, pp. 77, 79-80.

22. Michael M. Atkinson, "Policy Interests of Provincial Backbenchers and the Effects of Political Ambition," *Legislative Studies Quarterly*, 3 (November 1978), pp. 629-46.

23. Michael M. Atkinson and Kim Richard Nossal, "Executive Power and Committee Autonomy in the House of Commons: Leadership Selection, 1968-1979," *Canadian Journal of Political Science* (June 1980).

24. Richard J. Van Loon and Michael S. Whittington, *The Canadian Political System*, 2nd ed. (Toronto: McGraw-Hill Ryerson, 1976), p. 322.

25. Kornberg and Mishler, *Influence in Parliament: Canada*, p. 238.

26. Diane Pothier, "Parties and Free Votes in the Canadian House of Commons," *Journal of Canadian Studies*, 14 (Summer 1979), pp. 80-96.

27. For anecdotal appreciation of the process, see Gordon Aiken, *The Back-bencher* (Toronto: McClelland and Stewart, 1974), pp. 114-23.

28. In the United Kingdom the existence of procedural devices, such as Early Day Motions, and party factions which organize propaganda campaigns provide opportunities which do not exist in Canada to examine back-bench opinion. See S. E. Finer, H. B. Berrington, and D. J. Barth-olomew, *Backbench Opinion in the House of Commons, 1955-59* (Oxford: Pergamon Press, 1961), and Robert J. Jackson, *Rebels and Whips* (London: Macmillan, 1968).

29. Heinz Eulau, "The Legislator as Representative: Representational Roles," in John Wahlke *et al.*, *The Legislative System* (New York: John Wiley and Sons, 1962), pp. 267-86.

30. Kornberg, *Canadian Legislative Behaviour*, pp. 106-08.

31. Hoffman and Ward, *Bilingualism and Biculturalism in the Canadian House of Commons*, pp. 66-77.

32. Kornberg and Mishler, *Influence in Parliament: Canada*, p. 94.

33. Kornberg, *Canadian Legislative Behaviour*, p. 109.

34. Hoffman and Ward, *Bilingualism and Biculturalism in the Canadian House of Commons*, pp. 70-72.

35. Heinz Eulau and John C. Wahlke, *The Politics of Representation*, p. 14.

36. The information presented in this section is drawn largely from Alistair Fraser, "Legislators and Their Staffs," a paper presented to a Confer-ence on Legislative Studies in Canada, Simon Fraser University (Febru-ary 1979). See also Alan Clayton, "The Information Revolution Comes to Parliament," *Optimum*, 10 (1979), pp. 5-16.

37. Fraser, "Legislators and Their Staffs," p. 16. Mark MacGuigan offers an insider's view of the problem: "A few members manage to assign one of their Ottawa staff permanently to the role of an assistant to help in legislative tasks in Ottawa. I have found that impossible. My need for secretarial assistance is such that the entire energies of my four-person staff (in the two offices) are devoted to secretarial and constituency business." Mark MacGuigan, "Parliamentary Reform: Impediments to an Enlarged Role for the Backbencher," *Legislative Studies Quarterly*, 3 (November 1978), p. 677.

38. Grant Mitchell, "Research Facilities and the Backbench Member of Parliament," in Gaboury and Hurley, *The Canadian House of Commons Observed*, pp. 155-63.

39. Hoffman and Ward, *Bilingualism and Biculturalism in the House of Commons*, pp. 83-86.

40. Kornberg and Mishler, *Influence in Parliament: Canada*, p. 82.

41. Harold D. Clarke and Richard G. Price, "A Note on the Pre-Nomination Role Socialization of Freshmen Members of Parliament," *Canadian Journal of Political Science*, 10 (June 1977), pp. 391-406.

42. R. V. Stewart Hyson, "The Role of the Backbencher: An Analysis of Private Members' Bills in the Canadian House of Commons," *Parlia-mentary Affairs*, 28 (1974-75), pp. 262-72, and Marie Cordeau, "Private Members' Hours," in Gaboury and Hurley, *The Canadian House of Commons Observed*, pp. 57-67.

43. Kornberg and Mishler, *Influence in Parliament: Canada*, p. 253-55.

8. Evaluating Legislative Activity

The evaluation of political institutions has been a traditional and fundamental part of political philosophy. Based on assumptions about the nature of man and the political community, students of politics have continuously offered prescriptions for more suitable political organization. However, in the 1950s and 1960s, as more scholars began to lend their support to the idea of a "science" of politics, there developed a marked tendency to avoid political evaluation. Indeed, many empirically oriented political scientists claimed that the evaluation of policies or institutions lay outside the ambit of a value-free social science. Evaluations require standards of value, and the establishment of such standards is a subjective exercise, unamenable to scientific procedures or arbitration. Clearly this type of attitude has had some positive ramifications for the discipline of political science, but it has also meant that the tools of social science have been applied only randomly to the evaluation of political structures and public policies. A complementary attitude exists among some members of parliament. It is not uncommon to hear the view that the very nature of legislative institutions disqualifies them from evaluation by social scientists. The predominance of competing ideologies and personalities, it is argued, makes political, not rational, discourse the order of the day.

The attitudes of political scientists and politicians seem to be changing. In recent years the absence of explicit and systematic evaluations of political systems has been condemned by political scientists[1] and, in Canada, more academics have been employed in the development of ideas and judgments about political institutions. In fact, the data assembled by social scientists are now considered an absolute necessity for the task of evaluation.

There are basic problems in the application of social science to the reform of political institutions. While there is general agreement that evaluation involves the measurement of success in achieving a stated purpose or objective,[2] it is practically impossible to secure agreement on the purposes of legislatures. In the United States it has been pointed out that "the evaluation of Congressional performance has been fragmentary and disappointing"[3] and "the reformers' premises concerning the proper functions of Congress remain unarticulated or indistinct, or even contradictory."[4] In Canada lack of agreement on the purpose of parliament has been compounded by the fusion of the executive and legislative branches of government.[5] It is unclear whether parliament is supposed to emphasize the refining of legislation, for example, or the surveillance of the executive. In Chapter 2 we listed several functions that the legislative system may be expected to perform. In this chapter we are forced to limit our approach because, at present, few functions are amenable to systematic evaluation research. Ultimately, of course, all evaluations of legislative performance will depend on value judgments about the purposes of legislatures.

In theory, the methodology of evaluation research is the same as nonevaluation research. As Edward Suchman puts it, "ultimately the significance of the results will be determined according to the same scientific standards. . . ."[6] Science requires the formulation and testing of hypotheses and this often entails some element of quantification. For some the prospect of quantifying legislative activities is an anathema. Even advocates of more systematic evaluation have emphasized that the language of value is full of metaphors and allusions. Robert Dahl has pointed out that, "to those who love the language of value, operational measures rob their poetry of all its beauty, most of its subtlety, and a great deal of its meaning."[7] Eventually, however, evaluations will have to be made using quantitative techniques that permit comparison and scientific generalization. At present even tentative statements based on quantitative studies will complement the impressionistic approach on which students of the Canadian legislative system often rely.

This chapter provides a quantitative assessment of the lawmaking function in the legislative system. As such it is only a partial assessment of the performance of this system and only a partial assessment of lawmaking since no evaluation is made of the quality of legislative output.[8] In spite of this, and as we have emphasized throughout, the *manner* in which laws are made in Canada has enormous symbolic, as well as practical, consequence. The performance of other functions depends to some degree on how laws are made. Time spent at this task should be time well spent and a quantitative appreciation of this function represents a first step towards a reasoned judgment.

Parliamentary reforms have generally been directed at improving the efficiency of lawmaking. Most of these reforms have had other, unintended, consequences. The relation between reform proposals and their consequences is also an aspect of evaluative research and the latter part of the chapter is devoted to an examination of the impact of the 1968 procedural reforms on lawmaking in parliament.

LAWMAKING IN THE LEGISLATIVE SYSTEM

In evaluating lawmaking, considerable attention will be paid to how expeditious the legislature has been. The performance of legislative decisionmaking will frequently be expressed as the ratio of time to volume of legislative output. Time, in this sense, is assumed to represent an important resource for both parts of the legislative system: the government and the legislature. The idea of using time as an indicator of cost presumes there is a shortage of it. It must be possible for the legislature to use it more efficiently, which means the source of input cannot periodically dry up while the legislature is ostensibly performing this function. The fact that most conventional procedural weapons, regardless of who employs them, are directed at the time resource is an indicator of cost even in parliamentarians' evaluations of legislative decisionmaking.

The choice of indicators brings some of the problems of evaluative research into sharp relief. First, indicators that emphasize the volume and speed of lawmaking do not exhaust all that the concept of lawmaking implies. Abraham Kaplan[9] recounts the story of one of the subjects of Kinsey's study of sexual behaviour who complained, "No matter what I told him he just looked me straight in the eye and asked 'how many times?'" In this case the subject felt that the significance of his activity did not depend on its frequency. Clearly, the question of quality as well as quantity is important in assessing some activities. Unfortunately, it is difficult to develop a consistent, meaningful classification of legislation and almost impossible to achieve agreement on criteria suitable to measure the quality of legislation. Also, judgments based on the content or quality of decisions are often evaluations of governmental and not legislative decisionmaking.

The second problem comes in evaluating particular levels of legislative output. The reader will have to decide what is the "best" level of legislative output and whether a slow, methodical (and sometimes obstructive) legislature is to be preferred to one that is responsive (and sometimes overindulgent). If efficiency is the only value involved, then the more output produced in the same time, the better the performance of the lawmaking function. But rapidity is not the only consideration in lawmaking and functions other than lawmaking must also be performed. For example, parliament must take enough time to debate and consider legislation in order to perform a legitimation function. And if parliament is slow in lawmaking, the government may attempt to withdraw some of the opportunities available to perform other functions that compete for parliamentary time. These considerations should give pause to the eager evaluator, especially when he considers that a very high level of performance in one activity may be ultimately dysfunctional for the performance of others.

Since Confederation, parliament has been gradually working longer and achieving less in terms of gross legislative output.[10] The average number of bills passed per day between the 1st and 8th Parliaments (1867-72 and 1896-1900) was 1.39, but between the 19th and 27th Parliaments (1940-45 and 1965-68) the performance ratio fell to 0.54. However, as Kornberg has observed, the comparability of this data is suspect because the number of private and private members' bills was considerably greater in the nineteenth than in the twentieth century. Furthermore, the modern period is characterized by a government program in which legislation is longer and more complex than it was in earlier periods. Nevertheless, the fact that it now takes longer to pass legislation is an interesting comment on the argument often repeated in the scholarly literature that the government has manipulated parliamentary procedures to make the House of Commons a legislation factory.

In order to evaluate the modern parliament, postwar data have been assessed in more detail. The changes wrought by the Second World War and the continued development of the positive state make these data more compelling and predictive of future trends than less exhaustive treatments of earlier years.

Table 8-1 depicts legislative activity since 1945 by averaging data for consecutive groups of four sessions of parliament. In terms of the number of days required to pass a bill the evidence is straightforward: the trend is toward longer consideration for the average public bill. It

Table 8-1 THE LAWMAKING PERFORMANCE OF THE CANADIAN
HOUSE OF COMMONS, SESSION BY SESSION, 1945-1978

Years of four session intervals	Average no. of sitting days	Average no. of public bills enacted	Average no. of days to pass a bill	Number of pages of enacted legislation	Average no. of pages passed per sitting day
1945-47	82	40	2.1	356	4.3
1948-50	83	49	1.7	474	5.7
1951-52	89	52	1.7	425	4.7
1953-57	126	54	2.3	468	3.7
1957-60	111	44	2.5	382	3.4
1960-63	107	38	2.8	279	2.6
1964-68	177	53	3.4	614	3.5
1968-72	171	54	3.2	629	3.7
1973-78*	185	54	3.4	563	3.1

*Includes five sessions
SOURCES: House of Commons, *Debates*; Statutes of Canada.

now takes approximately twice as long to pass a bill as it did during the
first decade following the Second World War. As the number of pages
of enacted legislation suggest, part of the reason is that bills have
become longer — and probably more complex — especially since
1964.

An examination of output in terms of the volume of pages, rather
than the number of bills, produces a different trend line.[11] By treating
legislative performance as the ratio of pages of output to days of
deliberation we find, initially, a steadily declining performance ratio,
from a high of 5.7 in the sessions between 1948 and 1950 to a low of
2.6 between 1960 and 1963. The sessions between 1964 and 1968
produced a rise in the performance ratio to 3.5 and the next period,
1968 to 1972, reveals a further increase. Data on the most recent
period, which includes both the minority 29th Parliament (1972-74)
and three sessions of the majority 30th Parliament (1974-78), indicate
a slight decline in the rate of output.

It is impossible to know how different performance levels affect

Table 8-2 COMPARISON OF LAWMAKING PERFORMANCE IN
MINORITY AND MAJORITY GOVERNMENT SITUATIONS,
BY SESSION, 1945-1974

	Number of sessions	Average no. of sitting days	Average no. of public bills enacted	Average no. of days to pass a bill	Average no. of pages of enacted legislation	Average no. of pages passed per sitting day
Minority governments	9	137	40	3.4	398	2.9
Majority governments	25	112	51	2.2	467	4.1

SOURCES: House of Commons, *Debates*; Statutes of Canada.

attitudes toward parliament or parliament's capacity to perform other functions. But each performance level creates its own problems, and these evoke responses. When environmental changes make existing organizational procedures unsatisfactory, James March and Herbert Simon hypothesize that the rate of innovation will increase.[12] During the period between 1960 and 1963 when performance ratios were lowest on average, agitation did begin for a review of existing parliamentary procedures. And by 1965 special committees were studying procedure and organization. Dissatisfaction with organizational structures during this time indicates that at least some members perceived the legislature as having a low level of decisionmaking performance and that reforms were required.

One of the most fiercely debated explanations of trends in lawmaking performance is the presence or absence of minority government. According to some politicians minority governments result in a slow movement of legislation through the House. Governments may be more responsive to the House, but during these periods parliament is at its least expeditious. Some indication of support for this hypothesis is provided in Table 8-1. The three periods with the lowest performance ratios together contain eight of the nine minority government sessions in the postwar period. Table 8-2 provides a summary comparison of legislative output during nine minority government sessions and 25 sessions of majority government. On average it required more than a extra day to pass a bill in a minority session and the average number of pages passed per sitting day declined as well.

The downward trend in lawmaking performance and the specific

Table 8-3 LEGISLATIVE ACTIVITY, 1966-1979

Parliament (Session)	Sittings	Type of Gov't	Gov't Bills Intro'd.	Gov't Bills Passed*	Success Ratio (Bills Passed/ Bills Intro.)	Legislative Output (Bills Passed/ Day)
27 (1) 1966-67	250	Minority	104	97	0.93	0.42
27 (2) 1967-68	155	Minority	44	36	0.81	0.23
28 (1) 1968-69	198	Majority	64	56	0.88	0.28
28 (2) 1969-70	155	Majority	71	63	0.89	0.41
28 (3) 1970-72	244	Majority	71	59	0.83	0.24
28 (4) 1972	91	Majority	35	17	0.49	0.19
29 (1) 1973-74	206	Minority	56	48	0.86	0.23
29 (2) 1974	50	Minority	35	10	0.29	0.20
30 (1) 1974-76	341	Majority	118	102	0.86	0.30
30 (2) 1976-77	175	Majority	64	44	0.69	0.25
30 (2) 1977-78	151	Majority	74	34	0.46	0.23
30 (4) 1978-79	98	Majority	57	18	0.32	0.18

*Includes appropriations acts.
SOURCE: House of Commons, *Debates*; Statutes of Canada.

lack of efficiency during minority governments may be accounted for by the increasing complexity in legislative interaction. Technical considerations and the variety of demands raised by interest groups have contributed to the increasing intricacy of bills, estimates, and other matters. Minority governments compound the impact of such demands by requiring the government to entertain more withinputs from the minority parties. Although Diefenbaker and Pearson both resisted cooperation with these parties, during the 29th Parliament a desperate government, a single balancing party, and a set of structures which facilitated negotiation combined to produce an "informal understanding" between the Liberals and the NDP and several modifications to the government's legislative program.[13] Since electoral studies and public-opinion polls indicate that minority governments are likely to recur, reform proposals must counsel the type of institutional change which will promote high levels of performance even in the face of the increased complexity of inputs and withinputs in the legislative system.

Minority government is by no means the only influence on performance levels. A close examination of Table 8-3 shows that in two of the most recent minority parliaments legislative output, in terms of bills passed by day, was on average virtually the same as in the two majority parliaments that followed. More striking is that in each parliament the lowest performance levels appear during the final session of the parliament. Parliaments, it seems, become cantankerous as they get older and in recent years this pattern has appeared in both minority and majority parliaments.

To this point we have discussed only parliament's performance of the lawmaking function, but governments have the responsibility to secure the successful passage of their legislative programs. They must place before parliament legislation which is not so offensive that the opposition is required to devote all its energies to preventing enactment. They also have the responsibility to bargain for parliamentary time and to use this time wisely. Governments vary considerably in their ability to meet these requirements for legislative success.

Between 1945 and 1970, governments in Great Britain succeeded in enacting an average of 95 per cent of the legislation they introduced. In Germany 84 per cent of government bills were successful between 1949 and 1972.[14] Governments in Canada have occasionally surpassed the German average in a given session but, as Table 8-3 shows, these triumphs are more than offset by the disastrously low success levels registered on other occasions. The relative lack of success experienced by Canadian governments cannot be explained by the presence of minor parties since minor parties have been active in all three countries. The table indicates, moreover, that the failure of legislative programs occurs just as frequently in majority as in minority parliaments.

The pattern of success and failure seems to be closely related to the parliamentary cycle. As in the case of legislative output, governments appear to enjoy their greatest success during the early stages of their period in power. In the four parliaments covered by Table 8-3, the government succeeded in enacting an average of 88 per cent of the legislation introduced during the first session. By the final session, however, this average had dropped to 48 per cent.[15] A variety of interpretations might be placed on these trends. Governments, for example, may simply exhaust the projects to which they are committed or, as an election approaches, begin to introduce legislation to be used for campaign purposes. Parliaments may become increasingly difficult to manage and governments increasingly unable or unwilling to manage them. In any event, as long as governments are permitted to avoid commitment to their legislative programs, it is unlikely that they need to be concerned with the political ramifications of their failures.

THE CONSEQUENCES OF A REFORM POLICY

The above data are instructive about lawmaking efficiency in the House of Commons, but they do not provide any firm conclusions about how particular reforms will affect performance. To accomplish that objective the effects of policy changes on performance must be examined. An attempt to change the procedures of the House was made during 1968. It constituted a positional policy because it was aimed at affecting the process of policymaking rather than any substantive policy in that process. The evaluation of its effect on the performance of legislative decisionmaking provides an introduction to the problems of evaluating reform policies.

In this section we will limit the discussion to an evaluation of the success which the 1968-69 policy achieved in reaching its objectives. There are, of course, problems in deciding precisely what those objectives were. While general agreement may be obtained on the need for a new policy, there are usually different opinions about the goals and values that it embodies. For example, it might be argued that the major objective of the rule changes was to allow a more thorough legislative scrutiny of government proposals, or that it was to allow the government to meet its legislative commitments, or that it was both.

It is reasonable in this case to examine the objectives of the government since the final policy embodied only those reforms it felt were acceptable. The content of government objectives has been summarized by Donald S. Macdonald.[16] Unfortunately, his criticisms of the legislature were more explicit than his articulation of government objectives. Part of the reason may have been a desire to avoid discussing government intentions and to emphasize the role of parliament within the context of the new rules. According to Macdonald, there had been too much "politicking" in parliament and not enough attention to the careful examination of bills. The House had been too slow, members were bored by long, tedious sessions, and all of this was attracting public criticism. In his opinion the new rules would alleviate these problems.

Buried in these criticisms and proposals were three objectives. The first and primary objective was of intermediate range. The government wished to improve the performance ratio of the House of Commons. While it was not stated boldly by Macdonald, his explanation of the rule changes dwells heavily on the effect of protracted debates on government business. The proposals also embodied two short-range objectives intended to help accomplish the primary goal. First, the imposition of time restrictions on particular debates and the removal of repetitive and unnecessary motions were intended to give the House more time to debate public bills. Second, the abolition of Committee of Supply, the radical curtailment of Committee of the Whole, and the automatic referral of most bills to standing committees on second reading were intended to delegate a major proportion of the legislative workload to the committee system. The House was considered an inappropriate forum for some types of decisionmaking and it was assumed that, even though the new procedures would be more complicated, any disadvantages would be outweighed by the opportunity to have many items considered simultaneously. This would also increase legislative performance.

It is important to be aware of unintended consequences, particularly in the case of the second of these short-term objectives. The justifications the government offered for the rule changes did not include a clear statement of what was expected of the committee system. The Special Committee on Procedure (1967-68) which initiated the policy seemed preoccupied with improving proceedings in the chamber rather than in the committee system. Almost no steps were taken to prepare committees for the anticipated increase in workload. In assessing the impact of the reform it is therefore necessary to examine the performance of the committee system under the new procedures. The most suitable way to test the impact of a policy is to perform a controlled experiment where the stimulus is properly isolated and changes in performance may be attributed to its influence. In the case of parliamentary reform this approach is impossible. The only feasible procedure is to examine in some detail two sessions of parliament, one before and one after the new rules, and determine if the variation in performance can be attributed to the reforms.[17] In general terms these sessions illustrate the impact of a revitalized committee system.

Our discussion of Table 8-1 noted that an increase in legislative performance occurred immediately after the introduction of the provisional rule changes in 1965, followed by another increase in the 28th Parliament. However, neither increase was particularly dramatic and

Table 8-4 COMPARISON OF LAWMAKING PERFORMANCE, BY
SESSION, 1945-1968 AND 1968-1978

	Average no. of sitting days	Average no. of public bills enacted	Average no. of days to pass a bill	Average no. of pages of enacted legislation	Average no. of pages passed per sitting day
1945-68	111	48	2.5	428	3.9
1968-78	179	54	3.3	597	3.3

SOURCE: House of Commons, *Debates;* Statutes of Canada.

the latter came at a time when a majority government succeeded six sessions of minorities. Table 8-4 indicates that, during the four sessions since the rule changes were adopted, the performance ratio has remained, on average, lower than that recorded during the sessions between 1945 and 1968. Together these findings suggest that the intermediate objective of improving the performance ratio of the legislature met with little immediate success.

The government did succeed in activating standing committees and using them as legislative refineries. The second session of the 27th Parliament and the second session of the 28th Parliament each lasted 155 days; but, in the latter session, after the rule changes, the activity of the committee system increased dramatically. One of the most obvious bases of comparison is simply the number of meetings that was held in each of these sessions. In the second session of the 27th Parliament the committees held 218 meetings (excluding subcommittees and meetings adjourned because of the lack of quorum) but in the second session of the 28th Parliament 759 meetings were held. In the earlier session, while 21 committees were constituted, only 13 of them ever met. In the second session of the 28th Parliament each of the 18 committees met at least three times and one committee met over one hundred times. Similarly, in the second session of the 27th Parliament no meetings at all were scheduled during three months (April, August, and September), whereas in the later session at least one committee held meetings every month. Not only were committees more active than before 1968, but this activity was distributed more evenly throughout the committee system, and committees used more of the time available during the year.

Table 8-5   A COMPARISON OF THE ACTIVITIES AND LAWMAKING
PERFORMANCE OF THE COMMITTEE SYSTEM IN 2ND SESSION, 27TH
PARLIAMENT AND 2ND SESSION, 28TH PARLIAMENT

	2nd session 27th Parliament	2nd session 28th Parliament
No. of bills considered	18	86
Total volume in pages	93	461
Time spent examining bills (hours)	177	401
Ratio of time (hours) to volume (pages)	1.9	0.83

SOURCE: Minutes and Proceedings of the Standing Committees.

Table 8-5 indicates that only 93 pages of legislation were considered by committee in the second session of the 27th Parliament,
compared with a total of 461 in the second session of the 28th
Parliament. Even considering that the number of active committees
had increased, the average committee in the later session considered
about twice as much legislation as in the earlier session. Given this
heavy increase in overall workload, it is tempting to speculate that one
reason the reforms did not provide a higher performance ratio for the
legislature was the inability of the committee system to consider and
return bills to the House promptly. However, when the performance
ratio is calculated in terms of the number of hours of committee time
devoted to the consideration of one page of legislation it reveals an
improvement in committee performance. In the second session of the
27th Parliament, only six committees considered and reported legislation; for some committees it was a lengthy operation. The performance ratio of the committee system during this session was 1.9,
whereas in the second session of the 28th Parliament the performance
ratio of the committee system became 0.83 as the committees were
forced to handle a massive increase in workload (see Table 8-5). Our
analysis indicates that the government achieved the objective of transferring the consideration of legislation to committees without sacrific-
ing efficiency in committees during the sessions examined.

Why then, has the government been no more successful than before
the reforms in having its legislation passed promptly by the House of
Commons? This lack of success has occurred in part because the time

Table 8-6 COMPARISON OF TIME SPENT ON ESTIMATES BEFORE AND
AFTER THE 1968 RULE CHANGES

	2nd session 27th Parliament	2nd session 28th Parliament
No. of sitting days	155	155
No. of hours spent in Committee of Supply*	205	0
No. of hours spent on estimates in standing committee	46	219
No. of hours spent debating supply motions (S.O. 58)	0	106
Total time spent on estimates (hours)	251	325

*Includes six, two-day supply motions.
SOURCE: House of Commons, *Debates*; Minutes and Proceedings of the Standing Committees.

required to complete other activities has increased. Specifically, parliament now devotes more time to the consideration of estimates and supply debates and to the second reading stage of legislation.

As mentioned previously, the number of sitting days in the two sessions under consideration was 155. When one turns to the time devoted to the study of departmental estimates during these two sessions, the effects of the 1968 procedural changes are immediately evident. As Table 8-6 indicates, there is no means of comparing the amount of time spent in Committee of Supply for each session, since that body was no longer operative in the later session. However, the table shows that transferring the bulk of estimates examination to the committee system resulted in the investment of an extra 74 hours to the consideration of supply. The study of estimates in committee required approximately the same length of time as it did on the floor of the House in the earlier session. The additional hours in the later session were consumed by opposition motions under Standing Order 58. It might be argued that debates under Standing Order 58 do not apply to the study of estimates and therefore should not be included. However, such debates were intended to compensate for the loss of opportunity to challenge governmental policies during Committee of Supply and during the debates on supply motions. By transferring the considera-

Table 8-7 COMPARISON OF THE AMOUNT OF TIME DEVOTED TO
TYPES OF COMMITTEE BUSINESS TO 2ND SESSION, 27TH PARLIAMENT
AND 2ND SESSION, 28TH PARLIAMENT*

	2nd session 27th Parliament	2nd session 28th Parliament
Bills	177 hrs. (54%)	401 hrs. (26%)
Estimates	46 hrs. (14%)	219 hrs. (14%)
Miscellaneous	104 hrs. (32%)	950 hrs. (60%)
Total	327 hrs. (100%)	1570 hrs. (100%)

*Figures have been rounded to the nearest whole number.
SOURCE: Minutes and Proceedings of the Standing Committees.

tion of supply to committee and retaining for the opposition an opportunity to initiate resolutions under the heading of *Supply* in the House,
there was an absolute increase in the amount of time parliament
devoted to this aspect of surveillance.

The transfer of business to the committee also brought little relief to
the legislative timetable on the floor of the House. More time is being
spent at the report stage, despite the fact that bills have been subject to
detailed scrutiny in committees.[18] Similarly the time required to complete second-reading stage has been growing since the 1968 reforms.[19]
There is no doubt that government legislation is now being considered
more carefully but, as John Stewart has pointed out, there is a considerable waste of time and energy at this stage since only those who have
an intense interest in the measure will come to hear the minister deliver
a prepared statement on the bill.[20] And, as we have pointed out earlier,
the second-reading stage presently encourages the premature adoption
of rigid party positions — a source of frustration for the private member.

There have been other unanticipated consequences of reform. The
nature of committee preceedings has changed. In the second session of
the 27th Parliament the number of hours of committee time devoted to
the examination of legislation comprised 54 per cent of the total, but in
the second session of the 28th Parliament this task's hours had dropped
to 26 per cent of the total, despite a rather significant absolute increase
(see Table 8-7). It is in handling miscellaneous items that the committees have spent most of their time — 60 per cent in the later session
compared with 32 per cent in the earlier one. Those items assembled

under this heading include annual reports, white papers, the auditor general's report, and general investigatory references. Although the time devoted to these subjects declined in succeeding sessions, this finding is of considerable importance since it represents a marked change in the nature of committee activities that cannot be traced directly to procedural changes. The procedural changes which specified that both bills and estimates must be referred to standing committees have had the effect of strengthening the committee system and making it a more viable structure for handling general investigatory references.

In 1968, rule changes succeeded in providing the House with extra time to debate legislation and in transferring the detailed work on bills, estimates, and other matters from the House to the committee. In the short term it even improved the legislative performance of the House, but the performance level returned to its pre-1968 standard in subsequent sessions. The new procedures have been unable to dramatically reverse the trend toward lower performance ratios which was caused by the impact of intricate legislation and the prevalence of minority governments. The reforms produced considerable decentralization and proliferation of structures, but also allowed greater opportunities to reduce the flow of legislation.

Given these constraints it may be difficult to affect radically the level of legislative performance through reform measures. But the greatest problem with evaluating either the performance of the House of Commons or attempts to reform its activities is the absence of standards. Until Canadian politicians decide what parliament should achieve, scientific evaluation of legislative performance will continue to be a process of short uncertain steps.

NOTES

1. Robert Dahl, "The Evaluation of Political Systems," in I. de Sola Pool (ed.), *Contemporary Political Science: Toward Empirical Theory* (Toronto: McGraw-Hill, 1967), pp. 166-81; David Easton, "The New Revolution in Political Science," *American Political Science Review*, 63 (December 1969), p. 1052; Eugene Meehan, *Contemporary Political Thought: A Critical Study* (Homewood, Ill.: Dorsey Press, 1967), pp. 230, 232. Harry Eckstein, *The Evaluation of Political Performance* (Beverly Hills: Sage Publications, 1971); and Ted Gurr and Muriel McClelland, *Political Performance: A Twelve Nation Study* (Beverly Hills: Sage Publications, 1971).

2. Evaluation may also imply an examination of unintended as well as intended consequences, an evaluation of the objectives themselves or an attempt to ascertain why a particular policy met with success or failure. See Edward Suchman, *Evaluation Research* (Hartford, Conn.: Russell Sage Foundation, 1967), Chapter 3.

3. John Saloma III, *Congress and the New Politics* (Boston: Little, Brown, 1970), p. 5.

4. Roger Davidson, David Kovenock, and Michael O'Leary, *Congress in Crisis: Politics and Congressional Reform* (Belmont, Calif.: Wadsworth, 1966), p. 2.

5. Only one author has explicitly grappled with this problem in Canada. J. A. A. Lovink suggests five criteria which may be used to evaluate reform proposals. The criteria he suggests amount to five activities the author feels parliament engages in or should engage in. His evaluation of the impact reform proposals may have on these activities is an impressionistic one in the sense that he relies on no indicators beyond his own judgment. Lovink succeeds in covering many aspects of legislative performance, but not in such a manner that others may repeat his exercise and expect to arrive at his conclusions. See Lovink, "Parliamentary Reform and Governmental Effectiveness in Canada," *Canadian Public Administration*, 16 (Spring 1973), pp. 35-54.

6. Suchman, *Evaluation Research*, p. 12.

7. Dahl, "The Evaluation of Political Systems," p. 174.

8. Typologies of legislative output in Canada are rare, but examples include Paul G. Thomas, "The Influence of Standing Committees of Parliament on Government Legislation," *Legislative Studies Quarterly*, 3 (November 1978), pp. 691-99; and Allan Kornberg, David Falcone, and William Mishler, *Legislatures and Societal Change: The Case of Canada* (Beverly Hills: Sage Research Papers, 1973).

9. Abraham Kaplan, *The Conduct of Inquiry* (Scranton, Penn.: Chandler, 1964), p. 176.

10. Allan Kornberg, "Parliament in Canadian Society," in Allan Kornberg and Lloyd D. Musolf (ed.), *Legislatures in Developmental Perspective* (Durham, N.C.: Duke University Press, 1970), pp. 107-08.

11. Pages are not only a more precise measure of volume but perhaps a more realistic one, since bills must receive clause-by-clause scrutiny.

12. James March and Herbert Simon, *Organizations* (New York: John Wiley, 1958), p. 183.

13. Linda Geller-Schwartz, "Minority Government Reconsidered," *Journal of Canadian Studies*, 14 (Summer 1979), pp. 67-79. See also R. M. Punnett, *The Prime Minister in Canadian Government and Politics* (Toronto: Macmillan of Canada, 1977), pp. 129-36.

14. Gerhard Lowenberg and Samuel C. Patterson, *Comparing Legislatures* (Boston: Little, Brown, 1979), p. 267.

15. It must be allowed that two of these sessions were cut short by elections, but success levels in the other two sessions were also very low.

16. Donald S. Macdonald, "Change in the House of Commons: New Rules," *Canadian Public Adminstration*, 13 (Spring 1970), pp. 30-39.

17. For a similar study, see Ronald D. Hedlund and Keith E. Hamm, "Institutional Development and Legislative Effectiveness: Rule Changes in the Wisconsin Assembly," in Abdo I. Baaklini and James J. Heaphey (ed.), *Comparative Legislative Reforms and Innovations* (New York: State University of New York, 1977), pp. 173-213.

18. Thomas, "The Influence of Standing Committees," pp. 701-02.

19. John B. Stewart, *The Canadian House of Commons, Procedure and Reform* (Montreal: McGill-Queen's University Press, 1977), p. 270.

20. *Ibid.*, pp. 269-71.

9. Reform Design: Politicians and Policymaking

The first seven chapters have established the relations between the legislative system and society, the inner circle and parliament, the House of Commons and its committees, and the political actors and the roles they attempt to assume. Chapter 8 aggregated the data on members' activities by assessing legislative and committee performance. This synthesis has suggested that deficiencies exist in the legislative system and has permitted observations which are instructive in prescribing change and reform. In this chapter we concentrate only on the future directions that parliament could take.

The importance of accountability in a democracy lies in the need for the governed to be protected in some manner from the arbitrary use of power by the governors. Those who are trusted with the instruments of the state must be made to explain and justify their actions. The problem has always been — and remains — to devise an organizational and procedural regime which will secure for parliament a role in demanding that the executive explain and defend its actions without confining the executive to the point that it is unable to act at all.

One means of securing increased and adequate accountability is to enhance the independent authority of the legislature. This option is generally resisted by those who believe that the genius of the British constitutional system resides in a strong executive and that strengthening the legislature dilutes governmental authority. Those who defend this latter position argue that parliamentary activities should present a permanent election campaign among competing parties, and that the essence of accountability is the public acceptance of the responsibility of choosing a government from among these parties.

These critics of an increasingly powerful legislature believe that it is the opposition that needs to be induced to demand accountability from the government, and that the opposition will demand answers when it has a prospect of embarrassing the government. The idea of contributing to the efficient management of the public service or to the effectiveness of government programs has little or no appeal to the opposition, no matter how much they may protest their interest in honesty, probity, and good government.

In this volume we endorse the view that it is possible both to strengthen parliament and to exact a greater degree of accountability from government. In fact, until parliament is given the necessary powers, accountability will remain an unattained ideal. A strengthened parliament and a more responsive and responsible executive are more than compatible, they are mutually reinforcing. This is because parliament can be strengthened in certain respects only, enhancing not its ability to direct the affairs of the nation but its capacity to require the executive to account for its direction. Indeed, what is needed is a program of reform that does not stifle, but rather improves the quality of partisanship.

In such reforms there is a need to strike a balance between different conceptions of "efficiency." To the government, efficiency means the speed and cost-effectiveness of getting its legislation and financial matters through the House. To the opposition it means the ability to scrutinize proposals in as effective a manner as possible. Both sides define the concept to serve their own partisan interests. Bridging this gap by reason is not possible — only political compromise based on a solid public concern can build such bridges.

Conflicting arguments about reform should be the starting point for realistic appraisals. Unfortunately, this rarely happens. Since the publication of the first edition of this book, several party reports, royal commissions, and private interests[1] have come forward with reform proposals to strengthen parliament. Since all of them have ignored the implicit norms governing the possibility for success in this endeavour, we believe it is necessary to set down the rules which govern the likelihood of comprehensive change via parliamentary reform. First, no government will accept organizational or procedural changes regardless of the theoretical justifications unless it is assured that changes favourable to the government will also be adopted. Second, no reforms ought to be suggested on the naive assumption that partisanship will or should automatically be reduced by the existence of new structures. Third, a mixture of compulsion, rewards, and persuasion will be required to change politicians' attitudes and behaviour; one will not work without the others. Lastly, it is reasonably simple to adjust procedures and institutions, but immensely difficult to initiate change which will have a positive effect on performance levels.

If we are correct in our premise that these four basic rules govern the possibilities of success, then only proposals based on them have any hope of success. Comprehensive adjustments in institutions, linkages, and attitudes can be built on this foundation and eventually enhance the significance of the legislative system. Since incrementalism often leads to contradictory proposals, consistent reform depends on an articulation of and a commitment to long-range objectives or goals. At this juncture in the development of Canadian parliamentary institutions there should be three general objectives to reform:

1. *To improve the linkages within the legislative system.* Insufficient concern has been shown for the relations between the executive and legislative branches. Academics and political practitioners are too inclined toward a rigid separation of the functions of these two structures. Ministerial responsibility should be more clearly articulated and parliamentary surveillance of the executive made more systematic.

2. *To increase the policymaking role of the individual MP within the legislative system.* Reshaping the role of parliamentarians should not be at the expense of executive and political control. Attempts to make parliament into the major policymaking forum or to diminsh the resources of the inner circle are unlikely to be helpful, but more political and professional input at the appropriate stages in policymaking is essential.

3. *To enhance the image of parliament in the mass public.* A greater openness and honesty among politicians in both parts of the legislative system is required. The principle of full democratic accountability and guaranteed access to government information by all Canadians needs to be accepted.

These objectives will require the elimination of some old structures, the adjustment of some procedures, and the creation of some new institutions.

EXECUTIVE-LEGISLATIVE LINKAGES

Legislative and financial institutions in the preparliamentary stages of the legislative system should be restructured. In Canada the linkages have not been rationalized so that the stages for producing legislative items and the stages within the House are coherent. The two essential areas for reform are: the organization and preparation of the executive's approach to parliament and the approach itself.

The preparation of executive action has been aided by general goals, but ministers have not been committed to using them to force departmental response in the form of legislation. In fact, there has been a tendency to regard policy as separable from the legislative program. Some organizational changes would be helpful. In addition to instructing departments to list their legislative proposals in correspondence with government goals, an inventory of departmental legislation which has fulfilled established goals should be circulated within the public service. In Britain the ministries prepare documents for their ministers on how to implement the party platform. Such a practice would be a salutary, if sometimes embarrassing, addition to policymaking in Canada.

In the preparation of the legislative program, departments are too independent of cabinet control despite the efforts of the Privy Council Office. On occasion departments even circumvent cabinet intentions on the program. Failsafe procedures have not been developed, and sometimes the government has found itself without sufficient legislation to place before parliament. Draft bills are not circulated among departments; consequently, some policy considerations are often raised too late in the process. Lastly, no satisfactory means has yet been developed to allow feedback from parliamentary institutions into the preparliamentary process.

The solution to those difficulties associated with the preparation of the legislative program lies in a more thorough coordination of departmental policy memos and the drafting process, and more political input from ministers, caucus, and parliamentary institutions. The most direct means of producing such a result would be to appoint one minister responsible for the entire legislative system. Since the complexities of modern government require the prime minister to organize all the coordinating agencies, this new role should be assumed by another minister supported by a powerful cabinet committee structure. The development of a new, powerful "inner" cabinet might also provide the force necessary to coordinate the program.

The responsibilities of the Cabinet Committee on Legislation and House Planning should be increased. It should control the legislative program and form a bridge between parliament and the cabinet. To discharge these responsibilities the structure of the committee should be changed to provide for a Future Legislation Committee and a Current Legislation Committee. Ideally, the new responsible minister would be the chairman of both committees as well as government House leader. While he or she would have no departmental legislation to pilot through the House, the minister would be responsible for the composite program and its political thrust. This minister could retain the formal title of President of the Privy Council or a Minister of State position could be made the vehicle for this structural change.

On cabinet approval of priorities the minister would request from colleagues the legislative proposals which conform to government objectives. The minister's planning staff would perform the administrative duties now carried out by some sectors of the PCO. Plans for scheduling activities in departments and in parliament would be drawn up concurrently. The overall government priorities would, of course, remain the responsibility of the inner cabinet, serviced by the PCO. The administrative duties of the government House leader, such as office allocation, would be transferred to the chief government whip. The drafting office of the Department of Justice should be made responsible to the new minister's department, but it should be attached to parliament for administrative purposes. The new drafting office should be expected to act as a service agency for central government. It should draft bills according to the priorities set by the Future Legislation Committee or in exceptional situations by the government leader in the House. Draft bills should be immediately circulated to all departments for consideration and department solicitors should be drawn into a comprehensive framework for the legal consideration of all bills.

The Future Legislation Committee (or inner cabinet) would design the legislative program one year in advance of the session for which it was to be used.[2] The committee would receive advice from the departments, the PCO, draftsmen, the chief government whip, and the new minister's staff. This information would determine (subject to cabinet confirmation) the size of the program and the actual items to be included. If the committee rejected a bill, the sponsoring minister would be required to appear before the committee to argue for a reconsideration. Such an arrangement would limit departmental autonomy and individual ministerial control. The Future Legislation Committee could also supervise the writing of the speech from the throne. The chairman would have to be a tenacious administrator, however, since the integrity of the committee would depend on adherence to the shape and schedule of the legislative program as originally approved by cabinet.

The Current Legislation Committee would be assigned many of the tasks now undertaken by the Cabinet Committee on Legislation and House Planning. As in the United Kingdom, the new committee should not be required to examine the draft bills clause by clause to locate drafting errors. The sponsoring department, the drafting office, and the chairman's staff should advise the committee of the major political difficulties in the legislation (especially those that might prove embarrassing in the House) and help in the scrutiny of all projected expenditures and wide delegations of power. For practical and tactical purposes the precise timetable for the introduction and processing of legislation in the House should be left to the government House leader and chief whip, who would act in accordance with the wishes of the prime minister.

Lack of coordination in the timely production of legislation is paralleled in the executive by a general lack of adequate management and accountability in the financial affairs of government. The flaws in the process have been brilliantly described in the 1979 report of the Royal Commission on Financial Management and Accountability.[3] Many of their proposals in this field should be accepted. Not all. Unfortunately, the Commissioners made some basic errors in their report by basing their recommendations firmly on accepted practices in the management of private corporations. In doing so, they assumed that governments have clear and consistent goals, that parliamentarians rather than parties control parliament, and that majority governments persist in office for long periods. While all of these assumptions are incorrect, it would be unwise to overlook the very valuable service the Commissioners have done in suggesting the development of a fiscal plan.

It has been well known for some time that the role of the budget, the preparation of the estimates, and taxation have not been properly drawn together. Mitchell Sharp, after his tenure as minister of finance, admitted publicly that "we do separate too much the discussion of spending from the discussion of revenues."[4] While five-year revenue and expenditure forecasts have existed inside the government for a long time, they have not been made available to parliament. The Royal Commission suggests changing this process by having the minister of finance present to parliament a five-year fiscal plan which would provide estimates of revenues, expenditure ceilings, and predictions of the expected surplus or deficit. Ideally, we would like to see this plan and its annual updates tabled with or as part of the speech from the throne, as is the case with the legislative program. The combination of the government's philosophy or goals, the fiscal plan, and the legislative program in one package should provide a major vehicle for the discussion of the government's priorities, legislation, expenditures, and revenues.

In order to improve executive-legislative linkages the government should cultivate some new practices and attitudes in its approach to the House. Even though the new minister responsible for legislation would become the main link between the executive and the legislature, the administration of the whip's office could be improved and the government chief whip should be elevated to the status of a junior minister to permit his attendance at cabinet meetings on legislation. During the 30th Parliament, the Liberals allowed the Parliamentary Secretary to the President of The Privy Council, John Reid, to perform this role. The *ad hoc* approach compounded a charge that Mr. Reid knew about the budget before it was tabled. In view of the informality of this position, there will always be confusion. We would like to see such a position formalized.

The House leaders' meeting should remain the focal point of party negotiation, but a business committee composed of House leaders and the chairmen of standing committees should coordinate activities in the parliamentary part of the legislative system. The government should provide parliament with its own legislative schedule much farther in advance than is presently the case. Parliamentary planning should be based on a monthly rather than a weekly announcement. Items should not be added to the program during a session unless they are for extreme emergencies or unless they can be handled by a Second Reading Committee as discussed below. The addition of legislative items during a session diminishes the relation among goals, priorities, and bills, and ignores the need for adequate communication with parliament.

The government should return to the practice of placing a list of legislative proposals in the speech from the throne. In theory, all bills should be tabled at this time. No matter what date legislation is introduced, however, it should be accompanied by its detailed regulations. If parliament is not given a chance to debate the regulations (subordinate legislation) of a bill, they should not come into effect.[5]

The government should inaugurate a clear distinction between types of government publications by tabling green papers to illustrate government "ideas" and white papers on clear government "policy." Experiments with other types of papers will only harm public understanding of the policy process. The practice of introducing "trial balloon'' bills should also be dropped, to indicate the government's seriousness in developing a disciplined approach to the legislative program. Moreover, public servants should avoid the recent practice of writing two cabinet documents on each topic — one for the minister's eyes and a second, expurgated, version for tabling in parliament.

The executive should respond to initiatives from parliament and its committees. Substantive reports from parliamentary committees, for example, should be considered in departments, and ministers should provide answers to the criticisms and suggestions. This could be accomplished by the tabling of government green papers in response to House proposals. The government currently informs the Public Accounts Committee of the action it has taken on its recommendations. It should extend this practice by explaining the reasons why it has not been able to accept the recommendations. The government will naturally be reluctant to consume valuable time in the House debating all of these reports and responses, and some of the debate can safely be confined to committees. Nonetheless, the government should be unable to avoid an open debate and to that end the opposition parties should be prevailed upon to relinquish some of their opposition days. The links with the House should be seen as feedback mechanisms in which the executive absorbs ideas from the House in the same way that parliament reacts to cabinet initiatives.

Finally, the ambiguity which presently surrounds the principle of individual ministeral responsibility is regrettable. Neither ministers nor public servants should be able to invoke the principle when it pleases them and avoid it when it does not. Unfortunately, ambiguity. is probably unavoidable. No guidelines can be drafted which will define the precise range of a minister's responsibilities. These matters should be left to politicians who recognize both the importance of being able to vest elected officials with responsibility and the absurdity. of expecting ministers to resign in the face of administrative errors. Grey areas are best treated as such. In this respect, the Lambert Commission's proposal to divide responsibility between ministers and deputies by distinguishing between managerial and advisory activities should be examined closely and then shelved indefinitely.

INSTITUTIONS IN PARLIAMENT

Reforms in parliament should focus on those activities and institutions in which individual participation and organizational efficiency can be improved. Sympathy is widespread for the efforts of individual MPs who wish to satisfy personal aspirations and bring ideas to bear on the art of governing. Perhaps less obvious is the need for increased efficiency in the conduct of parliamentary business. Some proponents of parliamentary reform even consider it to be a contradictory goal.

There are two reasons for suggesting that efficiency, a value associated with the executive, be maximized in a reform of parliamentary proceedings. The first is a practical one. The government will be unwilling to permit the adjustment of parliamentary structures if no government priority is recognized. The idea of permitting free votes on the floor of the House or unlimited debate in committee would be opposed by any government because neither reform offers an incentive for abandoning the status quo. The second reason is that within a parliamentary system the political executive, the cabinet, should assume responsibility for leading the affairs of the legislature. Procedures that permit the government to avoid its responsibilities will have undesirable ramifications in the preparliamentary part of the system. They will also make it more difficult to assign responsibility for policy and hence will undermine the principle of democratic accountability. The government will not be made more responsive by making it more difficult to pass legislation. Political control of the legislative system requires that cabinet be provided with the means of achieving its objectives.

Obscure reform recommendations to do away with party discipline and cohesion come from many quarters. In a brief, *Parliamentary Government in Canada* prepared by Intercounsel Limited for the Business Council on National Issues, Thomas d'Aquino *et al.* advise "that the leaders of both the government and opposition parties recognize and adopt in practice a less stringent approach to the question of party discipline and rules governing confidence."[6] This is the wrong way to proceed. Recommendations must take the form of structural changes or rewards for compliance, not merely admonitions. The adoption, moreover, of such a proposal would eventually destroy party cohesion, require the government to declare some legislation or expenditures less important than others, and precipitate undesirable changes in the parliamentary system. As Lord Salisbury pointed out more than a century ago, "Combinations there must be — the only question is, whether they shall be broad parties, based on comprehensive ideas, and guided by men who have a name to stake on the wisdom of their course, or obscure cliques, with some narrow crotchet for a policy, and some paltry yelping shibboleth for a cry."[7]

The size of the House of Commons is too small for the legislative and constituency workload of members. It should be enlarged again so that no member will represent more than 50,000 constituents. The major purpose of this proposal is to construct a more stable House membership in order to develop a parliamentary career ladder and direct MPs' ambition to something other than membership in the cabinet. Moreover, sessions of the House of Commons last too long, making it difficult for most members of parliament to maintain permanent contact with their constituencies. Sessions should be roughly equivalent in length. They should begin in the fall and, if possible, be shortened.

In order to attract and keep intelligent parliamentarians, redundant and useless work should be eliminated. Examples would include eliminating some of the eight days used for the speech from the throne and the six debate days used for the budget. In the legislative process itself no speeches last more than 20 minutes. Technical parts of tax bills, like other legislation, should go directly to committees for examination rather than passing through The Committee of the Whole. This procedure would save time in the House and give MPs the benefit of technical opinions supplied by tax experts. The function of surveillance is not served by existing procedures. Some of the time now devoted to general debates could be reassigned to the discussion of matters raised in committees. Even Standing Order 43, which is often a useful means of embarrassing the government and sometimes forcing debate, should have a more stringent time limit imposed on it.

The above reforms would provide parliament with more time for legislation on the floor of the House. To further expedite business, parliament should agree to end the procedure whereby those bills which have not been passed during one session die on the order paper and must be reintroduced at the beginning of the next session. This is a process which inevitably results in the duplication of effort and permits the government to introduce "trial balloon" bills which they may have no intention of passing. Parliamentarians have the right to expect the government to remain committed to items that are on the legislative program. Failure to pass a bill should be a comment on the government's program, not on parliamentary inefficiency.

The government ought to have the means of terminating an opposition filibuster of legislation without recourse to closure. The present unfortunate wording of Standing Orders 75A, 75B, and 75C may not permit the government to set its own time limit. In fact, it may be possible for opposition parties under 75B to impose their time allocation on a majority government. On the strength of parliamentary convention, the government should be a party to any agreement regarding parliamentary time and minor changes are required to realize this objective.

Oral Question Period is presently a forum for unrelated assertions of fact and opinion. Order and continuity is required; for this purpose parliament should adopt, with some amendments, the British practice. This would terminate spontaneous questions by stipulating that those which require an oral reply must be on the order paper at least 48 hours in advance. The preparation of both queries and replies would thus become much more methodical. Members would still be motivated by political considerations, but questions would have to be worded carefully to solicit facts unflattering to the government. Excessive outbursts would be either ruled out of order or easily circumvented by an experienced minister. Replies would be drafted by departmental officials, but members would retain the right to ask a limited number of supplementaries. Ministers would no longer be able to stall their antagonists by arguing that considerable time is required to assemble the information. Members would lose the privilege of giving immediate expression to their inspirations, but the House would be saved the interruptions of the speaker's rulings and the inequities of a system in which most members are recognized by the speed with which they spring to their feet.

The new arrangement would be enhanced if certain days were set aside for the discussion of particular ministeries or particular policy areas. However, matters of urgency would not be dealt with immediately (placing more pressure on Standing Order 43) and it would be advisable, therefore, to supplement the revised question period with the present practice of permitting party leaders to initiate questions on current issues. Beginning with the leader of the opposition, each party should be permitted a single spontaneous question with supplementaries. It is anticipated that the retention of this feature of parliamentary questioning in Canada would further emphasize the clash between the prime minister and opposition party leadership. In order to prevent the ridiculous spectacle of Liberal ministers being able to avoid questions on the RCMP during the 30th Parliament, the rules should be changed to allow former ministers, who remain MPs, to answer questions on their previous activities.

The government should establish a continuous review of private members' bills and decisions should be taken regularly on which bills deserve to be passed. Precedence on the order paper should be established by a ballot among all members. Bills that are accorded priority and are discussed during private members' hour should be voted on at second reading. If they secure passage at this stage the committee system would provide a means by which MPs could solicit the opinions of the ministers and public servants responsible for the areas covered by the bill. If a bill is rejected at second reading the sponsoring member should be provided with an explanation of government policy and the reasons for the refusal. Private members' motions should be selected by a similar ballot procedure and be regarded as resolutions of the House, expressions of opinion not binding on the government. These motions should be permitted to come to a vote without the whip being applied. If they are adopted the government would not be formally required to act, but moral suasion would have been applied and backbenchers would have been granted another point of access in the legislative system.

The proposed changes are designed to rationalize and develop the main opportunites for efficiency and participation within the parliamentary part of the legislative system. The House of Commons requires, in addition, a preparliamentary policymaking capability. The denial of any formative policymaking role will probably hinder the performance of other ascribed functions. However, parliament cannot satisfy a policymaking role by perfecting tactics of legislative obstruction or by altering the policies which have already undergone detailed formulation and to which the government is openly committed. Policy input, if there is to be any, must come at a much earlier stage and certainly before legislation is within parliament. The committee system of the House of Commons has the most potential for this type of reform and a comprehensive alternative can be offered in this area.

A multifunctional committee system has been described earlier as one in which each committee is expected to assume responsibility for a variety of activities. In contrast to a system like Britain's, in which one type of committee is responsible for the parliamentary stages of lawmaking in a policy area while another type is responsible for scrutiny and surveillance, a multifunctional system has numerous subject-matter committees in which members acquire an expertise in all facets of a single policy area. Ideally, each activity should be performed when it is most likely to have an impact on the government and interested publics. In Canada, however, general investigation is often undertaken and advice offered when committees are ostensibly engaged in lawmaking. This means that the government's legislative program is delayed while witnesses are called and the committee investigates. Yet legislation is one of the final stages of policymaking and, when a majority government is committed to legislation, few major changes are ever achieved by backbenchers.

Canada should retain a multifunctional standing committee system, but investigation and advice should occur in the policy-creation stages. Committees often make valuable contributions to the refinement of legislation and they should retain the opportunity to offer detailed amendments.[9] Committee institutions should be developed so that members of parliament may participate in long-term planning. That is, the institutions should provide opportunities for backbench input into the government's goals and priorities. Moreover, adjustments in legislation and the criticism of spending patterns should be based on a comprehensive understanding of government policy in a particular area. The floor of the House, however, would remain the scene of eloquent debate and political manoeuvre.

To accomplish these objectives, legislation should go to committee with narrow terms of reference and, in all but the most exceptional situations, with no provision for other than departmental witnesses to be summoned. Committees which examine legislation should be charged, as they are in Britain, with the task of debating and amending details. The informal business committee, discussed earlier, should decide on the length of time each bill requires in standing committee. In short, the committee system should prepare itself to handle the government's legislative program in a thorough and expeditious manner. For its part, the government should formulate a projected legislative schedule, including the demands it intends to make on parliamentary and committee time for the consideration of legislation.

An adequate execution of ascribed functions depends on the opposition's capacity to offer comprehensive critiques and detailed amendments of government policy. However, as the pressure on parliamentary time increases, it becomes more difficult to create an atmosphere on the floor of the House in which both general and detailed criticism can be accommodated. The committees ought to develop into workshops where members can appreciate and criticize the most intricate and technical of legislative proposals. A relaxation of administrative secrecy and the provision of more professional advice to members of parliament are required. Moreover, in the committee forum, government and opposition members should interact under a different set of norms from those prescribed by the confrontation style of opposition. After the introduction of the new committee system in 1968, there were signs that such a development was underway. It is an extension, not a reversal, of this trend that would alleviate some of the problems in the legislative system.

Committees should be assisted in acquiring a much larger role in investigation. This could be accomplished partly through the existing estimates procedure, but new opportunities should be provided for members to initiate independent investigations into selected policy areas. Committees should automatically be granted wide terms of reference at the beginning of each session, and the government should automatically refer to committees the annual reports of all departments in order to give substance to these general references. If the experience of British select committees is an indication, the Canadian committees will choose issues and areas on which no firm policy commitments have been made by any party. Where possible the government should also table statements of policy intent in the form of green papers. It is envisaged that when the estimates are tabled the committees will have already chosen areas of concentration and members will have become sufficiently conversant with policy that a more effective surveillance function can be performed.

The estimates procedures call for special attention. In an era in which the first concerns of members of parliament are not cost reduction to the government, the mechanisms are inadequate. John Stewart has best summarized the situation: ''The spending estimates are important nowadays, not because of the wharves and runways to be built, or the salaries to be paid, but because of the impact of government spending on the nation's economy.''[10] In view of this fact, there are two basic problems with the procedures: no committee deals with cross-departmental comparisons of spending and the one-year framework is too short for adequate analysis. The proposed long-term fiscal-plan concept would alleviate the latter difficulty, but the first problem needs further consideration. Consolidated estimates which include government-wide and comparative data should be tabled as well as the individual estimates of each department. The new consolidated estimates should be presented in a comprehensive format and be examined by a new committee (also needed to scrutinize the fiscal plan) possibly called the Committee on Finance and the Economy. The individual department estimates should be referred to the normal subject-matter committee with an order which would encourage the investigation of government policy. Royal recommendations on bills should be drafted in wider terms, with only total expenditures included in order to provide procedural flexibility.

Because of the complexity of government (there are more than 400 departments, crown corporations, agencies, boards, and commissions), the committees should have broad powers to demand information and papers. A special committee on crown corporations and similar bodies should be established to investigate agencies such as Atomic Energy of Canada Limited, Air Canada, and the CBC. They should have to produce their financial statements and some working papers. The Public Accounts Committee should be given the power to request the auditor general to carry out studies for it.

A more specialized committee system requires government response to parliamentary initiatives. Procedures should be introduced to permit the discussion of committee reports on the floor of the House. Substantive committee reports should have concurrence moved and be debated during a specific committee time. In this regard, consideration should be given to allotting a specified number of committee days per session and permitting the speaker to choose the committee reports to be debated. Concurrence in such reports would not render them binding on the government. Nevertheless, the government should respond automatically to them by tabling a paper explaining why it agrees or disagrees with the recommendations. This would initiate another round of prelegislative policy study within the committee.

A committee system which offers expanded opportunities for personal initiative would encourage the continuity in membership necessary for specialization. Even with an enlarged House of Commons, it would be desirable to reduce both the number of committees and the size of their membership. In order to accommodate the two new committees — on finance and crown corporations — the whole system of names and duties of committees must be revised. The new committees should deal with inclusive topics rather than be organized on the department-by-department basis which is now the case. The 30- and 20-member committees should have their composition reduced to fewer than 15. To retain flexibility in membership change and at the same time discipline the procedure, members should be permitted to change committees only at specified and regular times. This could be accomplished by restricting changes to the beginning of a new session, or alternative lists could be drawn up from which substitutes could be selected. Since committees work best when they are small and have active members, the rules which govern quorums should be changed so that only about a quarter of the membership are required to be present at any one time. This practice will be especially significant when the committees divide into subcommittees more often in order to carry out the duties and responsibilities that this new committee system would require of all members of parliament.

Leadership in committees should be institutionalized. At the present time the chairman of a committee cannot even have a name plate on his office door to signify that he is an officer of the house. On the government side the role of partisan leader should be assumed by the parliamentary secretary who may have to be accorded some of the rights and duties of a junior minister. The chairman should be made an impartial, paid official and a panel of chairmen should be created with the government and the opposition each providing half the delegation. The speaker should be empowered to select chairmen from among the panel to serve on particular committees. The chairmen would administer research funds and represent committees in the House, but only on the direction of a majority of committees members. In a system which would place heavy emphasis on investigation and scrutiny, an impartial chairman would encourage cooperation among all members of the House. He would occupy a position of authority not effectively influenced by the government. Moreover, a panel of impartial chairmen, acting as a unit, may be able to secure important concessions from the government that are unobtainable by individual plea.

A professional research staff and a budget for committees are necessary additions to this type of committee system. Studies indicate that the lack of support facilities, including research assistance, has been a common complaint among members.[11] A fixed budget would be a radical feature of this new research scheme since it would provide the committee with the funds necessary to launch an independent investigation. In this way, staff could be hired and trips taken at the discretion of the committee. Another possibility is to hire a permanent staff which could be attached to the Research Branch of the Library of Parliament but assigned specifically to committee work. These reforms would have a cumulative effect on committees inasmuch as they would provide a new and separate source of information and an opportunity to conduct affairs with less fear of government interference. In order to bring about this collective enterprise committees would be forced to change their internal procedures. Norms which require that each member ask a witness questions for ten minutes produce an uncoordinated pattern of questions and answers. With the help of a professional staff, members ought to be able to prepare skilled and penetrating analyses and questions.

While some observers believe that the speaker of the House of Commons should be made an impartial spokesman, we do not believe that such changes are required. The last few speakers, including the incumbent Mr. James Jerome, have proven that the present system can work well. There is little complaint among MPs and we share this viewpoint. Most of the speaker's staff, the clerks, the table officers, and those charged with general housekeeping and administration do their job well — with tact and dispatch.

Since the publication of the first edition of this volume, considerable attention has been paid to the future of the Senate. As a response to provincial complaints and the ascendancy of the Parti Québécois in the province of Quebec, parties, provincial leaders, academics, and others have called for a new set of institutions in place of the present-day Senate.[12] Almost all the schemes appear to involve changes in the composition of that body. The most popular schemes appear to be those which take some power away from the federal government to make all appointments to the upper house. The Liberals would like the federal and provincial governments to share this responsibility; the Conservatives would give the provinces all the power to make appointments; and the New Democrats would abolish the upper house altogether.

We do not believe that the upper house should be abolished. In its day-to-day work it performs important tasks for the legislative system in refining bills, drawing attention to detailed problems, and promoting research on important topics such as finance and poverty. After examining the proposals to change the upper house into a body somewhat similar to the Bundesrat of the Federal Republic of Germany, we have come to a mixed view. One should first consider the motives behind the idea. If it is stimulated by the belief that the appointment of those familiar with provincial interests will promote a higher quality of legislation, it should be viewed with suspicion. If, on the other hand, the suggestion is made in the hope that the Senate will be strengthened in the performance of integration, representation, and legitimation functions, then constructing elaborate representation formulas is justified. In practical terms, the government rarely requires party stalwarts in the Senate and, as the current lack of partisanship indicates, there are possibilities for the development of regional and provincial loyalties if a different system of appointment is adopted. Offers of senatorships could also be extended to individuals in the arts and to other prominent Canadians who have had little or no prior association with politics. Major changes in composition would undoubtedly bring a reevaluation of Senate activities. The future of the Senate lies not in the acquisition of more lawmaking functions, but in the improvement of its status as a symbol of the nation. Changes in the committee system could increase the ability of senators to contribute to policymaking and to provide the government with an opportunity to conduct its business in a more orderly fashion. It is also possible that the type of improvements suggested will enhance the image of parliament among the mass public. As we have emphasized throughout, a reservoir of support for parliament is necessary for the performance of ascribed functions. Unfortunately, the impact of internal reforms on public attitudes toward parliament is difficult to assess. Even when efforts are consciously undertaken to improve parliament's status, the problem of evaluating the impact remains. This does not mean that reforms should not be made, only that their consequences—intended and unintended—ought to be carefully considered.

Parliament can improve its image if it is less remote from the average citizen. To this end committees should be encouraged to increase, not curtail, their travelling. When committees meet in different surroundings, citizens can see their representatives at work. Travel also stimulates a more thorough development of the subject-matter specialization on which the committee system should be predicated. Radio and television should be used to announce committee meetings and invite submissions. Witnesses who appear before parliamentary committees should be selected by a steering committee on which all parties are represented. Decisions of this committee should be made public by listing those who will be granted—and those who will be denied—access to committee deliberations. Parliament should investigate the protections available to witnesses in committee hearings. When sensitive personal matters are under discussion the committee should accept only sworn testimony and when necessary hold *in camera* meetings.

It is reasonable to assume that the image of the individual member of parliament would be enhanced if parliament were to adopt strict legislation in the area of conflict of interest. Conflict of interest legislation should clearly establish that membership in the House of Commons is a full-time activity. Those private financial interests a member retains should be carefully supervised by a parliamentary committee and by the courts. A green paper outlining proposed detailed legislation on conflict of interest for members of parliament was tabled in the House of Commons in July 1973. On the first attempt to pass legislation based on the green paper, the Senate blocked the proposal; on the second attempt, parliament was dissolved in 1979 before the bill reached second reading.

Efforts to control ministers were also undertaken by the Liberals. Prime Minister Trudeau issued guidelines for cabinet ministers in 1972. A registry of cabinet ministers' financial holdings was to be kept, and ministers could choose one of the following options:

1. Divest themselves of their financial holdings.
2. Place financial holdings in a blind trust (meaning, in theory, the ministers should not know what their holdings are).
3. Place them in a frozen trust (meaning that ministers could know what they are but not be able to change them).

Later, the Prime Minister said ministers could make a public declaration of their holdings and continue to control them. After the Judges Affair in 1976, Prime Minister Trudeau added that ministers could no longer contact judges on matters before the courts.

Codes of ethics announced in the House, or prime minister's guidelines, cannot replace legislation in this field. One of Joe Clark's first acts as prime minister was to expand the provisions of the guidelines. Such prime-ministerial discretion is not enough. Canada needs legislation (without frozen-trust provisions) to replace the existing guidelines, to define for all members the limits of their extraparliamentary activities, and to insure that privileged information is not used for private gain.

One of the basic criticisms of politicians and the legislative system in the past decade has been excessive secrecy in government. It was argued that a curtain of secrecy veiled matters of concern to the general public, and that legislation to provide freedom of information was required. We agree that public access to government information ought to be improved. Canada needs legislation which provides more public access to government documents.

In theory practically everyone can agree with this exhortation. The New Democratic and Progressive Conservative parties have argued such a viewpoint throughout the decade. The Liberal government, too, responded with various papers and directives. In 1973 the Trudeau government, for example, issued new guidelines about government information. Aside from 16 exemptions, the government declared itself prepared to make public as much factual information as possible, consistent with effective administration, the protection of the security of the state, rights to privacy, and other such matters. Two years later, the government's own Parliamentary Secretary to the Privy Council, John Reid, cited numerous cases where the guidelines had not been adequate in allowing "open government." The issue simply would not go away—or Ged Baldwin, the indefatigable Tory MP, would not let it go away. In 1977 the government tabled its own green paper, *Legislation on Public Access to Government Documents*, and in May 1978 discussion began in parliamentary committees.

If legislation is passed it must be congruent with other statutes and replace the patchwork of laws and government directives now in force. In our opinion much more information can, however, be made available even if legal and practical difficulties must be overcome. Virtually everything about the political process itself should be public (in fact, it should be taught in educational institutions!): cabinet committees, their membership, and the exact organization of central government are information that should be available to everyone. Only clearcut cases of national security or individual privacy should circumscribe the general rule.

Two extreme viewpoints must be rejected before an analysis can provide an operational system. First, no panacea for the problems of modern government is to be found by the release of more information. It is erroneous to assume that information is readily available and suitable to all desired purposes. Second, there is little but rhetoric in the notion that ministerial responsibility and our system of government will be destroyed simply because some public servants are required to publish more policy-related documents. This does not mean, on the contrary, that there is absolutely nothing to the argument that public servants must be frank in their advice to ministers or the system will not work. Nor does it mean that there need be no exemptions in cases of national security. A list of cabinet ministers or public servants studying organized crime or terrorism might be an example. Presently, the funds for security purposes are spread throughout the estimates so that no foreign powers can determine the size or scope of security operations. MPs find out about theses figures in *in camera* meetings only. Such information will have to remain confidential.

Legislation which provides more information for parliamentarians and the public will be complex and several important questions will have to be answered:

1. Which documents and papers should be exempted from public scrutiny? We think the limits should be as narrow as possible, subject to the need to keep private all cabinet deliberations and some policy-option papers of senior public servants as well as the need to keep in mind the individual right to privacy.[13]
2. How much will all of this cost? The costs should be reasonable. The Green Paper estimated an annual cost of $10 million, depending on the number of requests.
3. Is useful information readily available? Almost certainly not. There will have to be a proper and relevant classification and indexing system instituted.

A major question involves the complaint-review process. What system should be used to resolve disputes between the government and citizens about exempted papers and documents? The Conservative party favours a combination of parliament and the courts; the Green Paper, a parliamentary commissioner. This complaint-review process has been the subject of heated debate, especially in print between Murray Rankin and Richard French. Rankin favours court adjudication: "There is no compelling reason why the courts in Canada should not be entrusted with the responsibility to review all information requests which the government has denied."[14] We favour the approach of the Green Paper and Richard French,[15] and prefer a parliamentary commissioner.

Arguments against a court performing this role are legion. Resort to the judicial process would be quite expensive; litigation would increase and the costs would mount because of the need for legal counsel. An appeal under the American Freedom of Information Act costs an average of $10,000.[16] Secondly, private interests piggyback on the right to know philosophy by going to court to gather information, to benefit from policy studies carried out for the federal government, to stall the regulatory process, and even to seek private information about their competitors which has been stored by governments.[17]

The major reason that parliament should scrutinize the executive's response to the freedom of information legislation is that Canada should not legislate away to the courts a fundamental part of the responsibility of parliament, namely surveillance of the governors. If parliament is to increase its prestige, it is important that it improve its monitoring of the executive. Consequently, we endorse the Conservative government's plan to establish an information commissioner analogous to the commissioner of official languages, the human rights commissioner, or the auditor general. On complaint, the commissioner would examine, *in camera*, documents which the government had refused to release. As the Green Paper proposed, the commissioner should have the power to order the release of the document. Allowing complainants or the government to appeal beyond the commissioner to the courts will only duplicate the process and rob the commissioner's office of the authority and independence required to develop and to insist on guidelines which capture the spirit as well as the letter of the law.

Election expenditure by parties and candidates is increasing more rapidly than the cost of living. In January 1974, parliament approved an election-expense formula with high ceilings and rather weak supervisory mechanisms. It is to be hoped that over time inflation will reduce the impact of the allotments and that the officers appointed to oversee the regulations will be scrupulous in their endeavours to hold down election expenses and to plug any loopholes that may arise. If these factors are not present, public cynicism toward the legislative system may be a byproduct.

One means of encouraging devotion to parliamentary duties is to provide a level of remuneration high enough that members of parliament can remain independent of private sources of income. There is little excuse for the undignified controversy that surrounds every pay increase. After the 1975 salary raise, MPs received a fixed, taxable salary of $24,000 with the additional $10,000 of nontaxable income. Since then salaries have been automatically adjusted by an annual cost of living increase of up to 7 per cent and in March 1979 MPs could expect, at minimum, a $28,600 indemnity and a $12,700 expense allowance. In keeping with the government's own policy on taxable income, no provision for nontaxable funds should be included in the new formula. It is true that the needs of MPs differ and that not everyone requires additional research or secretarial aid. Nevertheless, as the Beaupré Report emphasized, a general improvement in the standard of facilities would probably increase the effectiveness of all MPs. The decision in early 1974 to provide constituency offices for members of parliament was a step in the right direction. These offices have helped to relieve the burden of requests and referrals to government agencies and have symbolized the member's continual role in the constituency. However, members need even more executive and technical support. Each member should have a research assistant both in parliament and in the constituency. These should be formal positions, not secretarial allotments. During the election campaigns, offices in public buildings should be provided for both incumbents and challengers.

In communicating with the mass public, institutions and individuals in the legislative system rely heavily on the mass media. In the first edition we advocated that parliament televise its own proceedings with its own technicians and allow broadcasters to employ the tapes and sound tracks as they wish. We argued that a national cable company should carry all parliamentary proceedings in the expectation that, if parliament were widely projected, an audience could be educated in the fundamentals of government and so support for parliamentary institutions could be generated.[18] Since that time parliament has done precisely that. While evidence is still mixed, it appears that this step was an important advance in communicating with the public. Certainly the introduction of live televised debates has signalled many changes in the behaviour of politicians in parliament. However, the process is still quite mysterious to many citizens, and improvements in the House's procedures are still required to reduce this confusion. More important, perhaps, some consideration should be given to allowing the television networks more independence to enhance the format of televised proceedings.

There have also been undesirable consequences of televising the House. Frontbenchers are inclined to monopolize debating time, especially during Question Period, and too many parliamentary buffoons behave childishly during debates. Because approximately 80 per cent of the proceedings are in English, and the French audience may resent the translation, more cabinet ministers are being obliged to confine their parliamentary remarks to the French language. Some of these difficulties may be overcome by existing legislative norms, but parliament should carefully monitor the impact of television and consider how it might adapt to the new technology without destroying parliamentary traditions.

Finally, parliament needs continual scrutiny from the public and the academic community. Parliament is much too important to the public purpose for its reforms to be left to bureaucrats and politicians — even if they are experts on the system and have all the good will in the world. An effective association of parliamentary experts is a necessity. The Canadian Study of Parliament Group was a step in the right direction. However, some members privately complain that the politicians monopolize the discussions and that the public servants are often afraid to speak openly and critically about their political masters. In Britain, politicians are not allowed to be members of the analogous body, and that might be worth considering in Canada. Another more positive approach would be to have two wings to the same organization, one for members of parliament and another without them. Furthermore, the groups should devote more time to research, as in the case of Britain, and less time in the preparation of conferences for generalists. Lastly, Canada is one of the few democracies without a journal of opinion about its parliamentary institutions. In the United Kingdom the Hansard Society assumes this task in addition to providing a forum for discussion about governmental reform. A Canadian institution could undertake similar duties.

NOTES

1. The many reform proposals are contained in these and other papers and books: *Royal Commission on Financial Management and Accountability* (Hull: Supply and Services, 1979); *Seminar on the Budgetary Process* (Ottawa: Queen's Printer, 1977); *Seminar on Accountability to Parliament* (Ottawa: Queen's Printer, 1978); and, *Parliamentary Government in Canada* (Ottawa: A Study Prepared for the Business Council on National Issues, 1979).
2. A similar cabinet committee in the United Kingdom aided the Labour government to accomplish its enormous legislative program between 1945 and 1951.
3. *Royal Commission on Financial Management and Accountability*, passim.
4. See Mitchell Sharp in *Seminar on the Budgetary Process*, p. 23.
5. The amount of delegated or subordinate legislation is simply phenomenal — between January 1, 1969, and September 14, 1977, a total of 6861 statutory orders, regulations, and other instruments were published, many of these authorizing appointments.
6. *Parliamentary Government in Canada*, p. 40.
7. Ronald Butt, *The Power of Parliament* (London: Constable, 1969), p. 72.
8. This structure would also diminish the need for those omnibus bills which are used solely to link minor adjustments in the law. Mitchell Sharp spoke about such a reform during the 30th Parliament. However, this procedural change should not be accepted unless it is part of a package arrangement. Instead, a short-run project would be to limit second reading to one day for some bills. Even this would probably be made unworkable by partisanship in the House.

9. The research is conflicting. For the differing conclusions, see Michael Rush, "The Committees of the Canadian House of Commons," unpublished paper (1973), and Allan Kornberg and William Mishler, *Influence in Parliament* (Durham, N.C.: Duke University Press, 1976), pp. 305-07 and concluding chapter.

10. John Stewart, *The Canadian House of Commons; Procedure and Reform* (Montreal: McGill-Queen's University Press, 1977), p. 278.

11. J. A. A. Lovink, "Who Wants Parliamentary Reform?", *Queens Quarterly*, 79 (Winter 1972), p. 510.

12. For a summary of the literature, see Colin Campbell, *The Canadian Senate* (Toronto: Macmillan of Canada, 1978).

13. The Official Secrets Act, for example, is too vague and unworkable. Furthermore, it attacks principles of free speech and assembly. See *The Globe and Mail* (April 24, 1974), p. 2.

14. T. Murray Rankin, *Freedom of Information in Canada: Will the Doors Stay Shut?* (Canadian Bar Association, August 1977), p. 155.

15. Green Paper: Canada, Secretary of State, *Legislation on Public Access to Government Documents* (Ottawa: Supply and Services, 1977); Richard D. French, "Freedom of Information and Parliament," a paper prepared for a Conference on Legislative Studies in Canada, Simon Fraser University (February 1979), pp. 17-32.

16. Harold C. Relyea, "The Provision of Government Information: The Federal Freedom of Information Act Experience," *Canadian Public Administration*, 20 (1977), p. 326.

17. French, *op. cit.*, p. 30.

18. Canada should consider adopting the computerized answering service now employed in the State of New York for those citizens who wish more information about parliamentary proceedings.

Index

217

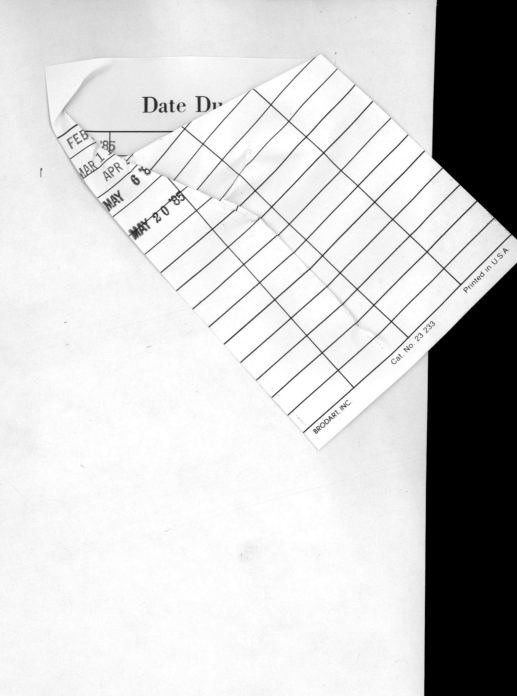

Date Due

FEB	'85										
MAR 1	'85										
APR 6											
MAY											
MAY 20	'85										

BRODART, INC.   Cat. No. 23 233   Printed in U.S.A.